Women and Sexuality

Recent Titles in
Women and Society around the World

Women and Violence: Global Lives in Focus
Kathleen Nadeau and Sangita Rayamajhi, Editors

Women and Health: Global Lives in Focus
AnnJanette Alejano-Steele, Editor

Women and the Military: Global Lives in Focus
Ruth Margolies Beitler and Sarah M. Gerstein

Women and Religion: Global Lives in Focus
Susan M. Shaw, Editor

Women and Sexuality

Global Lives in Focus

Kelly Campbell and M. L. Parker, Editors

Women and Society around the World

An Imprint of ABC-CLIO, LLC

Santa Barbara, California • Denver, Colorado

Library of Congress Cataloging-in-Publication Data

Names: Campbell, Kelly (Professor of psychology), editor.
Title: Women and sexuality : global lives in focus / Kelly Campbell and M. L. Parker, editors.
Description: Santa Barbara : ABC-CLIO, 2023. I Series: Women and society
  around the world I Includes bibliographical references and index.
Identifiers: LCCN 2022026438 I ISBN 9781440873041 (hardcover) I ISBN
  9781440873058 (ebook)
Subjects: LCSH: Women—Sexual behavior.
Classification: LCC HQ29 .W663 2023 I DDC 306.7082—dc23/eng/20220804
LC record available at https://lccn.loc.gov/2022026438

ISBN: 978-1-4408-7304-1 (print)
      978-1-4408-7305-8 (ebook)

27 26 25 24 23   1 2 3 4 5

This book is also available as an eBook.

ABC-CLIO
An Imprint of ABC-CLIO, LLC

ABC-CLIO, LLC
147 Castilian Drive
Santa Barbara, California 93117
www.abc-clio.com

This book is printed on acid-free paper ∞

Manufactured in the United States of America

Contents

Series Foreword

Women's roles in society and the issues they face differ greatly from those of their male counterparts. In some corners of the world, women may manage households but are deemed unworthy of an education; in other areas, women scientists are pioneers in their fields, juggling family life and their careers. Gender inequality looms in all aspects of life, from employment to education to opportunities in sports and the military. What are the challenges, issues, and achievements women around the world face?

The *Women and Society around the World* series looks at women's lives as they pertain to various issues. The volumes cover topics such as

- Health;
- Violence;
- Religion;
- Sexuality;
- The military;
- Sports;
- Education; and
- Technology, among others.

Each volume begins with an introductory background essay on the volume's topic and is followed by a general chronology of significant world events pertaining to the topic. Eight chapters follow, focusing on the world's regions: North America (United States and Canada), Latin America and the Caribbean, Europe, North Africa and the Middle East, Sub-Saharan Africa, Central and East Asia, South Asia and Southeast Asia, and Oceania. All chapters include a list of further reading resources, and a selected bibliography at the end of each volume provides students with additional print and electronic resources for further research needs.

The chapters examine women in each region with broad brushstrokes, highlighting specific examples of key customs and policies in specific countries that help to illuminate cultural nuances among countries within each region. They can be read alone or be reviewed cumulatively to make cross-cultural comparisons. The volumes are ideal for high school students doing projects, undergraduate students writing research papers, and even general readers interested in learning about women's lives.

The goal of the *Women and Society around the World* series is to depict the roles of women worldwide by exploring the major issues they face and the accomplishments they have made, especially in terms of bridging the gap in gender inequality and fighting for basic human rights. While readers will learn about the challenges that half of the world's population face, they will also discover the empowering ways women succeed and overcome social and cultural barriers in their daily lives.

Introduction

Women and Sexuality: Global Lives in Focus examines historical and contemporary issues pertaining to women's sexualities around the world. Each chapter addresses a different geographic region, including North America, Latin America and the Caribbean, Europe, North Africa and the Middle East, sub-Saharan Africa, Central and East Asia, South and Southeast Asia, and Oceania. The topics covered in each chapter include culture and attitudes toward sexuality, religion and sexuality, sexual violence, reproductive health and menstruation, marriage and partnerships, and the media and sexuality. This format enables readers to consider the experiences of women cross-culturally, evaluating how they are both similar and different. One construct that has heavily influenced women's sexuality in all regions is patriarchy. We begin by defining this and other constructs that are central to understanding the content in this book. After defining key terms, we review important theories that help explain and contextualize women's sexuality. Our hope is that the reader will refer back to these concepts and theories as they move through the chapters.

DEFINING KEY TERMS

Patriarchy

"Patriarchy" refers to a societal system in which men have more power than women. Power is defined as the ability to influence people. In patriarchal societies, men have more financial resources than women do, and they occupy a greater number of leadership roles. Nearly every country in the world is considered patriarchal (Kimmel 2017). It is impossible to discuss women's sexualities without addressing patriarchy, because in many countries, women are considered the property of men, and violence against them, including sexual assault and rape, is common. Consider that even in industrialized regions such as Australia, the United States, and the United Kingdom, women are "given away" by fathers to their husbands at the time of marriage (Rathus, Nevid, and Fichner-Rathus 2018). Societies that teach men to have power over women through patriarchal laws, rules, and customs lead men to feel entitled to such power. Men's rates of sexual violence vary by culture, with instances being lower in egalitarian societies such as Scandinavia, providing evidence that sexual exploitation is primarily rooted in cultural power dynamics rather than biological factors.

Biological Sex

The term "sex" refers to biological characteristics such as chromosomes, anatomy, and sex hormones that distinguish a person as a man or a woman. Sex is determined at the moment of conception by the male's sperm (Rathus, Nevid, and Fichner-Rathus 2018). In combination with the X chromosome contained by the egg, the sperm contains either an X chromosome, to produce XX for a girl, or a Y chromosome, to produce XY for a boy. Over the course of prenatal development, the baby's biological temperament is influenced by exposure to the woman's hormone levels (Kimmel 2017). The absence of androgens causes female genitalia to develop. Girls may exhibit more aggressive traits after birth when androgens are present during the prenatal period, which can occur for a variety of reasons such as compromised adrenal glands or supplements taken by the mother. The presence of androgens also increases the likelihood that girls will have ambiguous or male genitalia, despite their XX chromosomes. In such cases, the parents may opt to raise the child as a boy, and additional hormone treatment will be required to help establish secondary sex characteristics such as body hair and an enlarged Adam's apple. Individuals who are intersex exhibit biological traits that are typical of both men and women. It is estimated that approximately 1% to 2% of the population is intersex (Kimmel 2017).

Gender

The concept of sex is different from that of gender, with the latter referring to socialized, cultural expectations about what it means to be a man or a woman (Donnelly and Twenge 2017). Gender is often described using the terms "male" and "female." It includes culturally influenced ideas about how each sex should behave. The main agents of socialization are families, especially parents, but gender expectations are also learned from friends, teachers, the media, including social media, and institutions such as church, school, and workplaces. Gender expectations can be communicated through direct messages, such as when people say "Boys don't cry" or "Girls should be quiet." Yet expectations can also be communicated in subtle or indirect ways, such as when parents assign different chores to their daughters versus sons or give different privileges and freedoms to children based on their biological sex. Differences in the socialization of boys compared to girls is a major factor impacting gender differences in sexual behavior (Kimmel 2017). People who feel as though their sex and gender match are termed "cisgender" whereas those who mismatch are called "transgender" (Diamond 2018). Some transgender people alter their outward physical appearance by dressing according to their preferred gender, using surgeries, and/or preferring certain gender names and pronouns over others. People who do not adhere to culturally prescribed ideas about how their sex should behave tend to be heavily criticized.

Sexual Orientation

Sexual orientation refers to whether a person feels predominantly attracted to and pursues relationships with people of the same sex, different sex, or either sex (Diamond 2003). The term "heterosexual" is used to describe a person who is attracted to a different sex. "Homosexual" refers to people who are attracted to the same sex, and "bisexual" refers to attraction toward either sex. Other terms can also be used, such as "asexual," meaning a person does not experience feelings of attraction, and "pansexual," whereby attraction is not dependent on a partner's gender or biological sex. "Queer" is yet another term that has gained popularity in the LGBTQ+ community (lesbian, gay, bisexual, transgender, queer) and refers to people who do not subscribe to a heterosexual or cisgender identity. All over the world, people who espouse a nondominant sexual identity of LGBTQ+ are heavily discriminated against and are at greater risk of death by way of suicide or homicide (Badgett and Frank 2007; Human Rights Watch 2013). The most accepting countries toward LGBTQ+ tend to be in the Scandinavian region of Northern Europe, whereas the least accepting are predominantly in the Middle East, including Egypt, Saudi Arabia, and Bahrain, and the South Asian country of Bangladesh.

THEORIES

A variety of theories can be used to explain women's sexuality. The three most popular are reviewed here. The first, evolutionary theory, describes sex differences according to biological factors. Next, social structural theory explains sex differences according to macrosocietal characteristics, most notably the power differences that exist between men and women. The third perspective is attachment theory, which focuses less on the differences between men and women and more on how people develop styles of relating to others that are derived from their families of origin. The explanations of attachment theory consider how both biological and social factors influence behavior.

Evolutionary Theory

The predominant biological explanation for sex differences in sexual behavior is evolutionary theory. This orientation has mostly focused on heterosexual rather than same-sex partnerships. It contains many subtheories and concepts, which are too lengthy to outline here; however, some of the core concepts that relate to sexuality are described. Central to this orientation is the concept of natural selection, which refers to the idea that people who adapt well to their environments are more likely to survive and produce offspring to carry on those adaptive features (Confer et al. 2010). Adaptive traits are behaviors or characteristics that give a reproductive or survival advantage to people who possess them. One example of an adaptive trait is that around the world, women are perceived as more physically attractive if their waist is 30% smaller than their hips (Singh and Singh 2011). This waist-to-hip ratio is associated with health and fertility and signals to prospective partners that women may be successful at bearing children.

According to sexual selection theory, a subtheory of the evolutionary perspective, men and women have different reproductive goals, which causes them to seek different qualities in their mates (Buss 1989). Men have a goal of assuring a child is their own, a concept known as paternity certainty. As such, they tend to value women who are sexually restrained and feel especially jealous at the threat of sexual infidelity. Women have greater parental investment than men, because the time commitment for reproduction is lengthier (at least nine months compared to a few minutes), which causes them to seek partners who can provide long-term resources and care. As such, they tend to feel more jealous over emotional rather than sexual infidelity, because emotional attachments could lead their mate to commit himself to a sexual rival. Given that parental investment is longer for women, and the risk of engaging in casual or uncommitted sex is greater, women are theorized to be more selective than men when choosing among prospective mates.

Empirical research supports this proposition. In two separate studies, the first across 33 countries and the second across 52, Buss (1989) and Schmitt and Dovidio (2003) found that men prefer more sex partners than women do, prefer to have sex after a shorter time knowing a partner, and are more likely than women to seek short-term partnerships, irrespective of their current relationship status. Although evolutionary theories describe greater reproductive benefits for promiscuous men than promiscuous women—because promiscuous men will produce abundant offspring—researchers also identify at least one benefit for promiscuous women: By having sex with multiple partners during her fertile period, a woman can elicit sperm competition and enhance her chances of birthing optimal offspring (Pham and Shackelford 2015).

Sexual selection theory also describes gender differences regarding intra- and intersexual selection. According to the theory, men and women faced different challenges in their ancestral history, which led them to develop distinct strategies for reproductive success (Buss et al. 2017). Intrasexual selection involves competing with members of one's own sex for a potential mate, whereas intersexual selection refers to the manner in which each sex demonstrates its desirability to potential mates. Given that women value resources, status, and physical strength, particularly during their fertile period, men compete with each other on these traits by boasting about their financial accomplishments and demonstrating their physical prowess. Men are also expected to derogate their rivals on precisely these traits. Women, on the other hand, are expected to compete with each other on traits that men prioritize, such as those signaling youth and fertility. They are predicted to wear clothing that accentuates their figure and to invest in makeup, hair products, and even cosmetic procedures that will enhance their outward appearance. They derogate their rivals on the qualities valued by men, heavily criticizing for example, the outward appearance of other women (Buss 2012). Although the ideas stemming from this theory focus on gender stereotypes and do not often apply to same-sex relationships, research supports its propositions.

Social Structural Theory

Social structural theory, advanced by Eagly and Wood (1999), considers the role of biology in producing distinct mate preferences but mostly focuses on men and women's unequal power distributions in patriarchal societies. This perspective suggests that biological differences between men and women have historically caused the sexes to specialize in different roles. Given that women biologically bear children and in most societies are the primary caregivers, they are left with little time and effort to devote to noncaregiving duties such as work outside of the home. Biologically, men's bodies are physically bigger and stronger than women, which has historically caused them to seek out jobs relating to building, moving, and resource acquisition. Through their enactment of these different roles, members of a society start expecting women to specialize in caregiving and men to specialize in paid work. Sex differences therefore exist because of cultural expectations and social structures that grant opportunities to men and limit those of women.

As previously noted, a variety of expectations for men and women are conveyed through socialization. In most world regions, women are expected to be caring and kind, whereas men are expected to be dominant and assertive. People who do not comply with these gendered expectations experience backlash and criticism. Consider the example of transgendered people who experience discrimination at rates much higher than those who comply with gender role norms, including bullying, harassment, job loss, housing evictions, violence, and murder (Human Rights Campaign 2019). Gendered expectations and the resulting penalties for violating them lead each sex to develop skills that will help it optimally perform its roles. Those who meet society's expectations for their gender are praised, and those who do not are punished. Because gender expectations are governed by social norms, they vary across historical time and context. For example, during World War II, when men were called on to fight, women were required for labor. During this period, media images depicted women in men's attire, performing men's jobs. Yet the representation of women leading up to the war and in the postwar era was drastically different, providing evidence for the social construction and flexibility of gender role norms (Bradbury and Karney 2019).

In terms of mate selection, social structural explanations suggest that to optimize potential, each sex seeks complementary features in its partners. Younger women tend to have less money and resources than older women, so they prefer men with resources. By selecting for this trait, the power differential between men and women is amplified. Men's accommodation to roles with greater power encourage dominant behavior, and women's accommodation to roles with lesser power reinforces subordinate behavior. Eagly and Wood (1999) examined the cross-cultural data collected by Buss (1989) as well as data collected by the United Nations and found support for their proposition that power imbalance, more than biology, predicts gender differences. Cultures with traditional divisions of labor exhibited the expected complementary role pattern. Countries that were more egalitarian in their division of roles, such as Canada, Denmark, Finland, New Zealand, Norway, Sweden, and the United States did not adhere as strictly to complementary mate selection. Zentner and Mitura (2012) conducted a more recent analysis, which corroborated Eagly and Wood's (1999) findings. These studies demonstrate that biological sex is not as strong a predictor of sexual behaviors than the power associated with each sex in a given society.

Attachment Theory

Attachment theory describes people's general orientation toward relationships. It first emerged as an evolutionary framework but has since been adopted by social scientists. The essence of the theory is that everyone is born with the biological desire to form attachment bonds, but the particular style a person develops is based on the person's socialization (Bowlby 1982). Given that attachment styles are socialized rather than biologically determined, it is possible to change styles over the course of one's life. Usually, however, once people develop a certain style, they act in ways that cause others to respond according to their existing style, so it can be difficult to change, especially after a lifetime of reinforcement. There are four adult attachment styles that can be described along two dimensions: *anxiety* and *avoidance of intimacy* (Brennan, Clark, and Shaver 1998). In every culture, 50% to 75% of the adult population—with China at the low end and the UK at the high end—espouse a secure style, which is characterized as low on both anxiety and avoidance of intimacy (Bakermans-Kranenburg and van IJzendoorn 2009; Van IJzendoorn and Kroonenberg 1988). A secure style develops among children who have caregivers that consistently and responsively meet their needs. Having learned that people can be relied upon, the child therefore readily expresses desires. As adults, secure individuals easily form relationships, successfully bond with others, and have a relaxed trust.

The other three attachment styles are classified as insecure. Preoccupied attachment style comprises approximately 5% to 25% of the adult population, with the UK at the low end and Israel at the high end (Bakermans-Kranenburg and van IJzendoorn 2009; Van IJzendoorn and Kroonenberg 1988). These individuals are considered high on anxiety and low on avoidance. As children, they receive inconsistent care. Sometimes parents are warm and attentive, and other times they are not. As adults, they do not believe people can be consistently relied upon and are therefore nervous, clingy, and needy. The final two styles are both considered avoidant, but the avoidant category splits in two subtypes: fearful and dismissive. Approximately 5% to 35% of the world's adult population are classified as avoidant with Japan at the low end and Germany at the high end (Bakermans-Kranenburg and van IJzendoorn 2009; Van IJzendoorn and Kroonenberg 1988). These children receive neglectful and/or hostile treatment from caregivers. As adults, the fearful subtype is high on anxiety and avoidance. Individuals with fearful attachment desire close relationships but often respond by withdrawing in relationships to avoid getting hurt. The dismissing subtype is low on anxiety and high on avoidance. Individuals with dismissing attachment do not want to form relationships; they are independent and have realized they are most comfortable not being in a relationship.

People with secure attachment styles are more open to sexual exploration with their partners. They tend to be more monogamous than their insecurely attached counterparts (Parker and Campbell 2017). The avoidantly attached have the least sex of all groups, which is consistent with their desire to avoid intimacy (Favez and Tissot 2017). However, those who are high on attachment avoidance (i.e., fearful, dismissing) engage in more hookups or sex with no strings attached compared to the other attachment types (Schmitt and Jonason 2015). Individuals who are high on attachment anxiety (i.e., preoccupied) are the most likely to engage in extramarital sex. Men who are high on attachment anxiety and avoidance (i.e., fearful) are also at risk for infidelity. Overall, those with a secure orientation have better, more fulfilling sex lives (Mikulincer and Shaver 2013). Interestingly, when insecure partners are in relationships with responsive, validating partners, it is possible to decrease attachment anxiety (Mizrahi et al. 2016) and avoidance (Stanton, Campbell, and Pink 2017) and become more securely attached. Men's attachment anxiety is reduced by having a partner who expresses intimacy, whereas women's attachment anxiety is reduced by partners who verbalize their sexual desire.

AS YOU READ THIS BOOK

Now that the groundwork has been laid with key definitions and a description of the major theoretical frameworks regarding women's sexuality, we hope you will use these tools to interpret and evaluate the information contained in this book.

Women's experiences are different from those of men, and even among women, there is great diversity. However, as you will see, women are united by common experiences such as being the targets of prejudice and discrimination, sexual violence, sexual exploitation, and oppression. A recent report from the United Nations found that nearly 90% of the world's people are biased against women in one form or another and that nearly 30% think it is acceptable for a man to physically harm his wife (United Nations Development Programme 2019). How can this be explained, and why do even women espouse these negative views? The key lies in socialization and cultural norms all over the world that attempt to control and dominate women. Despite these efforts, women are resilient. They are bonded by their experiences of adversity but also connected by their strength, grace, fight for equality, and ability to mother. Men are physically dominant in stature, but it is women who have stronger immune systems and outlive men all over the world. We urge the reader to keep these assets and attributes in mind as they digest the material in this book. Women are amazing, and attempts to diminish their influence will only serve to motivate and push them forward.

REFERENCES

Badgett, Lee M. V., and Jeff Frank. 2007. *Sexual Orientation Discrimination: An International Perspective*. New York: Routledge.

Bakermans-Kranenburg, Marian J., and Marinus H. van IJzendoorn. 2009. "The First 10,000 Adult Attachment Interviews: Distributions of Adult Attachment Representations in Clinical and Non-Clinical Groups." *Attachment & Human Development* 11 (3): 223263. https://doi.org/10.1080/14616730902814762.

Bowlby, John. 1982. *Attachment and Loss: Vol. 1: Attachment*. 2nd ed. New York: Basic.

Bradbury, Thomas N., and Benjamin R. Karney. 2019. *Intimate Relationships*. 3rd ed. New York: W. W. Norton & Company.

Brennan, Kelly A., Catherine L. Clark, and Phillip R. Shaver. 1998. "Self-Report Measurement of Adult Attachment: An Integrative Overview." In *Attachment Theory and Close Relationships*, edited by Jeffry A. Simpson and William S. Rholes, 46–76. New York: Guilford Press.

Buss, David M. 1989. "Sex Differences in Human Mate Preferences: Evolutionary Hypotheses Tested in 37 Cultures." *Behavioral and Brain Sciences* 12 (1): 1–14.

Buss, David M. 2012. "Derogation of Competitors." *Psychologist* 25 (1): 24.

Buss, David M., Cari Goetz, Joshua D. Duntley, Kelly Asao, and Daniel Conroy-Beam. 2017. "The Mate Switching Hypothesis." *Personality and Individual Differences* 104 (January): 143–49. https://doi.org/10.1016/j.paid.2016.07.022.

Confer, Jaime C., Judith A. Easton, Diana S. Fleischman, Cari D. Goetz, David M. G. Lewis, Carin Perilloux, and David M. Buss. 2010. "Evolutionary Psychology. Controversies, Questions, Prospects, and Limitations." *American Psychologist* 65 (2): 110–27.

Diamond, Lisa M. 2003. "What Does Sexual Orientation Orient? A Biobehavioral Model Distinguishing Romantic Love and Sexual Desire." *Psychological Review* 110 (1): 173–93.

Diamond, Lisa M. 2018. "Contemporary Theory in the Study of Intimacy, Desire, Gender, and Sexuality." In *Gender, Sex, and Sexualities: Psychological Perspectives*, edited by Nancy K. Dess, Jeanne Marecek, and Leslie C. Bell, 271–94. New York: Oxford University Press.

Donnelly, Kristin, and Jean M. Twenge. 2017. "Masculine and Feminine Traits on the Bem Sex-Role Inventory, 1993–2012: A Cross-Temporal Meta-Analysis." *Sex Roles: A Journal of Research* 76 (9–10): 556–65.

Eagly, Alice H., and Wendy Wood. 1999. "The Origins of Sex Differences in Human Behavior: Evolved Dispositions versus Social Roles." *American Psychologist* 54 (6): 408–23.

Favez, Nicolas, and Herve Tissot. 2017. "Attachment Tendencies and Sexual Activities." *Journal of Social & Personal Relationships* 34 (5): 732–53.

Human Rights Campaign. 2019. "Violence against the Transgender Community in 2019." Accessed May 30, 2019. https://www.hrc.org/resources/violence-against-the-transgender-community-in-2019.

Human Rights Watch. 2013. "LGBT Rights." Accessed March 14, 2020. https://www.hrw.org/topic/lgbt-rights#.

Kimmel, Michael. 2017. *The Gendered Society.* New York: Oxford University Press.

Mikulincer, Mario, and Phillip R. Shaver. 2013. "The Role of Attachment Security in Adolescent and Adult Close Relationships." In *The Oxford Handbook of Close Relationships,* edited by Jeffry A. Simpson and Lorne Campbell, 66–89. New York: Oxford University Press.

Mizrahi, Moran, Gilad Hirschberger, Mario Mikulincer, Ohad Szepsenwol, and Gurit E. Birnbaum. 2016. "Reassuring Sex: Can Sexual Desire and Intimacy Reduce Relationship-specific Attachment Insecurities?" *European Journal of Social Psychology* 46 (4): 467–81.

Parker, Michele L., and Kelly Campbell. 2017. "Infidelity and Attachment: The Moderating Role of Race/Ethnicity." *Contemporary Family Therapy* 39 (3): 172–83. https://doi.org/10.1007/s10591-017-9415-0.

Pham, Michael N., and Todd K. Shackelford. 2015. "Sperm Competition and the Evolution of Human Sexuality." In *The Evolution of Sexuality,* edited by Todd K. Shackelford and Ranald D. Hansen, 257–75. Cham, Switzerland: Springer International Publishing. https://doi.org/10.1007/978-3-319-09384-0_12.

Rathus, Spencer A., Jeffrey S. Nevid, and Lois Fichner-Rathus. 2018. *Human Sexuality in a World of Diversity.* 10th ed. New York: Pearson Education.

Schmitt, David P., and John F. Dovidio. 2003. "Universal Sex Differences in the Desire for Sexual Variety: Tests from 52 Nations, 6 Continents, and 13 Islands." *Journal of Personality and Social Psychology* 85 (1): 85–104.

Schmitt, David P., and Peter K. Jonason. 2015. "Attachment and Sexual Permissiveness: Exploring Differential Associations Across Sexes, Cultures, and Facets of Short-Term Mating." *Journal of Cross-Cultural Psychology* 46: 119–33. https://doi.org/10.1177/0022022114551052.

Singh, Devendra, and Dorian Singh. 2011. "Shape and Significance of Feminine Beauty: An Evolutionary Perspective." *Sex Roles* 64: 723–31. https://doi.org/10.1007/s11199-011-9938-z.

Stanton, Sarah C. E., Lorne Campbell, and Jennifer C. Pink. (2017). "Benefits of Positive Relationship Experiences for Avoidantly Attached Individuals." *Journal of Personality and Social Psychology* 113 (4): 568–88. https://doi.org/10.1037/pspi0000098.

United Nations Development Programme. 2019. "Tackling Social Norms: A Game Changer for Gender Inequalities." Accessed March 14, 2020. http://hdr.undp.org/sites/default/files/hd_perspectives_gsni.pdf.

Van IJzendoorn, Marinus H., and Pieter M. Kroonenberg. 1988. "Cross-Cultural Patterns of Attachment: A Meta-Analysis of the Strange Situation." *Child Development* 59 (1): 147–56. https://doi.org/10.2307/1130396.

Zentner, Marcel, and Klaudia Mitura. 2012. "Stepping Out of the Caveman's Shadow: Nations' Gender Gap Predicts Degree of Sex Differentiation in Mate Preferences." *Psychological Science* 23 (10): 1176–85. https://doi.org/10.1177/0956797612441004.

Chronology

51 BCE

Cleopatra VII becomes co-regent with her father as the ruler of ancient Egypt, and she rules for nearly 30 years. Even though she is well known for using her beauty and sexual appeal to gain political power, many Egyptian sources say Cleopatra is highly intelligent. She speaks multiple languages and is well educated.

672 CE

Lady K'abel becomes the military ruler of El Peru-Waka. She rules for 20 years and is one of only a few Mayan women rulers. Hieroglyphics label her "Lady Snake Lord," associating her with the Snake Dynasty of Calakmul.

937

The year marks the first historical record noting the practice of Chinese foot-binding to make the feet appear smaller and more sexually attractive. Despite the excruciating pain and lengthy process, women and girls endure foot-binding as a symbol of elegance and prestige.

1431

As a leader on the battlefield during the Hundred Years' War, Joan of Arc defies traditional female roles of her time and helps Charles VII become anointed and crowned king of France. However, once this is achieved, Joan is imprisoned and sent to England, where she is sentenced to death by fire. Following her death, Pope Callixtus III rejects the charges and pronounces her innocent.

1553

Mary I, later known as Bloody Mary, becomes the first woman to be crowned queen of England and recognized as the sole ruler in her own right.

1788

Captain James Cook arrives in Australia, which leads to the invasion and settlement of Europeans in Australia and the imposition of the highly patriarchal European legal and value system on Indigenous women.

1845

Teri'itari'a II is the queen of Tahiti during the Franco-Tahitian War (1844–1847), during which she leads forces against the French in two separate battles to liberate the Leeward Islands. The journals of European soldiers describe Queen Teri'itari'a's commanding leadership and her courage in battle.

1857

Dr. William Acton, an English gynecologist, publishes his medical textbook *The Functions and Disorders of the Reproductive Organs in Childhood, Youth, Adult Age, and Advanced Life.* The book explains the pathology of female masturbation and sexual desire, associating the symptoms with nymphomania, which frequently leads to women being institutionalized.

1859

The Witchcraft Suppression Act is passed by the British government in the Cape Colony in South Africa, making divination illegal. Under the guise of promoting development and enlightenment, European colonialists, missionaries, and traders thereby undermine local African agency and impose European definitions of gender and sexual norms.

1870

The Married Women's Property Act is passed in the United Kingdom, allowing women to own property and have an income separate from their husbands.

1883

Dr. Joseph Mortimer Granville, an English physician, invents the first handheld electric vibrator.

1893

Kate Sheppard works with fellow suffragists to present a petition to the New Zealand Parliament, ultimately leading to New Zealand becoming the first self-governing country to grant national voting rights to women.

1903

Marie Curie (1867–1934), from Warsaw, Russian Empire (what is now Poland), becomes the first woman to be awarded the Nobel Prize in

Physics and Chemistry (1911) for discovering the elements of radium and polonium.

1911

Raichō Hiratsuka cofounds *Seitō*, the first women-led journal in Japan. The journal challenges traditional Japanese gender roles in the home.

1911

The first International Women's Day takes place on March 8. Over one million people from Switzerland, Germany, and Austria gather in support of women's suffrage and labor rights.

1915

The Austrian Expressionist painter Egon Schiele releases his controversial paintings, *Two Women Embracing* and *Two Girls Lying Entwined*. Due to the sexually explicit nature of his paintings, he is often considered a pornographer and labeled a degenerate by the court.

1916

Margaret Sanger opens the first birth control clinic in Brooklyn, New York. Birth control is illegal, and the clinic is raided several times. Eventually, she will close the clinic to begin the American Birth Control League in 1921, which will become Planned Parenthood.

1919

The right to vote for all adult citizens, or universal suffrage, is implemented in Azerbaijan. This legislation makes Azerbaijan the first Muslim-majority country to allow women the right to vote.

1933

In Germany, the Nazi Party establishes the "Law for the Prevention of Progeny with Hereditary Diseases," which mandates forced sterilization of individuals with diseases and disabilities. By the end of World War II, an estimated 320,000 Jewish and Roma women will be forcibly sterilized.

1937

The Nanjing Massacre, also known as the Rape of Nanking, occurs when the Imperial Japanese Army captures the city of Nanjing, the former capital of China. In addition to mass murder of civilians, the widespread rape of an estimated 20,000 to 80,000 Chinese women takes place over a six-week period.

1941
The reigning queen of Buganda Kingdom, Uganda, Irene Drusilla Namaganda, sparks controversy when she defies Buganda tradition by marrying Reverend Canon Peter Kigozi. Not only is Namaganda the widow of a king, and so considered married under Buganda customs, but Kigozi is *mukoopi*, or a commoner.

1944
The Educational Act of England and Wales serves to recast the educational system and assures even more standards of educational opportunity. Every local education authority is required to submit a development plan as well as a plan for the future. The essential features of the Education Act of 1944 will be reproduced in the Education Act of 1945, in Scotland, and in the Education Act of 1947, in Northern Ireland.

1946
The Commission on the Status of Women is established as part of the United Nations Economic and Social Council to be the first global intergovernmental commission charged with empowering women and gender equality worldwide.

1948
Dr. Gisella Perl, a Romanian Jewish gynecologist, releases her book *I Was a Doctor in Auschwitz*. The book describes her experiences as a prisoner in the Nazi concentration camp, performing abortions for other women who became pregnant as a result of rape, so the women would not also be killed.

1948
Women in South Korea are granted the right to vote, drive a vehicle, and own and inherit property and assets.

1949
The Prohibition of Mixed Marriages Act is passed in South Africa when the strict, racist system of apartheid is implemented.

1950
The Marriage Law of 1950 is established in the People's Republic of China and is intended to address issues of inequality among husbands and wives. The legislation prohibits concubinage, polygamy, bigamy, child betrothal, and interference with the remarriage of widows.

1956
The local council, Njuri-Ncheke of Meru, Kenya, unanimously places a ban on clitoridectomies (i.e., female genital mutilation). However, many

Njuri adolescent girls continue to defy the ban and perform their own clitoridectomies, as the custom is considered an important rite of passage.

1960
The U.S. Federal Drug Administration approves the first birth control pill, which helps make it possible for women to have more control over their reproductive health and delay childbearing to pursue educational and career goals.

1972
Nena and George O'Neill publish their book *Open Marriage: A New Life Style for Couples*, which introduces the concept of nonmonogamous relationships into mainstream American culture.

1973
Jane Roe wins a landmark case in the U.S. Supreme Court against the district attorney of Dallas County, Texas, Henry Wade (*Roe v. Wade*); the win protects a pregnant woman's right to choose to have an abortion despite the existing U.S. state and federal laws banning abortion.

1973
Dr. Connie Pinkerton-Uri, a woman of Choctaw and Cherokee heritage, conducts a study at a reservation hospital in Claremore, Oklahoma (among others), where she discovers the American government forcibly sterilized approximately 25% of Native American women without their consent. Estimates will be as high as 80% of the women on some of the reservations Dr. Pinkerton-Uri subsequently visits.

1975
The United Nations holds the first World Conference on Women in Mexico City. Attending the conference are 133 governments from across the world to define a World Plan of Action and develop a comprehensive set of guidelines for the advancement of women. Following the first conference in 1975, the conference will be held in Copenhagen in 1980, Nairobi in 1985, and Beijing in 1995.

1979
China introduces the controversial one-child policy to combat the rapidly growing population. It is more common for female fetuses to be aborted, as male children are considered more desirable in Asian cultures. The one-child policy has long-lasting effects, as the birth of a female child is seen as a misfortune by some families today.

1985

The New Zealand Rape Law Reform Act is passed to abolish the legal immunity of spouses in marital rape cases.

1992

In Botswana, Unity Dow wins a landmark court case in which women married to noncitizens gain the right to confer nationality to their children. She will later become Botswana's first female high court judge.

1993

The United Nations World Conference on Human Rights officially defines the term "violence against women" as any act of gender-based violence that results in or is likely to result in harm to women, that occurs in the family or within the general community, and that is perpetrated or condoned by the state.

1994

During the Rwandan genocide, an estimated nearly 9,300 women are raped, sexually violated, held in sexual bondage, forced into "marriage," and abused. Many women become pregnant, and the Rwandan National Population Office comes to estimate that between 2,000 and 5,000 children are born in the immediately following year.

1998

In El Salvador, abortion is made illegal under all circumstances, and a "right to life" is granted from conception.

2002

Mukhtār Mā'ī, a woman from Meerwala, Pakistan, survives a brutal gang rape by members of a different tribal clan. While cultural customs dictate that she commit suicide after being raped to avoid shame, she instead speaks out, at great risk to her safety, and brings international attention to the men's crimes. She goes on to found the Mukhtār Mā'ī Women's Welfare Organization for Pakistani women and girls.

2006

Tarana Burke begins the Me Too movement to raise awareness about the growing prevalence of sexual assault, which leads to a broader initiative in 2017, with the hashtag #MeToo, in support of sexual abuse survivors.

2014

Nadia Murad, a 19-year-old Yazidi woman living in northern Iraq, sees her village attacked by the Islamic State (IS), which massacres 600 Yazidi men and captures her to serve as a sex slave. After three months in captivity, she manages to escape to a refugee camp. She goes on to win the Nobel Prize (2018) for her work to end sexual violence as a weapon of war. She is now living in Germany.

2016

Zimbabwe Constitutional Court rules in favor of Loveness Mudzuru and Ruvimbo Tsopodzi, former child brides, stating that no one may be married before the age of 18.

2017

Same-sex marriage is recognized in Australian law when the definition of marriage as a union between "a man and a woman" is replaced by a union between "two people."

2019

Despite the political influence of the overwhelmingly Catholic and Protestant populations in Ireland, abortion and same-sex marriage are legalized in the country.

2019

Finance Minister Namgay Tshering, of Bhutan, submits the recommendation to Parliament to repeal sections 213 and 214 of Bhutan's penal code that outlaw "unnatural sex." The two sections are repealed by an overwhelming vote to decriminalize homosexual relationships.

2020

U.S. Supreme Court Justice Ruth Bader Ginsburg (born 1933) dies from complications of pancreatic cancer. Prior to her appointment as the first Jewish woman on the U.S. Supreme Court, Ginsberg argued several landmark cases of gender equality, resulting in the constitutional prohibition of discrimination based on gender.

2022

The United States Supreme Court overturned *Roe v. Wade*, the federal ruling that established a constitutional right to abortion in the United States since 1973.

ONE

North America

Kelly Campbell

In this chapter, sexuality in the countries of Canada and the United States is addressed. Mexico, which is a part of North America, will be covered in chapter 2 because it is culturally more similar to Latin and Caribbean countries than to Canada and the United States. The latter are more multicultural, meaning that many cultural groups reside there. Mexico's population consists of predominantly Indigenous and European descendants, as well as people who are a combination of the two. Canada and the United States contain Indigenous inhabitants and also include significant numbers of people from countries across the world (Marger 2015). Each year, approximately one million immigrants arrive into North America from other countries. In terms of geographic positioning, North America is located in the Northern and Western Hemispheres, with the Arctic Ocean along its northern border, the Atlantic on the east, the Pacific along the west, and the Gulf of Mexico and Caribbean Sea in the southeast.

Given that Canada and the United States are made up of people from many countries, a person's culture of origin must be considered in conjunction with dominant, mainstream norms when discussing sexuality. However, the numerous cultural groups residing in these countries prohibit the ability to describe each subculture in this chapter. Therefore, the focus will be on North American trends and averages, with notable ethnic/racial differences highlighted. Many of the sexual beliefs and practices in Canada and the United States are similar, but when they are different, those distinctions are highlighted as well. Most research on sexuality has been conducted with heterosexual, cisgender samples, so the information presented mostly pertains to those two groups. More research is needed to examine experiences among sexual- and gender-minority individuals. Until that time, it cannot be presumed that their experiences are similar *or* dissimilar to those of the dominant groups.

BRIEF HISTORY OF WOMEN'S SEXUALITY IN NORTH AMERICA

North American mainstream views have been principally shaped by northwestern European settlers who immigrated to the region in the 1500s. Upon their arrival, they encountered Native people who had been inhabiting the land for thousands of years (Takaki 2008). The Native people were and still are a diverse group of people, with over 500 tribes in the North American region alone. The settlers violently subordinated the Native people, causing the genocide of millions (Leiker, Warren, and Watkins 2007). Many of the Indigenous inhabitants who did not die from the violence succumbed to diseases that were brought by the settlers, such as smallpox, influenza, and measles, for which they did not have immunity. Women were considered especially threatening to the European power structure because they could reproduce and therefore repopulate the continent. Also, the societies of Native people were much more egalitarian than those of the Europeans, and the settlers wanted to maintain patriarchal control. They did not want European women to adopt or align with Native customs and challenge the power of men. As such, purposeful efforts were made to sexually torture and kill the Native women (Smith 2003).

The sexuality of Native Americans contrasted sharply with the beliefs and practices of northwestern Europeans, adding to their perceived threat. Given the abundance of Native tribes, wide variation existed and continues to exist in their cultural norms. Several tribes, including the Navajo and Chickasaw, are matrilineal, meaning that women hold more power and have greater sexual freedoms than men (Kimmel 2017). Among the Cherokee and Sioux tribes, women who married other women were historically considered warriors. These women were elevated to a higher status than other tribal members, and they occupied various leadership roles. Among tribes in the southern United States, unmarried women were held in especially high regard and expected to engage in a wide variety of sexual behaviors as they transitioned from girl to woman (Donohoe 2012). A common practice among Cherokee and Chocktaw wives was to switch husbands, as sex was considered primarily for the benefit of women, not men.

In addition to matrilineal societies, Native Americans also differed from the European settlers in terms of their gender conceptualizations. Several tribes historically recognized more than two genders. The Navajo have three: feminine women, masculine men, and *nadle*, which refers to people who espouse both traditionally feminine and masculine attributes (Kimmel 2017). The Mojave tribe has recognized four genders, and depending on their societal roles, people could switch genders through initiation ceremonies. A common phenomenon across various midwestern tribes is the two-spirit person. These individuals are biologically one sex but live in alignment with the other sex in the terms of their behaviors. Two-spirit people are more often men than women and are described as espousing a third gender, similar to the transgendered identity. These individuals are held in high regard and control valued tribal resources. They are considered fair and impartial, largely because they do not seek sexual gratification from women and can therefore lead objectively (Kimmel 2017). The gender fluidity afforded in Native tribes traditionally enabled people to live according to their preferences and skill sets rather than rigid, prescribed gender role norms. However, the European Christian belief system disrupted many Native customs and shifted their egalitarian, female-empowered societies toward a more male-dominant structure.

The goal of European conquest was to minimize or eradicate the Indigenous population because it was considered a threat to "civilized" life. During this time, the settlers forced their Christian religion, English language, values, education, work ethic, laws, and political systems on Native people (Takaki 2008). Ever since this period, northwestern European cultural norms have dominated mainstream society in North America and defined what most people consider to be "the standard" way of life (Marger 2015). The Native population never fully recovered from the oppression it experienced. To this day, Natives Americans' health and well-being are among the most compromised of all ethnic/racial groups in North America (Dressler, Oths, and Gravlee 2005). Together with African Americans, they have the highest infant mortality rates, the lowest life expectancy rates, the highest suicide rates, and the highest rates of sexual violence, including rape. To make sense of these trends, it is essential to understand the history, because present-day outcomes have been directly impacted by the past.

Another historical factor that greatly impacted North American culture was the transatlantic slave trade, which began in the mid-1600s. During this era, African people were forcibly transported to colonial America and other parts of the world for unpaid labor (Takaki 2008). From 1661 to

1808, approximately 500,000 Africans of the 12.5 million who were transported worldwide were brought to North America. In order to rationalize
this oppressive system, the power holders (e.g., white male politicians and
slave owners) promoted views of white people as good, rational, orderly,
and capable of exerting self-control. This perspective was contrasted with
nonwhite groups, who were characterized as bad, irrational (overly emotional), chaotic, violent, and childlike or incapable of self-control (Kincheloe 1999; Takaki 2008). These views were incorrect, unfounded, racist,
and oppressive. The discriminatory dichotomy informed women's sexualities and was used to portray white women as disciplined, virginal, and
pure, and all nonwhite women as wild, sensual, and promiscuous. These
stereotypes have persisted through to the present day.

In the United States, women were exploited not only for their labor but
for reproduction as well. Beginning in 1808, an international order was
enacted prohibiting the slave trade, which forced the existing slave women
to perpetuate the system by bearing children (Takaki 2008). In a letter,
Thomas Jefferson, the third president of the United States wrote, "A breeding woman had lost 5 children in 4 years because her slave master made
her work rather than care for her children. . . . She must be allowed to
watch over children because the labor of a breeding woman is no object; if
she can birth a child every 2 years, this profit will be greater than the crop
of the best laboring man" (Takaki 2008, chapter 3). This practice continued until 1865, when slavery was officially abolished. In addition to being
used for reproduction, the presence of a large biracial population in the
southern United States provided evidence for the sexual abuse endured by
slave women who were raped by slave owners. Although a less common
occurrence, white women engaged in sexual relations with Black male
slaves too. In such cases, if a pregnancy resulted or if the sexual activities
were uncovered, the women would claim rape, and the resulting children
risked death (Foster 2011; Leiker, Warren, and Watkins 2007).

The U.S. Civil War (1861–1865) resulted in the abolishment of slavery,
but oppression, discrimination, and prejudice toward nonwhite men and
women continued. Many African Americans began fleeing from the southern region to cities such as Chicago, Cleveland, Detroit, and New York in
order to escape extreme forms of discrimination, including lynching
(Takaki 2008). By 1930, two million African Americans had migrated to
northern cities. The Jim Crow period, which lasted from the end of the
Civil War to 1968, included laws enacted by local and state governments
to deny African Americans education, employment, housing, and the right
to vote. The laws enforced racial segregation and prohibited interracial

marriage. The civil rights movement of the 1950s and '60s had a goal of ending this discriminatory system. In the mid-1960s, several laws, such as the Civil Rights Act of 1964, were implemented at the federal level to make discrimination based on race and other demographic characteristics illegal (Marger 2015).

During the civil rights era, which was primarily focused on race, women were struggling for gender-based equality. Although women participated in the civil rights movement by leading events and organizations, they faced abundant gender discrimination and sexual harassment, and their efforts were overshadowed by men (Rathus, Nevid, and Fichner-Rathus 2018). It is perhaps not surprising that a revolution for women's rights followed the civil rights period. From the mid-1960s to the mid-1970s, the sexual revolution occurred. This movement resulted in widespread social change regarding sex, politics, the arts (e.g., music, cinema, fashion), and the sciences.

A key factor influencing women's sexuality during the sexual revolution was the advent of the birth control pill (Goldin and Katz 2002). Prior to this time period, most people waited for marriage before having sex, or they quickly married if a pregnancy resulted from premarital sex. Women had significant worries about pregnancy because they were reliant on men for financial support. Only one-third of women were working in the paid sector, and even those who were working would require time off to care for a child in the event of pregnancy. The widespread availability of birth control enabled women to delay childbearing in order to pursue educational and career goals. As such, they progressively moved toward equality with men regarding their sexual rights, careers, and social power. Drawing comparisons between the 1960s and today highlights the impact of birth control on women's lives. In 1960, 5% of babies were conceived out of wedlock, whereas today, 30% to 40% of births are to unwed mothers (Miller 2018). In 1960, 75% of mothers with preschool-age children stayed home to care for their children, whereas now approximately 30% stay home. Although gains have been made, women still earn less money than men in every U.S. employment sector, which underscores the need for continued progress in this domain.

CULTURE AND ATTITUDES TOWARD SEXUALITY

As noted, the sexual revolution of the 1960s and '70s was associated with fundamental change regarding norms and practices relating to sex and sexuality (Rathus, Nevid, and Fichner-Rathus 2018). The liberal views

The advent of the birth control pill greatly impacted women's sexual freedom and power. (Marion S. Trikosko, photographer. Library of Congress, Prints & Photographs Division, *U.S. News & World Report* Magazine Collection, LC-U9-19168-23A)

of the era enabled research to be conducted with less social resistance than had been encountered in the past. The first wide-scale studies on sexual behavior were conducted by Alfred Kinsey in the 1940s and '50s. Kinsey interviewed over 10,000 people about their sexual activities, and his findings were published in two books known as the "Kinsey Reports": *Sexual Behavior in the Human Male* (Kinsey, Pomeroy, and Martin 1948) and *Sexual Behavior in the Human Female* (Kinsey et al. 1953). Up until the release of these books, sex was rarely discussed in the public sphere. Kinsey's work sparked abundant discussion, even though some media outlets refused to report the findings, and attempts were made at censorship. His research advanced the perspective that women were sexual beings, which posed a threat to patriarchy and to conceptualizations of women as nonsexual. Despite efforts to suppress his message, both books were best sellers.

Masters and Johnson (1966) continued this line of work and empirically investigated sexual behaviors on a grand scale. They observed subjects of all sexual orientations having sex and conducted extensive interviews with them. They concluded that communication is a key factor for satisfying sex and that same-sex couples tend to have better communication than heterosexual couples and, by extension, better sex. Masters and Johnson were the first researchers to identify the stages involved in sexual response and to find that some women were multiorgasmic. Like Kinsey, their research challenged prior notions about sexuality and was criticized; however, the era in which they conducted their work was more accepting of sexuality studies and so they did not experience as much resistance as Kinsey. Ultimately, the products of these three U.S. researchers laid the foundation for the scientific field of human sexuality (DeLamater and Plante, 2015).

Although norms and attitudes regarding sexuality have become more liberal over time, North American views are still more conservative than those of other parts of the world, particularly in the United States. One large research study found that Americans' beliefs on topics such as unmarried sex were more conservative than in Canada, the United Kingdom, Germany, Israel, and Spain (Widmer, Treas, and Newcomb 1998). Within the United States, there are differences across subgroups. Asian and Latin individuals hold more conservative views than whites/Europeans and African Americans, and those with the most liberal attitudes tend to be younger, Democrat, and nonreligious (Pew Research 2017). Sociosexual orientation refers to the degree to which a person is comfortable having uncommitted sexual relations (Simpson and Gangestad 1991). People with an unrestricted sociosexual orientation feel that sex without commitment is acceptable, whereas those with a restricted orientation require commitment before sex. People with unrestricted orientations have more sex partners across their lifetime and prefer more sexual variety. In terms of gender differences, women are more likely to have a restricted sociosexual orientation, whereas men are more likely to have an unrestricted orientation (Simpson and Gangestad 1991).

One reason women espouse more restricted sociosexual orientations than men is that in North America, the sexes are socialized differently (Kimmel 2017). Boys and men are encouraged to express a significant interest in sex and regularly pursue sexual opportunities, whereas girls and women are often shamed for exhibiting these same sexual tendencies. This differential socialization leads to a variety of gendered outcomes regarding sex. In general, compared to women, men think about sex more, are more motivated and interested in sex, initiate sex more often, are more likely to pursue casual sex opportunities, desire a greater number of sex partners, and desire a greater variety of sexual behaviors with their lovers (Laumann 1994). Although men and women both engage in hookups, or casual sexual encounters, women are more likely than men to regret them (Galperin et al. 2013). It is worth noting that gains in women's societal power are associated with a reduction in these gendered differences, and the more women learn about their sexuality, the fewer differences are observed (Kimmel 2017).

Culture and attitudes toward homosexuality are becoming more accepting, and yet individuals with a nonheterosexual orientation still face abundant discrimination, including violence and murder. Approximately 3% to 5% of the North American population identifies as nonheterosexual (Gates 2017; Statistics Canada 2015). Over the years, these individuals have been denied the rights to marry, parent, and inherit property (Badgett and Frank 2007). This discrimination has been unwarranted, because empirical evidence demonstrates that same-sex relationships differ very little from heterosexual unions in terms of conflict, satisfaction, love, and general relationship functioning (Miller 2018). Further, the children of same-sex parents do not experience outcomes that differ from those of heterosexual couples in terms of health, emotional well-being, behavior problems, self-esteem, and academic achievement (Bos et al. 2016; Bos, van Gelderen, and Gartrell 2014; Goldberg and Smith 2013). Marriage between same-sex individuals was federally sanctioned in the United States in 2015, bringing it into alignment with approximately 25 other nations that permit gay marriage, including Canada (legalized in 2005), Australia, Brazil, Taiwan, and many European countries (Pew Research 2019).

RELIGION AND SEXUALITY

Christian religious influences have greatly impacted women's roles and sexualities in North America. Although both Canada and the United States promote freedom of religion (i.e., the right to practice any religion or no religion), the European settlers originally imposed Christianity on the population, and those values continue to shape mainstream views (Marger 2015). The Hebrew and Christian Bibles prescribe that sex only occur in the context of marriage, and that extramarital sex, same-sex sexual contact, and sex during menstruation are prohibited (Lewis 1980; Rathus, Nevid, and Fichner-Rathus 2018). Although not explicitly described in scripture,

In 2015, the United States federally sanctioned marriage between two people of the same sex. (Eric Limon/Shutterstock)

the church warned people about the seven deadly sins that could lead to additional sins. The "deadly sins" include lust, wrath, envy, sloth (i.e., laziness), pride, gluttony, and greed. Nearly two-thirds of the population in North America identifies with a Judeo-Christian orientation, and yet incongruencies exist regarding people's beliefs and practices (Campbell and Wright 2010). For instance, while many people may say they believe sex should only occur between married partners or that infidelity is unacceptable, more than 90% of North Americans engage in sex before they marry, and up to 30% engage in extramarital sex at some point in marriage. These disparities can be explained by views becoming more relaxed over time, younger generations being less religious than older generations, and people having different—including more liberal—interpretations of religious doctrines (Miller 2018; Rathus, Nevid, and Fichner-Rathus 2018).

Religious teachings have been used to control women. In general, Christian denominations are patriarchal and prescribe more restrictive sexual standards for women than for men (Masci 2014). Several biblical passages, such as those in Corinthians, Ephesians, Peter, and Timothy, mandate that women be submissive to and obey their husbands. Additionally, women not allowed to hold positions of power within the Roman Catholic, Southern Baptist, Mormon, Orthodox, and Jewish Orthodox traditions. In terms of religious prescriptions about sex, the general view is that sex be used only for procreation, not for pleasure (Jung, Hunt, and Balakrishnan 2005). Women with a strong religious commitment tend to experience more guilt, shame, and anxiety related to sex compared to those who are less religious (Abbott, Harris, and Mollen 2016). Because scripture dictates that women be quiet and submissive, some men use religion as justification for having sex with their wives without the wives' consent (Jung, Hunt, and Balakrishnan 2005). Given that religious traditions want to expand their reach, childbearing is encouraged. As stated in Genesis, God instructed man and woman to "be fruitful and multiply." Some fundamentalist Mormon sects not only advocate for abundant childbearing but also practice polygamy (i.e., multiple wives). Although this practice is illegal in North America, a recent bill in Utah, where many Mormons live, could reduce its penalty from a felony to infraction and thereby encourage its continuation (Kelly 2020).

SEXUAL VIOLENCE

The United States has the highest rates of reported rape of all industrialized countries, with approximately 20% of women and 2% of men affected (Breiding et al. 2014). Rape is typically enacted for power and control rather than for sexual gratification (Kimmel 2017). For example, studies have shown that men are more likely to engage in physical or sexual violence when they are unemployed or have experienced a personal loss compared to other times. Most sexual assaults occur between romantic partners, including spouses, rather than between strangers or acquaintances. Also, ethnic minority women are disproportionately affected by sexual assaults, including rape, compared to European/white women. Approximately 25% of women will experience sexual violence in their lifetime, but this figure jumps to 60% for Black women, and rates are even higher for American Indian women. Other forms of unwanted sexual contact, such as being inappropriately grabbed or forced to engage in sexual activities, affect approximately 75% of women and 25% of men in the United States (Breiding et al. 2014; Miller 2018). Canada has fewer instances of reported sexual offenses, with approximately one-third of women identifying as targets (Statistics Canada 2017). Some hypotheses for the lower rates in Canada include cultural values that promote less violence overall, more sex education programming, and an underreporting of assaults. Although sexual assaults in both Canada and the United States are underreported, it is estimated that only 5% of sexual violence instances are reported to the police in Canada, whereas up to 25% to 35% may be reported in the United States (National Institute of Justice 2010).

The outcomes of sexual violence are devastating and vary by gender. Men tend to use much more physical force than women, are more likely cause injuries, and are more likely to engage in severe forms of violence such as rape (Kimmel 2017). Women are just as likely as men to verbally coerce a partner into having sex, even when a partner is unwilling, and to use verbal abuse (e.g., insults, belittling) in their efforts to do so (Miller 2018). Sexual assaults adversely impact the mental and physical health of those affected. Responses can include depression, anxiety, sleep disruptions, reduced self-esteem, substance abuse, and suicide. The victims may also acquire sexually transmitted infections (STIs) and diseases (STDs) and incur unwanted pregnancy. When the perpetrator is an intimate partner rather than an acquaintance or stranger, the effects on health and well-being are amplified, especially because the assault is likely to occur repeatedly. Unfortunately, many sexual assaults go unprosecuted, because both women and men are worried, fearful, or embarrassed about pursuing charges, particularly when the perpetrator is an intimate partner (National Institute of Justice 2010). One type of sexual violence that is particularly underreported involves the assault of women by police officers during routine stops or arrests. Although such incidents are rarely documented, the little available research suggests that officer sexual misconduct toward women is somewhat widespread (Stinson et al. 2016).

REPRODUCTIVE HEALTH AND MENSTRUATION

In North America, the average age of menarche is approximately 12.5 years (Al-Sahab et al. 2010; Sarpolis 2011). Ethnic/racial groups vary in the onset of menstruation, with African/Black Americans at the younger end, Hispanic/Latin girls in the middle, and European/white girls at the older end of the continuum. The mean ages for these groups differ across studies, but in general, there is about one-year difference between African Americans and European Americans. These ethnic-racial differences in menarche may also apply to menopause, with some research indicating that African and Latin American experience the onset of menopause

The term "period poverty" refers to menstrual inequalities that disadvantage low-income groups, including students, incarcerated women, transgender persons, and homeless individuals. For these girls and women, sanitary products are often not affordable and as a result, they experience poor hygiene, feelings of shame, and restricted freedom during their monthly cycle. In one study, U.S. girls and women reported relying on rags, toilet paper, and paper towels taken from public restrooms to cope (Kuhlmann et al. 2019). Sanitary products are not covered by government programs and, in many states, carry a high sales tax. The recent awareness regarding period poverty has led to the proposed 2021 Menstrual Equity for All Act, which if passed would provide enhanced access to menstrual products for low-income groups.

slightly earlier than white women and with more severe symptoms. Across all groups, the average age for the onset of menopause is 50 to 52 years. Over time, the age of menarche has declined. In 1890, it was approximately 15 years, and by 1920, it was 13 years (Flaws et al. 2000). Reasons for the decline are unclear, but changes in nutrition, weight, and stress are likely contributors. Coontz (1997) notes that the earlier physical maturation of girls and boys today coincides with a unique historical trend whereby children are financially dependent on parents for longer than ever before. Their early maturation combined with the inability to be financially independent causes intense conflict between parents and teens. Teens feel physically ready to engage in adult behaviors, including sexual activity, while parents struggle to maintain authority, prevent early pregnancy, and keep their children safe.

Sexual behavior is an important component of sexual and reproductive health. Factors such as early sexual debut, unprotected sex, and multiple sex partners put people at risk for unplanned pregnancy, and STIs/STDs, including HIV/AIDS. The average age of first sexual intercourse (sexual debut) for boys and girls in the United States is approximately 17 years, whereas in Canada it is closer to 16 years (Hansen et al. 2004; Miller 2018). African American boys tend to have the earliest sexual debut, and Asian boys and girls have the latest. A majority of people (65% to 75%) use condoms the first time they have sex; however, approximately 35% of high school students do not regularly use any contraception, and the highest rates of STIs and STDs occur among 15- to 24-year-olds. Compared to other industrialized nations, the United States has among the highest teen rates of STIs. Although most young adults have had only one or two sex partners, approximately 15% of female high school students have had multiple sexual partners (i.e., four or more), and approximately one-third of high schoolers have had more than one partner in the past year (Eaton et al. 2008). Approximately 25% of HIV positive cases in Canada and the United States are women, and their main method of contraction is through heterosexual sexual intercourse. One of the most effective ways to protect against STIs and STDs is sex education.

Sex education programming varies widely across North America, and even within each country, variation exists. In Canada, every province teaches about sex, and the curricula covers a wide array of topics. In the United States, only 38 states have sex education laws, and of those, only 8 provide comprehensive programming. Curricula that cover an abundance of topics are most effective in helping youth make informed decisions that keep them safe and healthy (Cloninger and Pagliaro, 2002). Abstinence-based programming, which is implemented in 30 U.S. states, is known to be ineffective at protecting youth from unplanned pregnancies and STIs/STDs (e.g., Brewster et al. 1998). In fact, the United States has the highest teen pregnancy rate in the world. When abstinence is the only advocated method of birth control, youth do not prepare for sex by purchasing or acquiring contraception, and they experience unintended consequences as a result.

Half of all pregnancies in North America are unplanned, and approximately 40% end in abortion (Bonham 2013). In 1973, the case of *Roe v. Wade* led the U.S. Supreme Court to recognize abortion as a constitutional right. In 2022, they overturned this ruling, enabling individual states to establish the illegality of abortion. This was an unprecedented setback for women's rights because in at least 20 states, women lost the freedom to make decisions about their own bodies and in several states (e.g., Arkansas, Oklahoma, Texas), laws were triggered to prevent abortion even in cases of incest or rape (Guttmacher Institute 2022). Prior to the Supreme Court's ruling, approximately one-third of states disallowed abortions after 20 weeks, and in many places, although the law technically allowed for abortion, hurdles were created to prevent them. For example, in Alabama, doctors who performed abortions could be criminally penalized. Also, very few abortion clinics exist in many states, making the procedure unavailable to most people unless they can travel to a state that allows and performs abortion such as California. Those with low incomes are among the most heavily impacted by these hurdles and the new ruling because they lack the resources for travel. Unlike the

United States, Canada has consistently protected a woman's right to choose abortion through the Canada Health Act of 1984 and appears not to be wavering in this decision.

MARRIAGE AND PARTNERSHIPS

In North America, there are generally two types of love that provide the foundation for marriage: passionate and companionate (Miller 2018). Passionate love is characterized by intense attraction and frequent and sexual contact. People in this phase may experience sleeplessness, a heightened immune system, and obsessive thinking about their lover (Xu et al. 2012). Passion is tied to the chemical production of phenylethylamine, and the feeling in this stage is similar to being on drugs containing amphetamines. Passionate love can therefore be addictive. People in this phase of love tend to engage in cognitive distortions that involve minimizing or overlooking their partner's faults and exaggerating their positive attributes. For this reason, family and friends tend to be better than the person in love at predicting whether a relationship will last, because they see things more objectively (MacDonald and Ross 1999). Passion tends to decline over a two-year span because it is maladaptive to maintain for the long term. Although passion can be periodically ignited in long-term partnerships, only about 5% of couples sustain levels that parallel those found in new relationships; nonetheless, approximately one-third of people are able to sustain at least a moderate level of passion over the course of their relationship (Xu et al. 2012). It would be wise to avoid marrying a partner while in this stage of love because not all couples successfully transition from passionate to companionate love.

Companionate love is more stable and predictable than passionate love (Fehr 2015). It is characterized by moderate emotional intensity, deep intimacy, a strong friendship, and more routine sexual interactions than passionate love. Individuals in this type of love experience satisfying, long-term partnerships. The risk is that these relationships can become predictable and partners may become bored if they do not regularly engage in novel behaviors (Campbell and Kaufman 2015; Frederick et al. 2017). People are happiest when their relationships contain a mix of stability and excitement. As such, therapists recommend that those in companionate unions take part in new and exciting activities together, which stimulates passion and helps ensure the partners remain satisfied.

Gender differences exist regarding love in North America. Men tend to fall in love faster than women and report more passion early in their relationships (Miller 2018). This is because being in love causes serotonin levels to drop, which destabilizes mood, and men experience a greater drop than women do (Fisher 2006). Men also tend to hold more romantic attitudes than women, believing more often in love at first sight and that love conquers all (Miller 2018). Women are more cautious in love, more selective about whom they love, and they experience feelings of passion more slowly. In short, they tend to be more rational about love. Women are more likely to initiate breakups, but men report falling out of love faster than women do (Kimmel 2017).

As is common in most parts of the world, North Americans have elaborate customs and traditions related to marriage. Women have historically held bridal showers prior to their wedding day, whereas men have held bachelor parties (Campbell 2014b). Although these rituals are still practiced today, they are increasingly coed functions, and some couples elect not to have them at all. The original purpose of the shower was to socialize the bride into her upcoming status as wife, allow her network to demonstrate approval of her nuptials, and provide her with homemaking and sexual gifts (Montemurro 2006). Typical gifts have included small kitchen appliances, dishes, linens, and lingerie. Even though most women now work outside the home, and many remain childless, shower gifts still tend to focus on homemaking. Shower attendees also commonly play games that reinforce traditional gender roles such as counting the number of times the bride rips her gift wrap, which is thought to symbolize the number of children she will bear.

The counterpart to a bridal shower has historically been the bachelor party. Unlike the shower, which celebrates the upcoming marriage and role of the bride as a wife, the bachelor party celebrates the groom's single life and impending loss of sexual freedom (Campbell 2014b). These parties have included exotic dancers or visits to gentlemen's clubs and out-of-town vacations to locations such Las Vegas, as depicted in the movie *The Hangover*. More recently, men have been diversifying the manner in which they celebrate their upcoming nuptials. Many attend sporting events or go golfing, camping, or out for dinner with friends. As women have gained social power and sexual freedom, they too have been enacting bachelorette parties in addition to their showers (Montemurro 2006).

Although the power dynamics for men and women in North America are changing, men are still socialized to believe that marriage is less desirable than being single, whereas women are socialized to pursue marriage as a life goal. This differential socialization is misguided, however, because research demonstrates that married men are happier and experience greater benefits from marriage than women do (Kimmel 2017; Miller 2018). Married men also live longer, are more likely to be employed, earn more money, use fewer drugs, and engage in fewer criminal activities than their unmarried counterparts. One reason for these gendered outcomes is that while men receive emotional, social, and sexual benefits from their romantic relationships, women obtain much of their nonsexual support from friends and family members (Kimmel 2017). Also, given that the North American economy is now dual-earner based, both partners generally work outside the home, yet women enact a majority of the housework. Prior to marriage, men prepare their own meals and clean their own homes. After marriage, men's housework is reduced by one-third, whereas women's domestic work increases by 15% to 20%. It is important to highlight that the number of hours men devote to family and domestic responsibilities is on the rise. Approximately one-fifth of men share 50% of the housework, and they tend to be the happiest in their marriages (Kimmel 2017; Miller 2018). Couples who are involved in equitable partnerships are much more satisfied than those who adhere to traditional gender role norms. Further, one of the strongest predictors of happiness for women is the extent to which their partners assist with domestic duties.

Most people believe that sex is an important component of a satisfying romantic relationship. Satisfying sex is good for health and well-being in that it reduces stress, improves mood, and protects from disease (Jakubiak and Feeney 2017). The boost in mood results from the release of oxytocin and vasopressin that can last for several days after a sexual experience. Individuals' overall relationship satisfaction is strongly predicted by their degree of sexual satisfaction, especially for men. In general, sexual satisfaction is tied to frequency, with more sex leading to greater satisfaction, up to a certain point. People who have infrequent or no sex are particularly dissatisfied, but sexual satisfaction does not continuously improve for couples having sex more than once a week. Again, the link between sex frequency and satisfaction is especially strong for men. It is important to note that partners who are more satisfied overall typically desire more sex, and so the association between frequency and satisfaction is bidirectional.

People who are unable to experience sex in their relationships despite wanting to do so are termed involuntarily celibate and, not surprisingly, this group of people are especially dissatisfied (Donnelly and Burgess 2008).

Sexual frequency varies depending on the relationship type. On average, cohabiting partners have sex three times per week, married couples have sex once per week, and single individuals have less sex than these two groups (Willetts, Sprecher, and Beck 2004). An examination of the amount of sex people are having now compared to 25 years ago shows that rates are declining (Twenge 2017). Reasons for declines include increased work demands that provide less time and energy for sex, unfair division of household chores that adversely impacts sexual desire, particularly for women, and more widespread use of pornography, particularly among men, that leads to negative perceptions of and unrealistic expectations for partners. Although men view pornography more than women, and their viewing habits tend to negatively impact the relationship, the use of pornography by women is associated with greater sexual satisfaction (Poulsen, Busby, and Galovan 2013). When partners view pornography together, they also tend to experience enhanced sexual satisfaction.

In terms of age, younger couples tend to have more sex than older couples, which is due in part to declining feelings of passion as people get older as well as physical changes such as decreased lubrication for women and decreased circulation for men (DeLamater 2012). Although sexual frequency is at its height during the first year of a relationship, with notable declines in the second year and then a leveling off after year two, people continue to have sex into old age. Data from the National Poll on Healthy Aging indicates that three-quarters of older North Americans are sexually satisfied and that older men more than women believe sex to be an important component of a romantic relationship and an important contributor to quality of life (National Poll on Healthy Aging 2018).

Gay men engage in more sex than individuals of other orientations; however, it is important to contextualize this information. Given that sex drive is predicted by testosterone, particularly for men, two men are likely to desire more sex than other matches containing at least one woman (Miller 2018). Heterosexual partners experience moderate levels of sexual frequency, and lesbian couples are on the lower end. Again, these differences are influenced by the varying levels of testosterone within each relationship type. Also, lesbian women are more likely than other people to define nonorgasmic behavior, including cuddling and kissing as sexual.

Such behaviors are not typically included in researchers' definitions of sex, which may result in low estimates of sexual frequency for lesbian couples.

Sexual fluidity refers to a person's degree of flexibility with respect to sexual desires (Diamond 2016). There are individual differences regarding fluidity; some people are highly fluid whereas others are not. Although fluidity does not change a person's sexual orientation, it provides an added layer of complexity. Both sexes experience fluidity, but women are prone to greater fluidity than men. Diamond notes that "many women report a markedly late, unexpected, and abrupt onset of same-sex sexuality as well as fluctuations over time in their attractions, behaviors, and identities" (2016, 1). It is worth noting that attraction between two women is more culturally accepted in North America than intimacy between two men, which likely contributes to women's higher rates of fluidity as well as their willingness to admit to same-sex attraction on social surveys. Women also experience greater sexual arousal than men when presented with stimuli relating to their nondominant gender preference. That is, heterosexual and lesbian women experience blood flow to their genitalia when presented with male or female sexual stimuli, whereas most men only experience this type of physiological response when presented with stimuli that matches their gender preference (Diamond 2016).

Other factors, beyond frequency, predict sexual satisfaction. The most sexually satisfied tend to be in committed relationships with only one sex partner. A major reason why the most satisfying sex is experienced in the context of committed partnerships is because trust and communication are higher than among uncommitted partners (Masters and Johnson 1966; Schoenfeld et al. 2017). Egalitarian relationships, in which the power is shared between partners, also have greater sexual satisfaction (as well as higher relationship satisfaction overall), compared to partnerships with traditional gender role norms (Sanchez, Fetterolf, and Rudman 2012). Sex is less satisfying in relationships with traditional norms because women are expected to be submissive, leading to less communication and less satisfying sex. In general, same-sex couples are more likely than heterosexual couples to have egalitarian relationships.

People who experience frequent orgasm through their sexual experiences tend to be more satisfied than those who infrequently experience orgasm. And men's, but not women's, satisfaction is tied to the number of times a partner reaches orgasm (Frederick et al. 2017). One reason for why this association may not be as strong among women is because men's rates of orgasm (75%) are much higher than women's rates (25%). Men also take less time to reach orgasm, with an average of four minutes compared to 10 or more minutes for women (Laumann 1994). Sexual variety predicts satisfaction, with both women and men reporting greater satisfaction when they incorporate a variety of behaviors, such as massage, sex toys, and new sexual positions, into their sex lives. Finally, the more time spent engaging in sexual activities as well as the amount of time cuddling afterward are both predictive of sexual satisfaction across the sexes.

Consensual nonmonogamy refers to relationships in which partners agree about engaging in sexual and/or emotional intimacy with people outside of their primary relationship (Bradbury and Karney 2019). These relationships require open and honest communication as well as healthy boundary setting to function optimally. Various agreements can be negotiated between partners, such as open relationships in which each person is able to pursue sexual activities with other partners; swinging, in which committed couples engage in sexual activities with other couples; and polyamory, which is literally defined as many (poly) loves (amory). This latter relationship type refers to engaging in multiple romantic relationships with the consent of all involved persons. Consensual nonmonogamy is associated with positive outcomes such as enhanced relationship, sexual, and life satisfaction (Campbell 2014a). Although jealousy may occur, partners are more likely than those in monogamous relationships to openly discuss and manage these emotions. Most women who engage in nonmonogamous relationships are bisexual, whereas most men are heterosexual. Estimates indicate that approximately 20% of people have participated in a consensually nonmonogamous relationship at some point (Bradbury and Karney 2019).

Infidelity refers to extradyadic sex without the consent of the primary partner (Campbell, Wright, and Flores 2015). The outcomes of infidelity are different than consensual nonmonogamy because infidelity involves partner betrayal, which breaks trust and can lead to hurt feelings, depression, violence, and reduced self-esteem. Infidelity is hard to define because, although most researchers agree that sexual intercourse is included, some also believe that emotional bonds with another person qualify. To resolve this concern, researchers sometimes ask participants about "affairs" or use umbrella terms that allow for subjective interpretations (Campbell and Wright 2010). An added problem with studying infidelity is that participants may respond to questions based on how they think the researchers want them to respond—a concept known as socially desirable response bias—rather than providing an accurate assessment, which leads to an underreporting of such behaviors.

Despite the aforementioned concerns, the most reliable estimates suggest that about 20% to 25% of married women and 30% of married men have been unfaithful at least one time in their relationship (Laumann 1994; Tafoya and Spitzberg 2007). As these percentages indicate, gender is among the predictors of infidelity, with men being more likely than women to engage in it, and of those who have had affairs, men are more likely to have had a greater number of sexual partners. Women, however, are more likely to switch partners as a result of having an affair (Buss et al. 2017). The sex ratio in a given population is predictive of infidelity. When there are more men than women in a society, the sex ratio is considered high. High sex ratio cultures tend to espouse conservative or traditional gender role norms. For example, they promote virgin brides, encourage women to stay home and raise children, and discourage divorce. When the sex ratio is low and there are more women than men in a population, such as in North America today, unmarried sex is promoted, women are encouraged to work outside the home, unmarried motherhood is common, and divorce rates are higher (Miller 2018). These sex ratio fluctuations are hypothesized to exist because men, who have historically held economic and political power, encourage an agenda suited to their interests: when a society has an abundance of women, men prefer sexual promiscuity, but when women are in short supply, they want to secure a partnership.

MEDIA AND SEXUALITY

Media is an incredibly powerful conveyer of gender and sexual expectations. Nearly 100% of homes have a television, approximately 90% have a computer, and many people spend almost their entire waking hours interacting with some form of media (Lauricella, Wartella, and Rideout 2015). One large-scale study of the 30 most popular U.S. television programs found that approximately 20% contained sexual content, 25% contained humor about sexual organs, and only a fraction included content relating to contraception or the consequences of sex, including STDs and STIs (Rathus, Nevid, and Fichner-Rathus 2018). Magazines, books, and music represent additional forms of media that are differentially targeted toward and consumed by men and women. Except for sports and war genres, women read more books and magazines than men do (Kimmel 2017). The most popular men's magazines, such as *Maxim* and *FHM*, feature sexually provocative photos of women and articles on how to please a woman sexually. One of the most sexually exploitive forms of media is music, with rock and rap among the top offenders. The lyrics and music videos in these genres are often misogynistic and, in the case of rap, largely portray women who are willing to exchange sex for money. Music is an especially powerful form of media because individuals' identity tends to be informed by their preferences. As such, music has the potential to influence other aspects of life, including what to wear, whom to befriend, and how to behave in romantic relationships (Kimmel 2017).

Video games represent a widely popular form of media, with approximately 50% of Canadians and 60% of Americans having played them (Entertainment Software Association 2019; Entertainment Software Association of Canada 2018). In 2018, U.S. video game revenues were over $40 billion. The most popular games pertain to military and fighting (i.e., *Call of Duty*) or sports (*Madden NFL*), and are predominantly played by men (Kimmel 2017). Women are more likely to play life skills games—such as *The Sims*—that require players to secure a job, get married, and have children. Video games generally contain characters with sex-stereotyped features such as men with exaggerated muscles and women with big breasts and tussled hair. There is a long-standing debate about whether video games cause people to become more aggressive, violent, and/or misogynistic. Research demonstrates that people who are drawn to such games tend to be more violent and misogynistic already; however, playing these games exaggerates their attributes (Kimmel 2017).

Pornography is another popular form of media that impacts sexual views and practices. In the United States, pornography revenues range from $10 billion to $15 billion per year (Kimmel 2017). This form of media is gaining popularity, with viewership increasing approximately 2,000% since the mid-1990s. Both men and women consume pornography, but men make up at least two-thirds of the market. The themes depicted in adult films largely reflect men's rather than women's fantasies, and women are portrayed as subservient. Like video gaming, porn watching has the potential to negatively impact the consumer. People, especially men, who watch this content are more likely than nonviewers to perceive women as sexual objects, misjudge women's interest in sex, hold unrealistic expectations for women regarding sex, and perceive their own sex lives as boring by comparison. The impact of porn viewing for women is mixed, with some reporting feelings of inadequacy and others indicating that they feel more comfortable with themselves after having watched porn (Ashton, McDonald, and Kirkman 2017). The adult film industry has a reputation for mistreating its predominantly female workers, and little regulation exists to protect their rights. In 2016, California's Proposition 60, which would have mandated condom use and other protections for adult film workers, was rejected by a vote of 54%; other states have yet to put such regulations on the ballot (Chappell 2016). In general, the female performers are young, inexperienced, and financially stressed. They are therefore vulnerable and unlikely to complain about poor or abusive working conditions, which can include sex without protection. A major reason for the demeaning portrayal and treatment of women across these various forms of media is that women do not hold industry power. In the key employment sectors of media, technology, politics, and finance, men grossly outnumber women. An important step toward creating change will involve having more women in positions of power within these industries.

More recently, women have been taking charge of their media representations and fighting back against oppression in this and other domains. In 2020, a California judge "ordered a pornography company [GirlsDoPorn] to pay $13 million to 22 young women, finding that they were tricked into performing in videos that threw their lives off course and led several to attempt suicide. . . . The company is also the subject of a separate criminal case in which its owners and employees face federal sex-trafficking charges" (Shammas 2020). Although many women remain at risk in the adult film industry, the settlement and media attention this case garnered will likely encourage women to come forward and take action against exploitation in the future. In the music arena, Rihanna was violently assaulted by her R&B singer boyfriend Chris Brown in 2009. The incident was widely covered by the media. Since that time, she has been fighting back against misogyny through her work. As Hobson (2015) details, "in the wake of Chris Brown's assault . . . Rihanna has refused the 'victim' image foisted on her and instead boldly engages with violent narratives to reposition herself in terms of power and survival. Her *Man Down* video, which invited controversy for its depiction of a rape survivor gunning down her assailant, is one such example."

The Me Too movement represents a recent and impactful example of women claiming power over their bodies and lives (https://metoomvmt. org). This movement was initiated by Tarana Burke on social media in 2006. Her goal was to draw attention to the countless women who had been sexually abused and harassed. The movement gained momentum in 2017 when U.S. film producer Harvey Weinstein was accused of sexually assaulting over 100 women. During the media coverage of the case, actress Alyssa Milano tweeted, "If you've been sexually harassed or assaulted

The Me Too movement was initiated in 2006 by Tarana Burke and went viral in 2017. Me Too highlighted the millions of women's experiences of sexual harassment and raised awareness that led to the firing of many high-profile men. (Andrei Gabriel Stanescu/Dreamstime.com)

write 'me too' as a reply to this tweet." Women followed suit, the hashtag of Me Too went viral, and sexual harassment came into the public domain in a way that had never occurred before. This awareness caused the firing of many high-profile men, including journalist and television host Bill O'Reilly and actor Kevin Spacey.

Although progress is being made, an article in the *New York Times* describes the magnitude of and difficulty with eradicating sexual harassment: "Sexual harassment has hardly been erased in the workplace. Federal law still does not fully protect huge groups of women, including those who work freelance or at companies with fewer than 15 employees. New workplace policies have little effect without deeper cultural change. As the Supreme Court confirmation battle over Brett Kavanaugh showed, Americans disagree on how people accused of sexual misconduct should be held accountable and what the standard of evidence should be" (Carlsen et al. 2018). Unfortunately, the Kavanaugh case demonstrated that little had changed since 1991, when Anita Hill courageously detailed the sexual harassment inflicted upon her by Clarence Thomas. In both the Kavanaugh and Thomas cases, men's accounts took precedence over women's, and the men were confirmed to serve as U.S. Supreme Court judges. Another example of men not being held culturally accountable for sexual harassment is the election of Donald J. Trump to the office of president. During his 2016 campaign, the public heard recordings of him stating, "Grab them by the pussy. You can do anything [to women]," and yet he was still elected to serve, with a majority of white women voting for him. At present, the Me Too hashtag is being used all over the world to represent not only sexual harassment but also the marginalization and oppression of women in different spheres.

CONCLUSION

This chapter has outlined how women's sexuality in North America has been shaped by northwestern European cultural and religious norms. The patriarchal system governing all aspects of life in Canada and the United States is associated with negative outcomes for women, including shame regarding their sexual expression and high rates of sexual violence. The sexual revolution that began in the 1960s and coincided with the advent of the birth control pill greatly impacted women's power in their relationships and lives. Today, more women work than ever before, and many romantic relationships are characterized by egalitarian norms. Partners in egalitarian relationships are much happier than those with traditional, gender-stereotyped norms. As they have done throughout history, women are fighting back against oppression with notable gains. The Me Too movement has been transformative in its impact on women's power and sexual rights. There is still a long way to go in achieving gender equality, particularly because conservative activists are threatening women's freedoms, but the gains being made in spite of those efforts provide optimism and hope that a more equitable society will be achieved. The following chapters outline similar themes of oppression and strength regarding women's sexuality. Around the world, women are bonded by their common struggles and desire for equality.

REFERENCES

Abbott, Dena M., Jeff E. Harris, and Debra Mollen. 2016. "The Impact of Religious Commitment on Women's Sexual Self-Esteem." *Sexuality & Culture* 20: 1063–82. https://doi.org/10.1007/s12119-016-9374-x.

Al-Sahab, Ban, Chris I. Ardern, Mazen J. Hamadeh, and Hala Tamim. 2010. "Age at Menarche in Canada: Results from the National Longitudinal Survey of Children & Youth." *BMC Public Health* 10: 1–8. https://doi.org/10.1186/1471-2458-10-736.

Ashton, Sarah, Karalyn McDonald, and Maggie Kirkman. 2018. "Women's Experiences of Pornography: A Systematic Review of Research Using Qualitative Methods." *Journal of Sex Research* 55 (3): 334–47. https://doi.org/10.1080/00224499.2017.1364337.

Badgett, Lee M. V., and Jeff Frank. 2007. *Sexual Orientation Discrimination: An International Perspective*. New York: Routledge.

Bonham, Adrienne D. 2013. "Why Are 50 Percent of Pregnancies in the U.S. Unplanned?" Accessed February 28, 2020. http://shriverreport.org/why-are-50-percent-of-pregnancies-in-the-us-unplanned-adrienne-d-bonham.

Bos, Henny, Loes van Gelderen, and Nanette Gartrell. 2014. "Lesbian and Heterosexual Two-Parent Families: Adolescent-Parent Relationship Quality and Adolescent Well-Being." *Journal of Child and Family Studies* 23 (2): 1–16.

Bos, Henny M. W., Justin R. Knox, Loes van Rijn-van Gelderen, and Nanette K. Gartrell. 2016. "Same-Sex and Different-Sex Parent Households and Child Health Outcomes: Findings from the National Survey of Children's Health." *Journal of Developmental & Behavioral Pediatrics* 37 (3): 179–87.

Bradbury, Thomas N., and Benjamin R. Karney. 2019. *Intimate Relationships*. 3rd ed. New York: W. W. Norton & Company.

Breiding, Matthew J., Sharon G. Smith, Kathleen C. Basile, Mikel L. Walters, Jieru Chen, and Melissa T. Merrick. 2014. "Prevalence and Characteristics of Sexual Violence, Stalking, and Intimate Partner Violence Victimization—National Intimate Partner and Sexual Violence Survey, United States, 2011." *Morbidity and Mortality Weekly Report: Surveillance Summaries* 63 (8): 1–18.

Brewster, Karin L., Elizabeth C. Cooksey, David K. Guilkey, and Ronald R. Rindfuss. 1998. "The Changing Impact of Religion on the Sexual and Contraceptive Behavior of Adolescent Women in the United States." *Journal of Marriage and Family* 60 (2): 493–504. https://doi.org/10.2307/353864.

Buss, David M., Cari Goetz, Joshua D. Duntley, Kelly Asao, and Daniel Conroy-Beam. 2017. "The Mate Switching Hypothesis." *Personality and Individual Differences* 104 (January): 143–49. https://doi.org /10.1016/j.paid.2016.07.022.

Campbell, Kelly. 2014a. "Swinging: Socially Deviant or Genetically Advantageous?" In *Encyclopedia of Social Deviance*, edited by Craig J. Forsyth and Heith Copes, 716–19. Thousand Oaks, CA: SAGE.

Campbell, Kelly. 2014b. "Wedding Showers." In *The Social History of the American Family*, edited by Marilyn J. Coleman and Lawrence H. Ganong, 1434–36. Thousand Oaks, CA: SAGE.

Campbell, Kelly, and James C. Kaufman. 2015. "Do You Pursue Your Heart or Your Art?: Creativity, Personality, and Love." *Journal of Family Issues* 38 (3): 1–25. https://doi.org/10.1177/0192513X15570318.

Campbell, Kelly, and David W. Wright. 2010. "Marriage Today: Exploring the Incongruence between Americans' Beliefs and Practices." *Journal of Comparative Family Studies* 41 (3): 329–45.

Campbell, Kelly, David W. Wright, and Carlos Flores. 2015. "Newlywed Women's Marital Expectations: Lifelong Monogamy?" *Journal of Divorce and Remarriage* 53 (2): 108–25.

Carlsen, Audrey, Maya Salam, Claire Cain, Denise Lu, Ash Ngu, Jugal K. Patel, and Zach Wichter. 2018. "#MeToo Brought Down 201 Powerful Men. Nearly Half of Their Replacements Are Women." Accessed February 22, 2020. https://www.nytimes.com/interactive /2018/10/23/us/metoo-replacements.html.

Chappell, Bill. 2016. "Condom Mandate for Porn Industry Falls Short in California." Accessed February 20, 2020. https://www.npr.org /sections/thetwo-way/2016/11/09/501405749/condom-mandate -for-porn-industry-falls-short-in-california.

Cloninger, Devon, and Susan Pagliaro. 2002. "Sex Education: Curricula and Programs." Accessed February 28, 2020. https://advocatesforyouth .org.

Coontz, Stephanie. 1997. *The Way We Really Are: Coming to Terms with America's Changing Families*. New York: Basic Books.

DeLamater, John. 2012. "Sexual Expression in Later Life: A Review and Synthesis." *Journal of Sex Research* 49 (2–3): 125–41. https://doi .org/10.1080/00224499.2011.603168.

DeLamater, John, and Rebecca F. Plante. 2015. *Handbook of the Sociology of Sexualities*. New York: Springer.

Diamond, Lisa M. 2016. "Sexual Fluidity." In *The SAGE Encyclopedia of LGBTQ Studies*, edited by Abbie E. Goldberg, 1053–55. Thousand Oaks, CA: SAGE Publications.

Donnelly, Denise A., and Elisabeth O. Burgess. 2008. "The Decision to Remain in an Involuntarily Celibate Relationship." *Journal of Marriage and Family* 70 (2): 519–35. https://doi.org/10.1111/j.1741-3737 .2008.00498.x.

Donohoe, Felicity. 2012. "To Beget a Tame Breed of People: Sex, Marriage, Adultery, and Indigenous North American Women." *Early American Studies: An Interdisciplinary Journal* 10 (1): 101–31. https://www.jstor.org/stable/23546683.

Dressler, William W., Kathryn S. Oths, and Clarence C. Gravlee. 2005. "Race and Ethnicity in Public Health Research Models to Explain Health Disparities." *Annual Review of Anthropology* 34 (1): 231–52.

Eaton, Danice K., Laura Kann, Steve Kinchen, Shari Shanklin, James Ross, Joseph Hawkins, William A. Harris, et al. 2008. "Youth Risk Behavior Surveillance—United States, 2007." *Morbidity & Mortality Weekly Report*, no. 57, 1–131.

Entertainment Software Association. 2019. "2019 Essential Facts about the Computer and Video Game Industry." Accessed February 28, 2020. https://www.theesa.com/esa-research/2019-essential-facts-about -the-computer-and-video-game-industry.

Entertainment Software Association of Canada. 2018. "The Canadian Video Game Industry." Accessed February 28, 2020. http://theesa .ca/wpcontent/uploads/2018/10/ESAC18_BookletEN.pdf.

Fehr, Beverley. 2015. "Love: Conceptualization and Experience." In *APA Handbook of Personality and Social Psychology*. Vol. 3, edited by Mario Mikulincer, Phillip R. Shaver, Jeffry A. Simpson, and John F. Dovidio, 495–522. Washington, DC: American Psychological Association. doi:10.1037/14344-018.

Fisher, Helen. 2006. "The Drive to Love: The Neural Mechanism for Mate Selection." In *The Psychology of Love*. 2nd ed., edited by Robert J. Sternberg and Michael L. Barnes, 87–115. New Haven, CT: Yale University Press.

Flaws, Jodi A., Fady I. Sharara, Ellen K. Silbergeld, and Anne N. Hirshfield. 2000. "Environmental Exposures and Women's Reproductive Health." In *Women and Health*, edited by Marlene B. Goldman and Maureen C. Hatch, 625–33. San Diego, CA: Academic Press.

Foster, Thomas A. 2011. "The Sexual Abuse of Black Men under American Slavery." *Journal of the History of Sexuality* 20 (3): 445–64.

Frederick, David A., Janet Lever, Brian J. Gillespie, and Justin R. Garcia. 2017. "What Keeps Passion Alive? Sexual Satisfaction Is Associated with Sexual Communication, Mood Setting, Sexual Variety, Oral Sex, Orgasm, and Sex Frequency in a National U.S. Study." *Journal of Sex Research* 54 (2): 186–202.

Galperin, Andrew, Martie Haselton, David Frederick, Joshua Poore, William Hippel, David Buss, and Gian Gonzaga. 2013. "Sexual Regret: Evidence for Evolved Sex Differences." *Archives of Sexual Behavior* 42 (7): 1145–62.

Gates, Gary J. 2017. "In U.S., More Adults Identifying as LGBT." Accessed May 30, 2019. https://news.gallup.com/poll/201731/lgbt-identification -rises.aspx.

Goldberg, Abbie E., and Julianna Z. Smith. 2013. "Predictors of Psychological Adjustment in Early Placed Adopted Children with Lesbian, Gay, and Heterosexual Parents." *Journal of Family Psychology* 27 (3): 431–43.

Goldin, Claudia and Lawrence F. Katz. 2002. "The Power of the Pill: Oral Contraceptives and Women's Career and Marriage Decisions." *Journal of Political Economy* 110 (4): 730–70.

Guttmacher Institute. 2022. "An Overview of Abortion Laws." Accessed July 11, 2022. https://www.guttmacher.org/state-policy/explore /overview-abortion-laws.

Hansen, Lisa, Janice Mann, Sharon McMahon, and Thomas Wong. 2004. "Sexual Health." *BMC Women's Health* 4 (1): S24.

Hobson, Janell. 2015. "Rhianna Unchained." Accessed July 11, 2022. https://msmagazine.com/2015/07/08/rihanna-unchained/.

Jakubiak, Brittany K., and Brooke C. Feeney. 2017. "Affectionate Touch to Promote Relational, Psychological, and Physical Well-Being in Adulthood: A Theoretical Model and Review of the Research." *Personality and Social Psychology Review* 21 (3): 228–52. https:// doi.org/10.1177/1088868316650307.

Jung, Patricia B., Mary E. Hunt, and Radhika Balakrishnan. 2005. *Good Sex: Feminist Perspectives from the World's Religions.* New Brunswick, NJ: Rutgers University Press.

Kelly, Mary Louise. 2020. "Utah Government Poised to Decriminalize Polygamy." Accessed February 29, 2020. https://www.npr.org /2020/02/27/810095467/utah-government-poised-to-decriminalize -polygamy.

Kimmel, Michael. 2017. *The Gendered Society.* New York: Oxford University Press.

Kincheloe, Joe L. 1999. "The Struggle to Define and Reinvent Whiteness: A Pedagogical Analysis." *College Literature* 26 (3): 162–94.

Kinsey, Alfred C., Wardell B. Pomeroy, and Clyde E. Martin. 1948. *Sexual Behavior in the Human Male*. Philadelphia: W. B. Saunders.

Kinsey, Alfred B., Wardell B. Pomeroy, Clyde E. Martin, and Paul H. Gebhard. 1953. *Sexual Behavior in the Human Female*. Philadelphia: W. B. Saunders.

Kuhlmann, Anne S., Eleanor Peters Bergquist, Djenie Danjoint, and Lewis L. Wall. 2019. "Unmet Menstrual Hygiene Needs among Low-Income Women." *Obstetrics & Gynecology* 133: 238–44.

Laumann, Edward O. 1994. *The Social Organization of Sexuality: Sexual Practices in the United States*. Chicago: University of Chicago Press.

Lauricella, Alexis R., Ellen Ann Wartella, and Victoria J. Rideout. 2015. "Young Children's Screen Time: The Complex Role of Parent and Child Factors." *Journal of Applied Developmental Psychology* 36: 11–17.

Leiker, James N., Kim Warren, and Barbara Watkins. 2007. *The First and the Forced: Essays on the Native American and African American Experience*. Lawrence: University of Kansas Press. Accessed February 28, 2020. https://kuscholarworks.ku.edu/handle/1808/29360.

Lewis, Myrna I. 1980. "The History of Female Sexuality in the United States." In *Women's Sexual Development*, edited by Martha Kirkpatrick, 19–43. Boston: Springer.

MacDonald, Tara K., and Michael Ross. 1999. "Assessing the Accuracy of Predictions about Dating Relationships: How and Why Do Lovers' Predictions Differ from Those Made by Observers?" *Personality & Social Psychology Bulletin* 25 (11): 1417–30.

Marger, Martin N. 2015. *Race and Ethnic Relations: American and Global Perspectives*. Belmont, CA: Cengage/Wadsworth.

Masci, David. 2014. "The Divide over Ordaining Women." Accessed February 20, 2020. https://www.pewresearch.org/fact-tank/2014/09/09/the-divide-over-ordaining-women.

Masters, William, and Virginia Johnson. 1966. *Human Sexual Response*. New York: Bantam.

Miller, Rowland S. 2018. *Intimate Relationships*. New York: McGraw Hill Education.

Montemurro, Elizabeth. 2006. *Something Old, Something Bold: Bridal Showers and Bachelorette Parties*. New Brunswick, NJ: Rutgers University Press.

National Institute of Justice. 2010. "Reporting of Sexual Violence Incidents." Accessed May 25, 2019. https://www.nij.gov/topics/crime/rape-sexual-violence/Pages/rape-notification.aspx.

National Poll on Healthy Aging. 2018. "Let's Talk about Sex." Accessed May 28, 2019. https://www.healthyagingpoll.org/report/lets-talk -about-sex.

Pew Research. 2017. "Support for Same Sex Marriage Grows, Even among Groups That Had Been Skeptical." Accessed February 17, 2020. https://www.people-press.org/2017/06/26/support-for-same-sex -marriage-grows-even-among-groups-that-had-been-skeptical.

Pew Research. 2019. "Same Sex Marriage around the World." Accessed May 31, 2019. https://www.pewforum.org/fact-sheet/gay-marriage -around-the-world.

Poulsen, Franklin O., Dean M. Busby, and Adam M. Galovan. 2013. "Pornography Use: Who Uses It and How It Is Associated with Couple Outcomes." *Journal of Sex Research* 50 (1): 72–84.

Rathus, Spencer A., Jeffrey S. Nevid, and Lois Fichner-Rathus. 2018. *Human Sexuality in a World of Diversity*. 10th ed. New York: Pearson Education.

Sanchez, Diana T., Janell C. Fetterolf, and Laurie A. Rudman. 2012. "Eroticizing Inequality in the United States: The Consequences and Determinants of Traditional Gender Role Adherence in Intimate Relationships." *Journal of Sex Research* 49 (2–3): 168–83. https://doi.org/10.1080/00224499.2011.653699.

Sarpolis, Karn. 2011. "First Menstruation: Average Age and Physical Signs." Accessed February 23, 2020. https://www.obgyn.net/sexual -health/first-menstruation-average-age-and-physical-signs.

Schoenfeld, Elizabeth A., Timothy J. Loving, Mark T. Pope, Ted L. Huston, and Aleksandar Štulhofer. 2017. "Does Sex Really Matter? Examining the Connections between Spouses' Nonsexual Behaviors, Sexual Frequency, Sexual Satisfaction, and Marital Satisfaction." *Archives of Sexual Behavior* 46 (2): 489–501. https://doi .org/10.1007/s10508-015-0672-4.

Shammas, Brittany. 2020. "Judge Awards $13 Million to Women Who Say They Were Tricked into Pornography." Accessed February 22, 2020. https://www.washingtonpost.com/business/2020/01/03 /judge-awards-million-women-who-say-they-were-tricked-into -pornography.

Simpson, Jeffry A., and Steven W. Gangestad. 1991. "Individual Differences in Sociosexuality: Evidence for Convergent and Discriminant Validity." *Journal of Personality and Social Psychology* 60: 870–83.

Smith, Andrea. 2003. "Not an Indian Tradition: The Sexual Colonization of Native Peoples." *Hypatia* 18: 70–85.

Statistics Canada. 2015. "Same-Sex Couples and Sexual Orientation . . . by the Numbers." Accessed May 30, 2019. https://www.statcan.gc.ca /eng/dai/smr08/2015/smr08_203_2015.

Statistics Canada. 2017. "Self-Reported Sexual Assault in Canada, 2014." Accessed May 28, 2019. https://www150.statcan.gc.ca/n1/pub/85 -002-x/2017001/article/14842-eng.htm.

Stinson, Philip M., John Liederbach, Steven P. Lab, and Steven L. Brewer. 2016. "Police Integrity Lost: A Study of Law Enforcement Officers Arrested." Accessed September 10, 2020. https://www.ncjrs.gov /pdffiles1/nij/grants/249850.pdf.

Tafoya, Melissa A., and Brian H. Spitzberg. 2007. "The Dark Side of Infidelity: Its Nature, Prevalence, and Communicative Functions." In *The Dark Side of Interpersonal Communication.* 2nd ed., edited by Brian H. Spitzberg and William R. Cupach, 201–42. Mahwah, NJ: Erlbaum.

Takaki, Ronald. 2008. *A Different Mirror: A History of Multicultural America.* New York: Back Bay Books.

Twenge, Jean. 2017. "Declines in Sexual Frequency among American Adults, 1989–2014." *Archives of Sexual Behavior* 46 (8): 2389–2402.

Widmer, Eric D., Judith Treas, and Robert Newcomb. 1998. "Attitudes toward Nonmarital Sex in 24 Countries." *Journal of Sex Research* 35: 349–58.

Willetts, Marion C., Susan Sprecher, and Frank D. Beck. 2004. "Overview of Sexual Practices and Attitudes within Relational Contexts." In *The Handbook of Sexuality in Close Relationships*, edited by John H. Harvey, Amy Wenzel, and Susan Sprecher, 57–85. Mahwah, NJ: Erlbaum.

Xu, Xiaomeng, Lucy Brown, Arthur Aron, Guikang Cao, Tingyong Feng, Bianca Acevedo, and Xuchu Weng. 2012. "Regional Brain Activity during Early-Stage Intense Romantic Love Predicted Relationship Outcomes after 40 Months: An FMRI Assessment." *Neuroscience Letters* 526 (1): 33–38.

TWO

Latin America and the Caribbean

Jessica Gomez

The region commonly labeled "Latin America" refers to an area of the Western Hemisphere that includes Central America, South America, and the Caribbean. Countries of Central America include Belize, Costa Rica, El Salvador, Guatemala, Honduras, Mexico, Nicaragua, and Panama. Mexico is technically a North American country but will be included in discussions of Central America due to its similarity to and fit within Latin American culture. South America is comprised of Argentina, Bolivia, Brazil, Chile, Colombia, Ecuador, the Falkland Islands, French Guiana, Guyana, Paraguay, Peru, Suriname, Uruguay, and Venezuela. The Caribbean includes the islands of Anguilla, Antigua, Aruba, Bahamas, Barbados, Barbuda, the British Virgin Islands, Caribbean Netherlands, Cayman Islands, Cuba, Curacao, Dominica, Dominican Republic, Grenada, Guadeloupe, Haiti, Jamaica, Martinique, Montserrat, Puerto Rico, Saint Barthelemy, Saint Kitts and Nevis, Saint Lucia, Saint Martin, Saint Vincent and Grenadines, Sint Maarten, Trinidad and Tobago, Turks and Caicos, and the U.S. Virgin Islands. A wide range of diversity exists within this region in language, politics, culture, and geography. The predominant languages spoken are Spanish, French, and Portuguese. It is estimated that Indigenous peoples make up just over 10% of the population and speak over 30 dialects in Mexico and Central America and 350 in South America. Geographical features include mountain ranges, grasslands, fjords, rainforests, islands, and volcanoes. The majority of individuals (88%) in Latin America claim religious ties to Christianity, often in the form of

Catholicism (69%) (Pew Research Center 2014). This is a long-standing historical trend, with 90% of the Latin American population identifying as Catholic only 50 years ago (Pew Research Center 2014). This pervasive Christian influence has undoubtedly contributed to sexual attitudes, beliefs, and behaviors of the women in Latin America.

A BRIEF HISTORY OF WOMEN'S SEXUALITY IN LATIN AMERICA

There are three key divisions that should be highlighted when considering the history of sexuality in Latin America: Indigenous cultures precolonization, Christian (specifically Catholic) beliefs that became the norm and majority postcolonization, and the influences of the transatlantic slave trade. It is important to note that during both the European colonialization and the transatlantic slave trade, conversion to Catholicism from tribal/Indigenous religions was often forced—sometimes at threat of death.

Beginning with the older histories in Latin America, the region was occupied by Indigenous peoples prior to the Spanish colonization of the early 1500s. These groups consisted largely of the Aztecs (Mexico), the Mayans (Central America), and the Incas (Andes Mountains region). While there were certainly other Indigenous cultures in Latin America, these three groups are the ones that formed the most prolific civilizations and whose history and traditions have been best documented. A brief discussion of sexual beliefs among the ancient Aztecs proves difficult, as a wide range of attitudes from very liberal to very conservative have been proposed (Bueno 2017; Evans 2008; Jimenez 2004; Nichols and Rodriguez-Alegria 2017). More information is known about the Mayans and Incas, however. Among the Mayans, there was a belief in an entire world of gods and

---

Many Indigenous cultures of Latin America had a three-gender system. This third gender consisted of those who were assigned male at birth (amab) but engaged in roles, behaviors, and duties that were considered "feminine" by their cultures. They were not considered female or male and were free to adopt male or female gender roles in their everyday lives. The term *berdache* was traditionally used, originating from Spanish conquistadors and colonizers, but many Indigenous peoples today consider it offensive due to its linguistic links with the word "sodomy." The term "two-spirit," *muxe*, or other regional designations are now preferred.

goddesses who were sexual beings. The Mayan culture did not impose many restrictions or sexual shame upon individuals, and sexuality was viewed as an important and powerful element of one's life. In fact, the ability to enjoy sex was seen as a gift from the gods and goddesses (Houston and Taube 2010). Similar views were held by the Incas, with no prohibitions on same-sex behaviors or nonmarital sex. Following mass forced conversions to Catholicism, the Mayan people modified their beliefs about sexuality, embracing a more conservative view of sexual restriction and purity that is still prevalent today (Tavarez 2017). The Incan peoples became more conservative for a time, partially due to threats of physical punishments or even execution if caught violating certain sexual restrictions, but the remaining Incan people in Peru today (referred to as Quechua) have again become more relaxed in their views on sexuality (Vecchio 2004).

Moving forward in history to the prevailing views of Latin American women's sexuality after colonization requires an introduction to the long-standing concept of "marianismo." Marianismo is the idealized female gender role, primarily derived from Catholic beliefs about the Virgin Mary, that incorporates moral and spiritual strength, feminine passivity, submission, nurturing tendencies, self-sacrifice, attachment to family, and purity—specifically, sexual purity and chastity (Castillo et al. 2010). Maintaining virginity until marriage is equated with an avoidance of shame for oneself and one's family, and sexual passivity is henceforth expected within marital relationships (Castillo et al. 2010). These beliefs have been linked to sex guilt, lower condom usage, and higher sexually transmitted infection (STI) risk (Espinosa-Hernandez, Vasilenko, and Bamaca-Colbert 2016; Noblega 2012; Moreno 2007). While there is a great deal of debate regarding the prevalence of marianismo culture in Latin America today, its historical influence on how Latin American women viewed their own sexuality cannot be discounted.

Examples of this premise are evidenced in studies of social norms and sexual behaviors among young Latin American women. Young Latinas tend to have restricted access to information regarding sexuality, leading to a silencing of any sexual issues that may arise (Faulkner and Mansfield 2002). Questions about sexual health and sexual activity are often discouraged, as this is considered a private—even embarrassing—topic. Women are expected to be guarded in their discussions of sexual desire, with prior sexual activity often spurring feelings of guilt (Faulkner and Mansfield 2002). While they are not encouraged to discuss their own desires, wives are expected to be attentive to their husbands' sexual wishes, submitting to and prioritizing the husbands' needs, even if it means sacrificing their own (Castillo et al. 2010; Rudman, Fetterolf, and Sanchez 2013). Levels of sexual assertiveness among Latina women are, and have traditionally been, rather low. In addition to the psychological distress that emerges from lacking sexual autonomy, there are additional adverse consequences associated with sexual submissiveness. Coerced sexual activity among Latin American women is tied to unintended pregnancy, unsafe termination of these pregnancies, increased risks of STIs, and intimate partner violence (Alvarez, Bauermeister, and Villarruel 2014; Goicolea et al. 2010).

The long-standing cultural norm of silencing Latin American women's sexuality is evidenced by the lack of sex research from Latin American countries. Some scholars have proposed that this gap may be explained by the continued stigmatization of sexuality in Latin America—that it is a facet of humanity to be regulated rather than studied and discussed (Araujo and Prieto 2008; Caricote 2006; Puentes 2008). Attempting to disentangle sources, influences, and time lines of gender inequalities in previous generations of Latin Americans has proven complicated, with most explanations returning to the underlying theme of an honor/shame thought process (Hutchinson 2003). In fact, the honor/shame paradigm held such significant influence in Latin American history that bringing shame upon one's family could ultimately be life threatening.

Women who engaged in extramarital sex were often seen as compromising their familial and marital honor in one of the most shameful ways possible. In early Peruvian Incan cultures, a woman could legally be starved to death by her husband as punishment for adultery, and Mexican Aztec law permitted execution by stoning or strangulation (Goldstein 2002). Bringing shame of this magnitude upon one's family and husband continued to be seen as such an egregious offense that the murder of "adulterous" women by their partners or male family members became a significant concern in Brazil from 1910 to the 1930s (Besse 1989). Under Portuguese law during Brazil's colonial period, many of these murders were legally permissible, given that a married man had the right to kill not only his "cheating" wife but also her lover. Even after the law was changed in 1940, the social acceptability of this practice remained (Corrêa 1981). While this is only one example from the history of one country in Latin America, it does convey an important historical fact: Latin American culture has traditionally upheld a strong honor/shame paradigm, especially when evaluating the sexual behaviors of women. Even today, women in some Latin American countries, such as Haiti, can be faced with time in prison if found guilty of adultery.

Another important consideration of the history of Latin America, particularly the Caribbean, involves the transatlantic slave trade that spanned the 1660s to the early 1800s. Although the slave trade is frequently discussed in the context of slaves being brought to the United States, less than 5% of those forced across the Atlantic ended up in North America (Miller 2018). A large percentage of individuals were sold to work in the sugarcane fields of Brazil, and most others were sold into labor in the Caribbean. Fewer women were sold into slavery than men were, with an estimated one woman for every two

During the transatlantic slave trade, many slaves were brought to Latin America (especially Brazil) and the Caribbean. Women were abused not only for their labor but also for reproduction. (Library of Congress, Prints & Photographs Division, LC-USZ62-15385)

to three men, but there were large numbers of female slaves nonetheless (Digital History 2019). Little is known about the sexual partnering or sexual activity of these enslaved women during this time period. However, it is known that sexual interactions between white male slave owners and their female slaves were common. These interactions were often forced, as the rape of slaves by their owners was not uncommon (Hallam 2004). Given that slaves were considered property, having sex with a slave owned by another man (whether consensual or forced) was considered a violation of that man's property. The fact that this act was the violation of a human woman was far less important, if it was considered at all.

Although there are some historical accounts where sexual interactions between slave women and their owners were portrayed as consensual, this is difficult to evaluate, as there is also evidence of slave women being whipped and beaten for refusing their masters' sexual advances (Hall and Thistlewood 1999). Knowing that sexual refusal would result in physical violence casts doubt on how truly "consensual" any of these relationships may have been. There are indications, however, that some slave women may have cooperated with sexual activity in order to gain a favored status with their male masters, resulting in a more comfortable life. In this way, female slaves may have seen their sexuality as one of the only tools at their disposal to improve their living conditions.

CULTURE AND ATTITUDES TOWARD SEXUALITY

The history of slavery plays an important role in the diversity that exists between many parts of mainland Central/South America and the islands of the Caribbean today. As freed slaves began forming their own culture by integrating African and British morality norms, many acknowledged that sexual activity and pleasure were a natural component of human life. Although natural, there was still an obligation to enact one's sexuality respectably (LaFont 2001). Many of these women were facing racist colonial stereotypes about Black female sexuality. White colonials frequently conceptualized the Black community as completely free and open with their sexuality, as not restraining themselves in any way. This was used to paint a negative picture of the Black woman being a powerful, undiscerning seductress, willing to engage with a lover at any time and in any place (such as finding a place in the jungle) and bearing more children than she could ever possibly care for (Fanon 1967). This racist stereotype, which has been traced back to the beginnings of the transatlantic slave trade, was used as justification for the rape of slaves. The conceptualization of Black women as promiscuous and sexually manipulative has been labeled "the Jezebel stereotype" and remains active today. Although analyses of the impact of the Jezebel stereotype on the justification of sexual assault have not centered on Latin America specifically, historians have suggested that this harmful ideology has continued to influence both victim blaming and a minimization of the seriousness of sexual violence against Black women (Rosen 2009; White 2001).

Influenced in part by this history, there are regions of the Caribbean that continue to prioritize "respectability" in a way that aligns with the traditional honor/shame paradigm but that hold guidelines of "respectable" sexual behavior that are less strict than in many of the Catholic-dominated

Latin American regions. There are also age-based trends seen today, wherein many adolescents and young adults are rebelling against conservative sexual attitudes. For example, on the island of Barbados, sexual norms among teenage girls are changing, with multiple partnering and early sexual initiation becoming more common (Barrow 2005). Likewise, 30% to 40% of Jamaican young women acknowledge engaging with multiple sexual partners, and 36% of Brazilian young women report being sexually active by age 15 (Figueroa 2006; World Health Organization 2006). Of course, one could question whether multiple partnering and earlier ages of consensual sexual initiation are actually increasing or social acceptability is simply allowing more women to feel comfortable discussing their sexual activities. Either way, this trend suggests that young women in some regions of Latin America are becoming more comfortable with an increased level of sexual autonomy over previous generations.

An important note about attitudes toward sexual partnering in Latin America involves the tolerance of transactional, economically beneficial sexual interactions. Interestingly, some nations of the Caribbean are more culturally accepting of multiple partnering if it is tied to economic gain (Senior 1991; Chevannes 2001). There are three primary methods in which sex is exchanged for goods, money, or other useful resources within Latin American culture: prostitution, tourist-oriented prostitution/romance, and transactional sex. To begin with the obvious, standard prostitution is rather common in many areas of Latin America and the Caribbean. This is the most direct form of exchange, where a person, most often a woman, has sexual interactions with a partner who provides an economic benefit during the same encounter without any further obligation. In Latin America, there are three varieties of legalized prostitution. In a "decriminalization" situation, there are no legal penalties for prostitution. "Full legalization" occurs when prostitution has not only been declared legal but is also regulated by the government in some form. "Abolitionism" occurs when prostitution has been declared legal for individuals but organized activities such as pimping or brothels remain illegal. Prostitution is permissible in one of these three ways in nearly every country of Latin America (with some countries allowing individual cities/states/regions to determine legality without a nationwide mandate), with the exceptions of French Guiana, Grenada, Guyana, Haiti, Jamaica, Saint Kitts and Nevis, Saint Lucia, Saint Vincent and the Grenadines, Suriname, and Trinidad and Tobago. Within these countries, prostitution is often widespread despite being illegal (Kempadoo 2000; Bailey and Figueroa 2016).

While it would be irresponsible to portray prostitution as a completely healthy, beneficial employment option for Latin American women, the reality that sex work has provided many with options for bettering their livelihood cannot be dismissed. An important example of this can be seen in Venezuela. For many years, Venezuela has been experiencing a severe economic crisis, with mass emigrations from the country for those who can afford to leave. The poverty is so widespread that a large proportion of citizens cannot meet their basic needs for food and shelter, and over half of Venezuelans are living in a state of extreme poverty (United Nations OHCHR 2018). Neighboring Colombia, however, is in a far better financial and economic state. Many women from Venezuela cross the border into Colombia and engage in sex work to make the money needed for escaping their potentially life-threatening poverty. Given that prostitution is legal in Colombia, these women are eventually able to apply for work visas, listing sex work as legitimate employment. For many, an hour of sex work in Colombia garners the same wages that a month of employment would yield in Venezuela (*The Economist* 2017). Some women report that their earnings from one day of sex work in Colombia are enough to send home to support their entire families in Venezuela for more than a full month (Moloney 2018). While there are women in Latin America who consider the option of legal prostitution a valuable tool for their economic freedom, the ability to buy and sell sex cannot be presented without also considering the negative impacts. For example, although women from Venezuela have benefited from the legalization of prostitution in Colombia, it must also be acknowledged that many young girls have been harmed by the same legalization.

Latin America is a primary supplier of girls and women for global sex trafficking, with only five countries acting in full compliance with international trafficking protection, reporting, and prosecuting guidelines (U.S. Department of State 2019). Some areas in Latin America function as "sex tourism" hot spots, a designation given to countries that are so lax in their prostitution laws that people will travel there specifically for the purpose of purchasing sex. Countries that are known as sex tourism sites often have high rates of sex trafficking, particularly of minors. Forced child prostitution has become so prevalent in Colombia that it is a destination for pedophiles seeking child sex tourism, and the country functions as a major supplier of women and girls who are trafficked to other parts of the world. Another example is Ecuador, where women and girls from Indigenous groups are the most frequent victims of trafficking, being forced to take on the role of sex worker after they have been captured (Moloney 2017). The families are typically told that these girls or young women will be relocated for educational or employment opportunities as domestics or farm-workers or a combination of both. Once they have agreed to go with their captor, they are intimidated into cooperation by threats of harm to their family. Costa Rica is another Latin American country known for sex tourism due to the legality and popularity of prostitution. Those who are forced into sex work in Costa Rica are often trafficked from other countries in Latin America, with high rates of both sex trafficking and child prostitution. Even though officials are aware of this issue, prostitutes who have been attacked and seek medical care are often ignored.

Tourist-oriented prostitution/romance is a different category than general prostitution. In this situation, a woman will enter into a relationship with an individual on vacation, typically from Europe or North America (Kempadoo 2004). Sometimes these are one-time encounters, with the consumer finding a sex worker in a way that almost resembles a tourist activity (e.g., fulfilling a "sex on the beach" fantasy or making a stop at a city center or hotel that is known for having sex workers available). But in other cases, the encounters may evolve into longer-term partnerships. Some women who engage in this type of sexual interaction are hoping to establish relationships that lead to marriage or an opportunity for a better life. Even if such planning does not ultimately lead to improved living conditions, women may still benefit from engaging in tourist romance. During the tourist's stay and even on future visits, women may gain access to high-end, vacation-oriented establishments in the region—places that would otherwise not be financially feasible to stay outside of such an arrangement (Morgan 2013). It is important to differentiate between tourist-oriented prostitution/romance and sex tourism. Many nations are hot spots for sex tourism and exploit prostitutes acquired through trafficking or other forced means. Sex tourism is more accurately classified as sexual victimization rather than consensual romance. While consensual interactions between locals and tourists do take place in areas that are known for sex tourism, sex tourism and tourist-oriented prostitution/romance are separate domains.

Finally, transactional sex can be among the most difficult to categorize and assess. Most women who engage in these associations would not label their interactions as prostitution. They acknowledge that their sexual relationship involves a material or economic benefit, but due to the long-term, consistent nature of these relationships, the participants do not consider them prostitution. The most common transactional arrangement involves young women with older men. In Jamaica, 24% of young women have engaged in transactional sex by age 19 (Whitehorne-Smith and Irons-Morgan 2015). In Nevis, it is not uncommon for those who are 15 or 16 years old to have experienced transactional relationships (Curtis 2009). Sometimes the economic benefit involves small luxury items, such as high-quality clothing or shoes. In other cases, the benefits could include something as basic as transportation. Often these exchanges serve as a woman's primary means for paying her day-to-day living expenses.

RELIGION AND SEXUALITY

Given the substantial majority of the Latin American population who identify with Catholicism, it is important to understand the backdrop of Catholic beliefs regarding sexuality. The Catholic Church has traditionally held conservative views on sexuality, teaching that sexual intimacy should be reserved for marital relationships and for the purpose of conceiving a child (United States Conference of Catholic Bishops 2020). Premarital sex is viewed as sinful, and contraception is frowned upon because it is believed that God should determine the timing and spacing of children. Abortion is widely viewed as the equivalent of taking a life, a belief that has shaped a number of legal restrictions on pregnancy termination in countries throughout Latin America. The Catholic Church also has a long-standing tradition of opposing same-sex marriage. There are, however, those who argue for the Catholic Church to revise its views on sexual issues. Among Latin American Catholics, a median of 66% believe that the church should begin supporting birth control. This number jumps to approximately 80% in Argentina, Chile, Uruguay, and Venezuela (Pew Research Center 2014). When considering Christianity as a whole in Latin America, research has found that Catholics tend to be less conservative on sexual issues than Protestants, who are even more strongly opposed to birth control, same-sex relationships, premarital sex, and abortion (Pew Research Center 2014).

The impact of Christianity on political policies and social culture cannot be ignored. One country that is not heavily influenced by religion is Uruguay, where nearly 40% of the population either does not affiliate with a religion or identifies as agnostic or atheist (Pew Research Center 2014). This is double the rate of any other Latin American country. Uruguay is also the only Latin American country where a majority of the population (62%) supports same-sex marriage. Similarly, about half of the population

(54%) believes that abortion should be a legal option for women. This represents an approval rating over 10 times greater than that of Paraguay (5%), and nearly double that of most Latin American countries surveyed (Pew Research Center 2014). Among Christians, 80% or more of Catholics and Protestants believe that abortion should be illegal in most or all cases (Pew Research Center 2014). These numbers suggest that the Christian backbone of Latin American culture greatly impacts political and personal beliefs with respect to sexuality and reproductive health.

Although Christianity is by far the most prominent religion in Latin America, it is important to acknowledge the presence of Afro-Caribbean religions as well. Identifying the number of local religious practitioners can be difficult because many people identify with both a Christian denomination and a local tribal, folk, or Indigenous religion. For example, many Haitians practice Vodou as well as Catholicism (Central Intelligence Agency 2019). Similarly, 66% of Catholics in Panama engage in practices associated with Indigenous religions (Pew Research Center 2014). Throughout Latin America, at least 30% of the population reports holding beliefs related to, or engaging in practices associated with, Afro-Caribbean or Indigenous religions, except in Paraguay, where only 25% of the people adhere to such beliefs.

The Virgin Mary is a core symbol in Catholicism that has influenced views regarding women's sexuality, including feminine passivity, purity, and self-sacrifice. (Peeterson/Dreamstime.com)

Although Santeria includes women and recognizes the importance of female priestesses, female practitioners face restrictions while menstruating. Due to the religion's view of the significance of blood, some rituals and ceremonial activities are not permitted during menstruation. It is believed that if a woman plays one of the ceremonial drums, known as *batá*, her menstrual blood could weaken the spiritual power of the drum, and she could be cursed with infertility as a consequence of her actions.

A discussion of the norms regarding women's sexuality in all of the Afro-Caribbean religions would constitute an entire book in itself because the variation is immense. However, these religions do share common origins. Afro-Caribbean religions evolved as a result of African religions combining with Christian traditions, largely when African individuals were transported to Latin America as slaves (Murrell 2010). The majority of these slaves experienced forced religious participation in Catholicism. As such, the adoption of Christian themes, saints, language, symbolism, and imagery to refer to elements of their home religion allowed them to continue practicing subversively. Perhaps because these religions were born out of periods of extreme adversity and oppression, they are often perceived as a safe refuge for those who feel marginalized, including those who identify as gay, lesbian, bisexual, transgender, or nonbinary/gender fluid. Some of the Afro-Caribbean religions, such as Santeria, also emphasize the importance of female priestesses, while others, such as Winti, acknowledge female goddesses along with male gods (Santeria Church 2012; Wooding 1972). Haitian Vodou acknowledges the presence of a spirit who functions as the patron of lesbians (Prower 2018). Many of these religions allow participants to make their own decisions regarding the enactment of sexuality in ways that offer more liberty than Christianity, but some impose restrictions on sexual interactions during time periods leading up to or following specific ceremonies, holidays, or rituals.

SEXUAL VIOLENCE

An examination of the prevalence of sexual violence in Latin America, particularly in the Caribbean, can be difficult for two reasons. First, statistics about sexual violence and domestic violence are often combined. Second, it is estimated that only 11% of sexual violence incidents against women and girls are reported (Center for Reproductive Rights 2017). Data from 15 Latin American countries indicate that 47% of women report experiencing some form of sexual assault at some point in their lives (Morrison, Ellsberg, and Bott 2005). Other reports have demonstrated lower frequencies and wide disparities across the Latin American countries, with Paraguay on the low end at 10.3% and Haiti on the high end at 27.2%. In some cases, these numbers can be broken down by age group, demonstrating an alarmingly high rate of sexual violence experienced by teenagers. For example, in Jamaica, approximately one in five teenage girls between the ages of 15 and 19 have been victimized (Whitehorne-Smith and Irons-Morgan 2015). Sexual violence is often perpetrated by an intimate partner (Bott et al. 2012). Several young women report that their first instance of intercourse was forced, with the highest rate being 21% in Haiti. When the wording of the question is changed to specifically include coerced sex, these numbers increase significantly, reaching nearly half of all young women (45%) in Jamaica (Bott et al. 2012) and 40% in Barbados (Drakes et al. 2013).

Regardless of the specific dataset used, the trend remains that Latin America has the highest rate of sexual violence worldwide when considering noncouple-based sexual crimes (Essayag 2017). Part of this prevalence is due to the normalization of sexual violence toward women. Another contributor is the way in which sexual violence has been used as a tool of control, threat, and intimidation on a systematic level during periods of political upheaval. There have been instances in which females of all ages—from younger girls to older women—have endured rape and other forms of sexual assault by groups who were trying to instill fear as a way to control the actions of the populace. Examples of this were seen in Haiti in the 1990s and in Chile in the 1970s. In some instances, males of all ages were forced to watch females endure rape and torture. The goal was to cause fear that similar harm would be done to family members or loved ones if they did not cooperate. These and other instances caused sexual violence to be perceived as a tool for control and intimidation through the present day.

There has traditionally been a practice of minimizing the severity of violence toward women in Latin America—a trend that persists among young adults today. For example, a survey of eight countries focusing on teenagers and young adults aged 15 to 25 uncovered several attitudes that downplay the significance of sexual assault (Ruiz and Sobrino 2018). Approximately 40% of males believed a woman was to blame for being raped if she was drunk, and 65% of teenage boys believed that a female who says no to sex is playing hard to get and wants to have sex. Surprisingly, 45% of teenage girls in the study also agreed with this idea. Approximately 70% of teenage boys thought that women should not be dressed "provocatively," with the majority also believing that women were responsible for their own sexual assaults because of how they were dressed.

REPRODUCTIVE HEALTH AND MENSTRUATION

A discussion of women's sexual health in Latin America must consider not only reproductive health but also the prevalence of STIs. The Caribbean region has the second highest rate of HIV infection worldwide, and in some areas, such as Jamaica, young women have higher rates of new infections than young men do (United Nations Programme on HIV/AIDS 2009). For many years, teenage girls in Jamaica had a risk of HIV infection approximately 2.5 times higher than teenage boys. Although this inequality has leveled in recent years, the trend of adolescent girls having a higher rate of HIV acquisition than teenage boys still persists in places such as Brazil (Brazilian Ministry of Health 2011). The degree of gender inequality in these regions with respect to HIV/AIDS—both past and present—demonstrates the need for examining women's sexual health in the Caribbean more closely.

Throughout the Caribbean, sexual relationships between younger women (including teenagers) and older men are a cultural norm. In Barbados, for example, approximately 35% of sexually active teenage girls aged 15 to 19 have engaged in sex with someone at least 10 years older (Drakes et al. 2013). These young women often benefit economically from these partnerships and feel dependent on them (Wood et al. 2011). As such, they typically yield to their respective partners' preferences regarding condom usage—or lack thereof. Pregnancy is a bigger concern for these women than STIs, so many will compromise and allow a withdrawal method (which offers only a slight risk reduction for pregnancy and no protection against STIs) rather than insist on condom usage (Wood et al. 2011). A similar trend exists in Brazil, where unprotected sex is more common among teenage girls than boys (Sanchez et al. 2013). Individuals from lower socioeconomic groups are especially at risk for unsafe sex, with the cost of condoms and relational power dynamics as contributing factors. Teenage girls from impoverished areas also receive less education on safe-sex practices, which adversely impacts condom use. For these reasons, and because of the high numbers of women involved in sex work, the risk of STI in Latin America and the Caribbean is high. In fact, strains of antibiotic-resistant gonorrhea have been documented in some areas due to the high rates of antibiotic treatment for bacterial STIs (Garcia, Benzaken, and Galban 2011). A complete understanding of the sexual health concerns among women in this region is difficult because the women minimize and under-report their sexual risk-taking behaviors due to shame and social norms that discourage reporting (Whitehorne-Smith and Irons-Morgan 2015).

Although in some Latin American countries (i.e., El Salvador, Guatemala, Honduras, and Panama), nearly half of the population believe that contraception is morally wrong, a majority of countries are not opposed to artificial means of birth control. Most countries approve of modern methods of hormonal birth control, condoms, and sterilization surgeries—at least to some extent. Rates of contraceptive disapproval are fairly equal between men and women (Pew Research Center 2014). Despite the disapproval of some individuals, a large majority (74%) of married Latin American women aged 15 to 49 use some form of contraception (Population Reference Bureau 2019). Variation exists across regions, with South America showing 79%, Central America 67%, and the Caribbean 58% in the use of contraception. This number varies greatly across countries, as well, with Haiti and Bolivia showing the lowest rates at 31% and 35%, respectively. Other countries such as Brazil, Colombia, Costa Rica, Cuba, and Paraguay have a contraceptive usage rate of over 70% (de Leon et al. 2019). Tubal ligation (female sterilization) is the most commonly used method of family planning. There is some concern, however, that sterilizations are often forced. Many Latin American women (23% in one study) have reported that they felt coerced into the procedure by their health-care provider (Kendall and Albert 2015). Sterilization rates are especially high among those who are HIV positive. Setting those cases aside, there are vast differences between the rates of women versus men who are sterilized in Latin America. Even though male sterilization is a safer and less invasive procedure with a shorter recovery time, there are only 6 male sterilizations for every 100 female sterilizations in Mexico (United Nations 2014). The explanations for this inequality again pertain to the cultural responsibilities placed upon women. Contraception is considered the woman's responsibility, and male sterilization is stigmatized and perceived as emasculating (Ulloa Pizarro 2014; Vega-Briones and Jaramillo-Cardona 2010).

Should a woman's plan for contraception fail and result in an unintended pregnancy, her options for pregnancy termination are limited or nonexistent. In Latin America, an overwhelming majority of the population believe that abortion should be illegal (Pew Research Center 2014). The most conservative views are held in Paraguay, with 95% being opposed to abortion in most or all cases. Less than 15% of the population approves of legal abortion in Dominican Republic (13%), El Salvador (10%), Guatemala (7%), Honduras (11%), Panama (14%), and Venezuela (12%). Uruguay is among the most liberal, with more than half (54%) approving of legalization. Many individuals oppose abortion due to religious beliefs suggesting that abortion is morally wrong. It is interesting to note that women are as likely as men to oppose abortion and in some countries are even more likely to believe that it is morally wrong.

One specific example of how current beliefs about abortion intersect with the policing of women's bodies is in El Salvador, where pregnancy termination is a crime, even in situations where the pregnancy is life-threatening to the woman. Since 1998–1999, abortion was made illegal under all circumstances, and a "right to life" is granted from conception. This firm cultural belief even causes miscarriages to be regarded with suspicion. Records show that dozens of women have faced homicide charges following a stillbirth or miscarriage, some being convicted of aggravated murder and sentenced to decades in prison. While many countries have loosened restrictions on abortion laws in recent years, three Latin American countries (El Salvador, Nicaragua, and Chile) have become more stringent (Provost 2014).

The discussion of contraception and abortion, especially among teens, is important, given that Latin America has the second-highest rate of adolescent childbearing in the world, and maternal mortality is one of the leading causes of death among girls aged 15 to 24 (United Nations 2019; Pan American Health Organization 2018). Throughout Latin America, less than half of all women receive the medical care needed for pregnancy complications, with approximately 7,000 women dying each year from issues related to pregnancy, abortion, miscarriage, or birth (Darroch, Audam, and Biddlecom 2017). A significant portion of these deaths are due to complications caused by early childbearing.

Among young women who are not even sexually active and therefore do not have concerns about STIs or pregnancy, reproductive health concerns still shape their daily lives. This is evidenced most clearly in difficulties surrounding menstruation—both in the myths that continue to persist regarding menstruation and in the logistics of acquiring and disposing of sanitary supplies. Young women in various Latin American cultures are often given instructions regarding activities that they should or should not do during menstruation. For example, young women in Mexico are told they should avoid doing strenuous physical activities, carrying heavy objects, drinking cold beverages, and eating spicy foods (Marvan and Trujillo 2009). Similar advice is given to young girls in Bolivia, where menstruation poses significant challenges to school-aged females. There is persistent fear and shame, mostly revolving around classmates noticing stains or odors due to inadequate access to sanitary materials (Long et al. 2013). The expense of sanitary pads is too high for many families to afford. Unsanitary conditions in school bathrooms (such as lack of trash cans or unlidded trash cans) cause many students to carry used menstrual supplies with them throughout the day and take them home for disposal. School bathrooms not only lack trash cans for disposal but also fail to provide hand soap for proper handwashing after handling saturated sanitary supplies. Due to the poor conditions, many young women report leaving the school grounds to find a private place for changing their menstrual cloths or pads (Long et al. 2013).

Not only do these young women struggle with hygiene during menstruation but incorrect cultural beliefs cause additional stress. A common myth about menstruation is that cancer can result from coming into contact with menstrual blood or through the burning of used menstrual supplies. Although these concerns are not valid, there are some genuine risks that arise from lack of hygiene and unsanitary handling and disposing of used menstrual supplies, such as skin irritations, urinary or genital tract infections, and bacterial infections. Some of these infections can be life-threatening if left untreated (e.g., urinary infections that spread to the kidneys) or can increase the risk of later developing cervical cancer, which can also be life-threatening. Hygiene issues that are compounded by inaccessibility to adequate facilities at school not only impact female students but female teachers, as well (Long et al. 2013). Throughout Latin America, many women, both teenagers and adults, experience "period poverty," wherein allocating money for sanitary supplies limits the ability to purchase food and other necessities.

In some Latin American folk religions, such as Hoodoo, menstruation is perceived much more positively. Rather than being a source of shame or uncleanliness, menstrual blood is believed to contain unique properties that make it a powerful element in magic rituals. Some of these are rituals are used for sex and sexuality, such as spells to attract or bind a lover/partner. Others focus on personal well-being and spiritual/psychological health. The principle of viewing menstruation as a benefit rather than a dirty, shameful source of stress represents an important alternate voice in a region where this natural biological process carries significant stigma.

MARRIAGE AND PARTNERSHIPS

There are many countries in Latin America that are shaped by conservative Christian norms and in which over half of the population believe that premarital sex is morally wrong (Pew Research Center 2014). This belief is generally split evenly between men and women, but some countries show a significant number of women being more opposed to premarital sex than men. This is the case in Colombia where 49% of women but only 38% of men believe premarital sex is morally wrong (Pew Research Center 2014). This gender difference is interesting, as there is a prevalent belief among adolescents and young adults that a woman's sexual desire is not as strong as a man's (Ruiz and Sobrino 2018). Strong ties to religion not only shape attitudes but also actions. Those who actively participate in religion are less likely to be sexually active outside of marriage (Drakes et al. 2013).

Several Latin American countries still stigmatize divorce. In countries such as El Salvador, Guatemala, Honduras, and Panama, over half of individuals are morally opposed to divorce (Pew Research Center 2014). Several other countries are added to this list when the sampling is restricted to Catholic and Protestant participants. These statistics are particularly interesting when considered in the context of women who are morally opposed to divorce even when their rights and experiences within marital relationships are not always positive. For example, in about half of the Latin American countries surveyed (Pew Research Center 2014), the majority of individuals believe that a wife is always obligated to be obedient to her husband. Only three countries surveyed (Argentina, Chile, and Uruguay) show that less than 40% hold this belief. Not surprisingly, men are more likely than women to agree with this viewpoint. However, in about half of the Latin American countries polled, at least 50% of women agreed with the principle of obligated obedience to their husbands. Taken together, this paints a pessimistic view for women who may be desiring to leave an unhappy or even abusive marriage. Not only may they face an overarching moral opposition to ending the marriage through divorce but the beliefs that get communicated regarding their marital responsibilities could likely center on submission and obedience.

Latin Americans tend to lean conservative in their opposition of same-sex marriage. As noted earlier, this can be traced back to a religious influence (Pew Research Center 2014). Uruguay is the only country wherein a significant majority of the population supports same-sex marriage, whereas approximately half of the population of Mexico (49%) and Argentina (52%) approve of the legalization (Pew Research Center 2014). As a result of this partial approval, Uruguay, Argentina, and parts of Brazil and Mexico have legalized same-sex marriage. These four countries are the only regions in Latin America where legalization has occurred; the rest of Latin America strongly opposes same-sex marriage. In El Salvador, Guatemala, Honduras, and Paraguay, 80% to 83% of the population are against such legalization. Not only are the majority of people against same-sex marriage but in most Latin American countries, there is also a strong, religion-based belief that same-sex attraction is morally wrong. Even among young adults (aged 15–25), a majority believe that women who identify as lesbian should not openly show their attraction in public (Ruiz and Sobrino 2018).

One country with a unique view on women's sexuality is Suriname, where some women practice what is known as "Mati work," defined as engaging in sexual/romantic relationships with other women without considering themselves to be bisexual or lesbian. Rather than identifying as lesbian or bisexual, these women categorize their sexual relationships with women as an activity they participate in rather than part of their identity. The phrases used are "doing the Mati work" or "I mati" (with "mati" as a verb) rather than "I am Mati." It has been estimated that approximately 75% of Creole, working-class women engage in Mati work at some point, with most of these women also engaging in relationships with men (Wekker 1999). Heterosexual relationships are seen as a necessity for women, both for childbearing and to avoid shame and stigma. One prevalent folk religion in Suriname, Winti, provides an important backdrop for this conceptualization of sexual relationships. Men and women are fully embraced as sexual beings with a variety of desires, and the fulfillment of their desires is seen as not only normal and healthy but also joyous (Blackwood 2000; Wekker 2006). The gender of one's partner is not prioritized within the Winti religion or the Surinamese culture. Given that these women are situated within a larger cultural framework that prioritizes and idealizes motherhood as the ultimate goal of womanhood, they perceive relationships with men as required for family and economic reasons. Outside of those practical needs, intimate relationships with other women are thought to provide an additional outlet for pleasure, joy, and companionship. In several other areas of Latin America, including Jamaica, Barbados, and Dominican Republic, same-sex relationships are often conceptualized as more of an activity than an aspect of one's identity (Sharpe and Pinto 2006).

A discussion of marriage in Latin America is incomplete without acknowledging child marriage. In Brazil, Dominican Republic, Guatemala, Honduras, and Nicaragua, a minimum of 30% of girls are married by the time they turn 18. In an additional 11 countries, between 20% and 30% are married by age 18. An additional 5% of girls throughout Latin America are married by age 15 (United Nations Children's Fund 2016). It is estimated that the overall rate of marriage prior to age 18 throughout Latin America and the Caribbean is just under 20%. Latin America is the only region globally where the prevalence of child marriage has not declined in the past 20 years (Davison 2019). Although many countries have established a minimum age for marriage, the laws are bypassed through loopholes or are simply not monitored or enforced. Parental consent is also used as a way to override the legal marriage age. In some areas of Mexico, girls as young as 14 can be married with parental permission. In Colombia, this age drops to 12.

Poverty is a significant factor in the child marriage trend, especially considering that husbands are on average five to seven years older than their teenager wives (Plan International and UNICEF 2014). While this is the average, differences of 10, 20, or even 25 years are not uncommon. Once a daughter can be married into another family, it means one less person to provide for, which is a key motivator for many impoverished families. However, there are other cultural issues at play. Given the stigma of teenage/unwed pregnancy, marriages also occur to avoid the shame of these situations (Girls Not Brides 2017). Similarly, restrictions and shame surrounding premarital sexual activity motivate young women to marry in order to explore their sexuality in an approved context (Girls Not Brides 2017). Also, elevated levels of respect are bestowed upon women in marital and motherhood roles, which encourages girls to enter marriage early and begin creating meaningful lives for themselves, especially when they feel trapped by poverty and perceive of limited options for the future (Garces and Vega 2016).

Although child marriage is prevalent and normalized in some areas, the negative consequences cannot be ignored. Early marriages often result in early childbearing, which create significant health risks. If a girl's hips have not yet widened, she can experience great difficulty pushing her baby out, if it is even possible. Without an emergency C-section, the mother and/or baby may not survive childbirth. If the mother was malnourished before and during pregnancy—a common occurrence for those living in poverty—she is unlikely to have a surplus of micronutrients built up in her body to nourish herself and the baby during pregnancy (Cherry and Dillon 2014). Malnourishment can lead to significant problems for the baby, some of which are life-threatening. Child marriage poses additional threats, including high rates of domestic violence comprising physical, sexual, psychological, and emotional abuse (Garces and Vega 2016). Once married, girls often leave school, which in turn leaves them with little education. If a marriage is arranged to a man outside of the immediate geographic area, the girl is expected to move away to be with her husband. The combination of low education and lack of familial support due to distance increases the risk for health and social issues. Finally, these girls often completely lose the opportunity to experience adolescence. They are suddenly responsible for maintaining a home, tending to a husband (recall that one of the wife's primary duties is to cater to her husband in most Latin cultures), and caring for children shortly after marriage. The important social, psychological, and emotional tasks of healthy adolescent development are pushed aside, as these girls find themselves functioning as fully grown, responsible adults.

MEDIA AND SEXUALITY

Some regions have credited American media with modifying sexual norms. For example, on the island of Nevis, many individuals claim that oral sex was not a common practice until recently, with some ascribing its popularity to HBO becoming available on the island (Curtis 2009). In fact, the Nevisian culture perceives the United States media as having such a negative influence on women's sexuality that avoiding U.S. programming—such as soap operas and the BET network—is strongly emphasized,

---

Until 1985, strict media censorship laws in Brazil did not allow films to contain explicit sex scenes. The Brazilian film industry got around this by developing a genre termed "Pornochanchada." These films began as sexual comedies, but the term later referred to any film with explicit, pervasive sexual content that pushed the boundaries of nudity without actually depicting sexual interactions. The debate over media censorship in Brazil is ongoing, with many accusations of discriminatory censorship of LGBTQ content.

Dance is an important component of Latin culture. However, the portrayal of women in the media is often hypersexualized and has contributed to their objectification. (Photosvit/Dreamstime.com)

particularly among the religious community. BET is mentioned specifically, given its popularity among young women who watch this channel for fashion and relationship advice. Some teenage girls have even reported using the content from BET as a form of sex education (Curtis 2009). The music videos featured on BET show men providing material goods or glamorous lifestyles in exchange for sexual favors from women, a message that reinforces the transactional sexual relationships often experienced among teenagers and young women in Nevis.

Others have expressed concerns about the ways in which Latina women are portrayed in media. The "spicy Latina" archetype is easy to find in many movies and television shows, often in such a way that the Latin American woman is depicted as a seductress with a quick temper (Brown 2015). The long-running television show *Sábado Gigante*, which began in Chile and later became an entertainment staple of Latin American television that aired for 53 years until its retirement in 2015, garnered concerns of an increasing trend where nearly every woman featured on air was provocatively dressed. Some of the ways in which the "hot Latina" stereotype were promoted were more subtle, such as in the comedy sketches where the female comedians would be scantily clad while the males would be given the comedic lines. Others were more overt, however, such as dancing competitions where the women would be in thong bikini bottoms while hosts and audience members critiqued their visual appeal (Miranda 2015). During carnival season in Brazil, each commercial break on the GLOBO broadcast network begins with a naked woman dancing while covered in glitter (Garcia-Navarro 2014). This stereotype is even seen in video games, with Latina women often being used to represent members of a minority class with sexualized bodies beyond those of other secondary characters and often relegated to a role of damsel-in-distress or love/sexual interest (Aldama 2018).

The media also has a positive impact on women's sexuality in Latin America. For example, television shows have been used as a form of activism in Nicaragua, inspiring discussions on topics that are often censored in schools and churches (Howe 2008). One popular show, *El Sexto Sentido* (The Sixth Sense), was originally aimed at adolescents and young adults but was often watched by families. The show tackled issues of rape, unintended pregnancy, teenage parenting, abortion, sexual abuse, and sexual orientation, including same-sex attraction between women. Viewers were concerned that the Nicaraguan government, influenced by the church, would remove the show from television or censor it, especially if it continued with abortion storylines. Their concerns did not ultimately come to fruition, which enabled the storylines to continue and the show to promote important conversations (Howe 2008).

The use of media for fostering conversations about sexuality is a meaningful step forward in Latin America. Many difficult topics need to be addressed by the general public, law enforcement, politicians, and religious leaders. Rates of poverty in regions across Latin America contribute to ongoing issues that threaten the sexual and reproductive health of women. Additional concerns result from cultural beliefs and norms that were reviewed in this chapter. It is difficult to describe women's sexuality in Latin America according to broad trends because of the abundant religious and cultural influences. Across the Caribbean and Central and South Americas however, one thing is for certain: effective measures for alleviating problematic issues must begin with addressing the widespread poverty and lack of opportunities that permeate the lives of countless Latina and Afro-Caribbean women.

REFERENCES

Aldama, F. 2018. *The Routledge Companion to Gender, Sex, and Latin American Culture.* New York: Routledge.

Alvarez, C., J. A. Bauermeister, and A. M. Villarruel. 2014. "Sexual Communication and Sexual Behavior among Young Adult Heterosexual Latinos." *Journal of the Association of Nurses in AIDS Care* 25 (6): 577–88. https://doi.org/10.1016/j.jana.2014.06.005.

Araujo, Kathya, and Mercedes Prieto. 2008. *Estudios Sobre Sexualidades en América Latina* [Studies on Sexualities in Latin America]. Quito, Ecador: Flacso-Sede.

Bailey, A., and J. P. Figueroa. 2016. "A Framework for Sexual Decision-Making among Female Sex Workers in Jamaica." *Archives of Sexual Behavior* 45: 911–21.

Barrow, C. 2005. "The 'At Risk' Behaviours, Sub-Cultures and Environments of Adolescent Girls in Barbados: Sexuality, Reproductive Health, and HIV/AIDS." UNICEF Caribbean Area Organisation (CAO). Accessed July 27, 2022. https://nanopdf.com/download/hiv-aids-unicef-report-title-page_pdf.

Besse, S. K. 1989. "Crimes of Passion: The Campaign against Wife Killing in Brazil, 1910–1940." *Journal of Social History* 22 (4): 653.

Blackwood, E. 2000. "Culture and Women's Sexualities." *Journal of Social Issues* 56 (2): 223–38.

Bott, S., A. Guedes, M. Goodwin, and J. A. Mendoza. 2012. *Violence against Women in Latin America and the Caribbean: A Comparative Analysis of Population-Based Data from 12 Countries*. Washington, DC: Pan American Health Organization.

Brazilian Ministry of Health. 2011. *Boletim Epidemiologico do AIDS/DST* (*Epidemiological Bulletin on AIDS/STD*). Brasilia: Ministerio da Saude.

Brown, J. 2015. *Beyond Bombshells: The New Action Heroine in Popular Culture*. Jackson: University Press of Mississippi.

Bueno, I. 2017. "Call of the Aztec Midwife: Childbirth in the 16th Century." *National Geographic History* 2 (6): 12–15.

Caricote Agreda, Esther. 2006. "Influencia de los Estereotipos de Género en la Salud Sexual en la Adolescencia [Influence of Gender Stereotypes on Sexual Health in Adolescence]." *Educere* 10 (34): 463–70.

Castillo, L., F. V. Perez, R. Castillo, and M. R. Ghosheh. 2010. "Construction and Initial Validation of the Marianismo Beliefs Scale." *Counselling Psychology Quarterly* 23 (2): 163–75. https://doi.org/10.1080/09515071003776036.

Center for Reproductive Rights. 2017. "Sexual Violence in Latin America and the Caribbean Takes Center Stage at the Inter-American Commission on Human Rights." October 26, Press release. Accessed Jul 27, 2022. https://reproductiverights.org/sexual-violence-in-latin-america-and-the-caribbean-takes-center-stage-at-the-inter-american-commission-on-human-rights/.

Central Intelligence Agency. 2019. "World Factbook: Haiti." December 5. Accessed December 14, 2019. https://www.cia.gov/library/publications/the-world-factbook/geos/ha.html#field-anchor-people-and-society-religions.

Cherry, A. L., and M. E. Dillon. 2014. *International Handbook of Adolescent Pregnancy: Medical, Psychosocial, and Public Health Responses*. New York: Springer.

Chevannes, B. 2001. *Learning to Be a Man: Culture, Socialization and Gender Identity in Five Caribbean Communities*. Kingston, Jamaica: University of West Indies Press.

Corrêa, M. 1981. *Os crimes da paixão*. Vol. 33. Sao Paulo, Brazil: Brasiliense.

Curtis, D. 2009. *Pleasures and Perils: Girls' Sexuality in a Caribbean Consumer Culture*. New Brunswick, NJ: Rutgers University Press.

Darroch, J. E., S. Audam, and A. Biddlecom. 2017. *Adding It Up: Investing in Contraception and Maternal and Newborn Health—Supplementary Tables*. New York: Guttmacher Institute.

Davison, T. 2019. "Latin America Has a Child Marriage Crisis." *Latin America Reports* (blog), April 29. Accessed June 22, 2022. https://latinamericareports.com/latin-america-has-a-child-marriage-crisis/1831.

de Leon, R., F. Ewerling, S. J. Serruya, M. F. Silveria, A. Sanhueza, A. Moazzam, F. Becerra-Posada, et al. 2019. "Contraceptive Use in Latin America and the Caribbean with a Focus on Long-Acting Reversible Contraceptives: Prevalence and Inequalities in 23 Countries." *Lancet Global Health* 72: e227–35. https://doi.org/10.1016/S2214-109X1830481-9.

Digital History. 2019. "Slavery Fact Sheet." Accessed February 29, 2020. http://www.digitalhistory.uh.edu/disp_textbook.cfm?smtID=11&psid=3807.

Drakes, N., C. Perks, A. Kumar, K. Quimby, C. Clarke, R. Patel, I. R. Hambleton, et al. 2013. "Prevalence and Risk Factors for Intergenerational

Sex: A Cross-Sectional Cluster Survey of Barbadian Females Aged 15–19." *BMC Womens Health* 13: 53. https:/doi.org/10.1186/1472 -6874-13-53.

The Economist. 2017. "Venezuelans Sell Sex in Colombia to Survive." July 20. Accessed December 27, 2019. https://www.economist.com/the -americas/2017/07/20/venezuelans-sell-sex-in-colombia-to-survive.

Espinosa-Hernandez, G., S. A. Vasilenko, and M. Y. Bamaca-Colbert. 2016. "Sexual Behaviors in Mexico: The Role of Values and Gender across Adolescence." *Journal of Research on Adolescence* 263: 603–9. https://doi.org/10.1111/jora.12209.

Essayag, S. 2017. *From Commitment to Action: Policies to End Violence against Women in Latin America and the Caribbean.* Panama: UN Development Programme and UN Entity for Gender Equality and the Empowerment of Women.

Evans, S. T. 2008. "Concubines and Cloth: Women and Weaving in Aztec Palaces and Colonial Mexico." In *Servants of the Dynasty,* edited by A. Walthall, 215–31. Berkeley: University of California Press.

Fanon, F. 1967. *Black Skin, White Masks.* New York: Grove Press.

Faulkner, S. L., and P. K. Mansfield. 2002. "Reconciling Messages: The Process of Sexual Talk for Latinas." *Qualitative Health Research* 123: 310–28. https://doi.org/10.1177/104973202129119919.

Figueroa, J. P. 2006. *Understanding Sexual Behaviour in Jamaica.* Kingston, Jamaica: The Chevannes Conference.

Garces, R. R., and C. V. Vega. 2016. *Reforming the Legislation on the Age of Marriage: Successful Experiences and Lessons Learned from Latin America and the Caribbean.* Panama: UN Women.

Garcia, P. J., A. S. Benzaken, and E. Galban. 2011. "STI Management and Control in Latin America: Where Do We Stand and Where Do We Go from Here?" *Sexually Transmitted Infections* 87: ii7–ii9.

Garcia-Navarro, L. 2014. "Which Place Is More Sexist: The Middle East or Latin America?" NPR, March 16. Accessed June 18, 2020. https://www.npr.org/sections/parallels/2014/03/11/289058115 /which-place-is-more-sexist-the-middle-east-or-latin-america.

Girls Not Brides. 2017. *Child Marriage in Latin America and the Caribbean.* London: Girls Not Brides.

Goicolea, I., M. Wulff, M. Sebastian, and A. Ohman. 2010. "Adolescent Pregnancies and Girls' Sexual and Reproductive Rights in the Amazon Basin of Ecuador: An Analysis of Providers' and Policy

Makers' Discourses." *BMC International Health and Human Rights* 10, article 12. https://doi.org/10.1186/1472-698X-10-12

Goldstein, M. A. 2002. "The Biological Roots of Heat-of-Passion Crimes and Honour Killings." *Politics and the Life Sciences* 212: 28–37.

Hall, D., and T. Thistlewood. 1999. *In Miserable Slavery: Thomas Thistlewood in Jamaica, 1750-86.* Kingston, Jamaica: University of the West Indies Press.

Hallam, J. 2004. *Slavery and the Making of America: Men, Women, & Gender.* New York: Thirteen/WNET.

Houston, S., and K. Taube. 2010. La sexualidad entre los antiguos mayas [Sexuality among the Ancient Mayas]. *Arqueologia Mexicana* 104: 38–45.

Howe, C. 2008. "Spectacles of Sexuality: Televisionary Activism in Nicaragua." *Cultural Anthropology* 231: 48–84.

Hutchinson, E. Q. 2003. "Add Gender and Stir? Cooking Up Gendered Histories of Modern Latin America." *Latin American Research Review* 38 (1): 267–87.

Jimenez, U. C. 2004. "How Much for Your Love? Prostitution among the Aztecs." Chacmool Conference, Calgary, Canada.

Kempadoo, K. 2000. "Sandoms and Other Exotic Women: Prostitution and Race in the Caribbean." In *Dispatches from the Ebony Tower: Intellectuals Confront the African American Experience*, edited by M. Marable, 75–89. New York: Columbia University Press.

Kempadoo, K. 2004. *Sexing the Caribbean: Gender, Race, and Sexual Labor.* New York: Routledge.

Kendall, T., and C. Albert. 2015. "Experiences of Coercion to Sterilize and Forced Sterilization among Women Living with HIV in Latin America." *Journal of the International AIDS Society* 181: 19462. https://doi.org/10.7448/ias.18.1.19462.

LaFont, S. 2001. "Very Straight Sex: The Development of Sexual Mores in Jamaica." *Journal of Colonialism and Colonial History* 23. https://doi.org/10.1353/cch.2001.0051.

Long, J., B. A. Caruso, D. Lopez, K. Vancraeynest, M. Sahin, K. L. Andes, and M. C. Freeman. 2013. *WASH in Schools Empowers Girls' Education in Rural Cochbamba, Bolivia: An Assessment of Menstrual Hygiene Management in Schools.* New York: United Nations Children's Fund.

Marvan, M. L., and P. Trujillo. 2009. "Menstrual Socialization, Beliefs, and Attitudes Concerning Menstruation in Rural and Urban

Mexican Women." *Health Care for Women International* 311: 53–67. https://doi.org/10.1080/07399330902833362.

Miller, J. C. 2018. *The Transatlantic Slave Trade.* Encyclopedia Virginia, August 2. Accessed February 29, 2020. https://www .encyclopediavirginia.org/Transatlantic_Slave_Trade_The#start _entry.

Miranda, C. 2015. "'Sábado Gigante' Has, for Better and Worse, Defined Spanish-Language TV." *Los Angeles Times*, April 18. Accessed June 18, 2020. https://www.latimes.com/nation/la-et-cam-sabado -gigante-for-better-and-worse-defined-spanish-language-tv -20150417-column.html.

Moloney, A. 2017. "Shame Silences Ecuador's Indigenous People Trafficked for Sex." Reuters, July 27. Accessed December 27, 2019. https://www.reuters.com/article/us-ecuador-humantrafficking -idUSKBN1AC2NU.

Moloney, A. 2018. "Venezuelans Sell Sex and Hair to Survive in Colombian Border City." Reuters, June 10. Accessed December 27, 2019. https://www.reuters.com/article/us-colombia-migrants-venezuela /venezuelans-sell-sex-and-hair-to-survive-in-colombian-border -city-idUSKBN1J703B.

Moreno, C. L. 2007. "The Relationship between Culture, Gender, Structural Factors, Abuse, Trauma, and HIV/AIDS for Latinas." *Qualitative Health Research* 173: 340–52. https://doi.org/10.1177 /1049732306297387.

Morgan, P. E. 2013. "Meet Me in the Islands: Sun, Sand and Transactional Sex in Caribbean Discourse." *Anthurium: A Caribbean Studies Journal* 101: 1–19.

Morrison, Andrew, Mary Ellsberg, and Sarah Bott. 2007. "Addressing Gender -Based Violence in the Latin American and Caribbean Region: A Critical Review of Interventions." *World Bank Researcher Observer* 22 (1): 25–51.

Murrell, N. S. 2010. *Afro-Caribbean Religions: An Introduction to Their Historical, Cultural, and Sacred Traditions.* Philadelphia: Temple University Press.

Nichols, D. L., and E. Rodriguez-Alegria. 2017. *The Oxford Handbook of the Aztecs.* New York: Oxford University Press.

Noblega, M. 2012. "Risk and Protective Factors for Physical and Emotional Intimate Partner Violence against Women in a Community of Lima, Peru." *Journal of Interpersonal Violence* 27 (18): 3644 –59. https://doi.org/10.1177/0886260512447522.

Pan American Health Organization. 2018. "PAHO Mortality Database." February 20. Accessed December 14, 2019. https://hiss.paho.org /pahosys/lcd.php.

Pew Research Center. 2014. *Religion in Latin America: Widespread Change in a Historically Catholic Religion*. Washington, DC: Pew Research Center.

Plan International and UNICEF. 2014. *Experiences and Accounts of Pregnancy amongst Adolescents*. Panama: Plan and UNICEF.

Population Reference Bureau. 2019. *2019 World Population Datasheet*. Washington, DC: Population Reference Bureau.

Provost, C. 2014. "El Salvador: Meet the Women Who Dare Challenge the Anti-Abortion State." *The Guardian*, April 17. https://www .theguardian.com/global-development/2014/apr/17/beatriz-case -resistance-el-salvador-abortion-law.

Prower, T. 2018. *Queer Magic: LGBT+ Spirituality and Culture from Around the World*. Woodbury, MN: Llewellyn Worldwide.

Puentes Rodrıguez, Yamira. 2008. "La Familia en la Educacion de la Sexualidad: un Enfoque Filosofico [Family in Sexuality Education: A Philosophical Approach]." *REV Sexologıa y Sociedad* 14 (38): 1–9

Rosen, H. 2009. *Terror in the Heart of Freedom: Citizenship, Sexual Violence, and the Meaning of Race in the Postemancipation South*. Chapel Hill: University of North Carolina Press.

Rudman, L. A., J. C. Fetterolf, and D. T. Sanchez. 2013. "What Motivates the Sexual Double Standard? More Support for Male versus Female Control Theory." *Personality and Social Psychology Bulletin* 392: 250–63. https://doi.org/10.1177/0146167212472375.

Ruiz, D., and B. Sobrino. 2018. *Breaking the Mould: Changing Belief Systems and Gender Norms to Eliminate Violence against Women*. Oxford: Oxfam International.

Sanchez, Z. M., S. A. Nappo, J. I. Cruz, E. A. Carlini, C. M. Carlini, and S. S. Martins. 2013. "Sexual Behavior among High School Students in Brazil: Alcohol Consumption and Legal and Illegal Drug Use Associated with Unprotected Sex." *Clinics* 684: 489–94. https://doi.org/10.6061/clinics/20130409.

Santeria Church. 2012. "The Importance of Women in Santeria." June 27. Accessed February 29, 2020. http://santeriachurch.org/the -importance-of-women-in-santeria.

Senior, O. 1991. *Working Miracles: Women's Lives in the English-Speaking Caribbean*. Bloomington: Indiana University Press.

Sharpe, J., and S. Pinto. 2006. "The Sweetest Taboo: Studies of Caribbean Sexualities; a Review Essay." *Signs* 321: 247–74.

Tavarez, D. 2017. *Words and Worlds Turned Around: Indigenous Christianities in Colonial Latin America*. Boulder: University Press of Colorado.

Ulloa Pizarro, C. 2014. Tensiones y conflictos en las políticas reguladoras de la salud sexual y reproductiva de las mujeres en México 2000–2012: El problema de la incorporación del principio de equidad y del derecho a la igualdad de género [Tensions and Conflicts in Regulatory Policies for Women's Sexual and Reproductive Health in Mexico 2000–2012: The Problem of the Incorporation of the Principle of Equity and the Right to Gender Equality]. *Sociológica México* 29 (82): 125–50.

United Nations. 2014. "World Contraceptive Use 2014." arch Accessed December 10, 2019. https://www.un.org/en/development/desa/population/publications/dataset/contraception/wcu2014.asp.

United Nations. 2019. *World Population Prospects: The 2019 Revision*. New York: United Nations Population Division.

United Nations Children's Fund. 2016. *The State of the World's Children*. New York: UNICEF.

United Nations OHCHR. 2018. *Venezuela: Dire Living Conditions Worsening by the Day, UN Human Rights Experts Warn*. Geneva, Switzerland: OHCHR.

United Nations Programme on HIV/AIDS. 2009. *Jamaica, 2010 Country Progress Report*. Geneva, Switzerland: United Nations.

United States Conference of Catholic Bishops. 2020. *Love and Sexuality*. Accessed February 29, 2020. http://www.usccb.org/beliefs-and-teachings/what-we-believe/love-and-sexuality/index.cfm.

U.S. Department of State. 2019. *Trafficking in Persons Report*. Washington, DC: U.S. Department of State.

Vecchio, Rick. 2004. "Erotic Ceramics Reveal Dirty Little Secret." *Los Angeles Times*, March 7. https://www.latimes.com/archives/la-xpm-2004-mar-07-adfg-pottery7-story.html.

Vega-Briones, G., and M. C. Jaramillo-Cardona. 2010. Percepciones y actitudes de los hombres de la frontera norte de México en relación con el uso de condones, práctica de la vasectomía y chequeos de próstata. *Revista Gerencia y Politicas de Salud* 9 (18): 50–77.

Wekker, G. 1999. "What's Identity Got to Do with It? Rethinking Identity in Light of the Mati Work in Suriname." In *Female Desires:*

Same-Sex Relations and Transgender Practices Across Cultures, edited by E. Blackwood, S. E. Wieringa, and S. Wieringa, 118–38. New York: Columbia University Press.

Wekker, G. 2006. *The Politics of Passion: Women's Sexual Culture in the Afro-Surinamese Diaspora.* New York: Columbia University Press.

White, E. F. 2001. *Dark Continent of our Bodies: Black Feminism and the Politics of Respectability.* Philadelphia: Temple University Press.

Whitehorne-Smith, P., and M. Irons-Morgan. 2015. *Strengthening Adolescent Component of National HIV Programmes through Country Assessments in Jamaica: Preliminary Report of Rapid Assessment.* Kingston, Jamaica: UNICEF Jamaica.

Wood, E. B., M. K. Hutchinson, E. Kahwa, H. Hewitt, and N. Waldron. 2011. "Jamaican Adolescent Girls with Older Male Sexual Partners." *Journal of Nursing Scholarship* 434: 396–404. https://doi.org/10.1111/j.1547-5069.2011.01418.x.

Wooding, C. J. 1972. "The Winti-Cult in the Para-District." *Caribbean Studies* 12: 51–78.

World Health Organization. 2006. *UNAIDS Fact Sheet: Latin America.* Geneva, Switzerland: UNAIDS.

THREE

Europe

Marissa A. Mosley and Tatjana M. Farley

In this chapter, the role of European women in history and modern times is explored, including what has stayed the same and what has changed. Given the large number of countries in Europe, the chapter is organized according to regions rather than countries. Specifically, northern Europe consists of the Aland Islands, Channel Islands (Guernsey, Jersey, Sark, etc.), Denmark, Estonia, Faroe Islands, Finland, Iceland, Ireland, Isle of Man, Latvia, Lithuania, Norway, Svalbard and Jan Mayen Islands, Sweden, and the United Kingdom of Great Britain and Northern Ireland. Eastern Europe includes Belarus, Bulgaria, Czechia, Hungary, Poland, Republic of Moldova, Romania, Russian Federation, Slovakia, and Ukraine. Southern Europe refers to Albania, Andorra, Bosnia and Herzegovina, Croatia, Gibraltar, Greece, Holy See, Italy, Montenegro, North Macedonia, Portugal, San Marino, Serbia, Slovenia, and Spain. Finally, Western Europe includes Austria, Belgium, France, Germany, Liechtenstein, Luxembourg, Monaco, Netherlands, and Switzerland (United Nations Statistics 1999).

A BRIEF HISTORY OF WOMEN'S SEXUALITY IN EUROPE

The Upper Paleolithic period began in ancient Europe approximately 40,000 years ago. During this era, women's bodies were sexualized and immortalized through art and sculptures. Women's sexuality was primarily conceptualized in terms of reproduction and fertility. Cave paintings and figurines presented women as goddesses or as ritualistic symbols that were controlled by men. Given that women were perceived according to their fertility and reproduction, their age and physical features were accentuated. Much of the artwork of the time suggests that women were viewed as a means of sexual pleasure for men, women, and themselves. For example, specific parts of female sexuality, including specific sex organs were displayed in iconography in countries such as France, Germany, and Austria. Scenes of masturbation and homosexual and heterosexual acts have been found in Greece, Spain, Russia, Portugal, Serbia, and Italy. Archaeological evidence and artistic remnants portray women in erotic forms and demonstrate the power differences between men and women. Ancient remnants also display women's roles and the rituals of that time (Sánchez Romero 2015).

During medieval times, from the 5th century up until the 15th century, religion dominated the lives of the people throughout Europe. Catholicism and Protestantism were two powerful Christian institutions that had a strong influence on women's roles. While Catholicism dominated, a German monk named Martin Luther wrote the "95 Theses" to highlight objections to the Catholic Church in the 16th century. As a result, the Protestant Reformation resulted in the development of a distinction between the Protestant faith and the Catholic faith by changes to the teachings and doctrines. The division of Catholics and Protestants was particularly impactful in challenging the social structure of countries in Northern Europe. For example, violence often resulted in countries such as England, Ireland, Scotland, and France, as the dominant religion of the country influenced the selection of leaders, how the people were governed, and the expectations of citizens. Despite the theological distinctions, Catholicism and Protestantism were fairly consistent in the treatment and governance of women.

Joan of Arc broke free from the traditional mold of women as a leader on the battlefield. Joan is best known for her role in the Hundred Years' War. She fought on the battlefield in order to help Charles VII get anointed and crowned king of France. Once this was achieved, Joan was imprisoned by a Germanic tribe and sent to England. Though she hoped to be saved by King Charles or through divine intervention, she was sentenced to death by fire. In her last demonstration of power, Joan neither screamed nor cried during her death; she only prayed (Heckel n.d.).

Adoration of St. Joan of Arc. (J. William Fosdick, Adoration of St. Joan of Arc, 1896, fire etched wood relief, Smithsonian American Art Museum, Gift of William T. Evans, 1910.9.8)

Under a Catholic-controlled state, women were expected to be celibate, to become nuns, or to become mothers (Richards 1994). The Protestant Reformation encouraged women to become wives and mothers rather than being either forced into the convent to become nuns or simply remaining celibate (Welborn 2017). Sexual activity and sexual desire outside the context of marriage were considered sins in both religions. Engaging in sex represented low morality and introduced the potential for health concerns. The medical world believed too much sex or too little sex put the health of men and women at risk through sexually transmitted diseases or by not keeping the body regular through sexual release. Women had to get married and have sex frequently in order to prevent this from happening; however, when this was not possible, physicians encouraged masturbation (Harvey 2018). The Catholic Church was morally opposed to masturbation as it was considered a sin, but the institutions trusted medicine enough to not condemn those engaging in masturbation. Regardless of which religion was ruling the country at the time, sex was not meant to be pleasurable and, if it was, it was considered sinful (Brundage 1987).

Through the Middle Ages, sexual activity was expected for the purpose of procreation. However, from a religious perspective, sex was considered morally wrong if it was occurring solely for pleasure. Women continued to be viewed mainly through their sexuality, which included the dichotomies of celibacy versus promiscuity and chastity versus adultery. These dichotomies were represented in art and literature. Virginity was of the utmost importance for women, both in terms of their bridal dowries and eternal salvation in the eyes of the church. Women were encouraged to either join the church as nuns and pay their dowry to the church, or use their virginity for higher dowries, thus making them more attractive to grooms (Heckel n.d.).

Strict rules were enforced regarding the rights and roles of women. Women had no right to serve in positions of public office, including the government and courts of law. They were living in patriarchal societies and considered possessions of their fathers and subsequently their husbands. Once they were married, women gained power inside the home and within their families of procreation. Although they were financially dependent on their husbands, wives were responsible for a majority of tasks and the maintenance of the home and children. It was through the performance of household duties that women accumulated their sense of power within their personal lives (McNamara and Wemple 1973).

As the Roman Empire declined, Germanic tribes began possessing previously occupied Roman territories, and the roles of women started to change. The new German oversight moved away from distinguishing between private and public lives. This meant that women coming from families with economic power were allowed to own and inherit property and occupy a role in the public sphere. While many women throughout Europe were still forced to marry a suitor chosen by the woman's parents, several countries moved toward allowing the bride to keep some, if not all, of her "bride gift." The bride gift consisted of money, goods, and/or property given to the family or bride in exchange for marriage. This practice still forced women into marriages with suitors they had not chosen but who provided the highest-quality bride gift. In England, arranged marriages and bride gifts were abolished in the early 11th century, and women were then able to select their own marital partners (McNamara and Wemple 1973).

Regarding sex and consummation of marriage, brides were given a "morning gift" from their husbands. Some examples of morning gifts included pieces of jewelry or small, valuable pieces of furniture to compensate for the bride's loss of virginity. Under Germanic rule, women were still expected to fulfill their domestic duties, including attending to spousal and reproductive obligations. Women acquired property through the bride gifts and morning gifts, although there is uncertainty as to whether women were allowed to keep this property for themselves or hand it over to their families. Some women were able to acquire considerable wealth and power through their husband's status or upon their husband's death (McNamara and Wemple 1973). Given that a woman's status was directly connected to her husband's position, women who remained single or wives who lost their husbands to death or separation would often support themselves through prostitution. Although prostitution was heavily frowned upon in the same manner as it is today, it was an active business that allowed women the opportunity to support themselves in lieu of spousal support. Women in dire financial positions even turned to prostitution to supplement their primary income (Heckel n.d.).

In the 10th century, social class played a larger role in the arrangement of marriages and women's roles. Men and women of higher classes were forced to marry and have children with those in the same social class. When a woman married outside of her class, she assumed her husband's position of power, whether higher or lower. This practice could determine a woman's social mobility, for better or worse. Across social classes, women were expected and encouraged to occupy standard gendered roles of housewife and mother. Even queens adhered to these roles and were expected to perform their wifely duties. Women who did not adhere to their roles were harshly criticized (McNamara and Wemple 1973).

Regardless of how women supported their families and themselves, they faced backlash from politicians and religious leaders. Women had the

Women throughout history understood the risks associated with sexual transgressions, including ostracism and even death. Queens were not excluded from these punishments if charged with adultery. Anne Boleyn was the second wife of King Henry VIII of England. She exercised much political power by encouraging Henry's succession from the Catholic Church and leading the country to the Reformation. She greatly impacted history but ultimately faced an early death. King Henry VIII lost interest in Anne and was disappointed in her for not producing a male heir, so he had her charged with adultery and incest with her brother.

legal ability to acquire land, and subsequently political power, upon the death of their husband. This right, supplemented with their power as the heads of families, created the opportunity for status and freedom. As women gained financial security, men criticized them for disrupting the traditional family system. Irrespective of such criticisms, women in the 9th to 11th centuries were able to exercise greater power than those of previous generations. They were increasingly involved in government, landowning, the church, and even the military (McNamara and Wemple 1973).

Toward the end of the Middle Ages and into modern Europe, a shift from Paganism toward Christianity occurred, and marriage and sexuality became more regulated. Marriage shifted from familial arrangements to consensual partnerships. Consummation was required to make marriage binding, and sex outside marriage was considered adultery, punishable by the courts. Churches were deeply involved in legal matters such that marital issues would be heard by both a church and a legal court. Records indicate that adultery trials typically focused on women's reputations. Although the number of women accusing their husbands of adultery in court was greater than the number of men accusing women, adulteresses were more often brought before the church. Prostitution, which was generally accepted earlier in the Middle Ages, became illegal in both England and France. Concubines were a point of legal contention. During the Roman Empire, "concubines" referred to women who lived with men instead of or in addition to a wife, whereas in the later Middle Ages, the term referred to any woman in a relationship with a man outside of marriage. It is worth noting that there is no comparable term for men who took residence with a woman outside the context of marriage, further highlighting the gender gap and power differentials between men and women across time (Karras 2011).

During this time period, women were considered "dangerous" due to their sexuality and menstruation. The medical community led the charge to gain insight and understanding about women's sexuality. It became popular to pathologize women for conditions, including nymphomania, menstrual madness, masturbation, and hysteria. In the 19th century, this movement led the medical community to remove the ovaries and clitoris because they were considered the offending organs responsible for these female disorders (Studd and Schwenkhagen 2009). Society went so far as to present women as monsters in images, books, and pamphlets. They were displayed as controlling men and engaging in sinful, sexual behaviors (Brenner 2009).

Witch trials, Germany 1555. (Everett Collection/Shutterstock)

Many people felt fearful of women during this time, which contributed to the witch hunts that were common from the later Middle Ages through to early modern Europe. Witch hunts began in the mid-1400s and escalated throughout the late 1600s. In total, 80,000 women were put to death due to suspicion and/or charges of being witches. Among the European countries, Germany had the most deaths, and Ireland had the fewest. People believed that women were working with the devil and, as a result, were filled with lust. Previously, women with perceived magical powers had been trusted and elevated by the people, but the spread of Christianity caused these same women to be perceived and persecuted as witches (Bailey 2006).

Once the witch-hunt hysteria calmed, women found new meaning and purpose in their roles. They worked to expand upon their occupations and activities, including through education and the arts. The development of industries allowed women to take positions as domestic workers (i.e., housekeepers) although they were still afforded little financial security or independence. Women were often forced to turn their earnings over to their husbands, who were the main financial providers. Women were also getting married at later ages than before. In the early Middle Ages, they had been forced to marry older men upon reaching puberty, whereas in the late 16th century, they were getting married in their 20s to spouses of a comparable age. This shift may have resulted from a recognition of women's household contributions, which encouraged their families of origin to keep them in the home for a longer period of time.

During this time, women also found new roles and meaning within the arts. Some individuals engaged in what were considered gender performances, with men dressing as women and women dressing as men both inside and outside of theatrical performances. Cross-dressing became widely accepted in England, France, Spain, and Italy in the late 16th and early 17th centuries, allowing women to assume acting roles in the theater that were previously reserved for men. Along with their roles in the theater, women were introducing their writing into the public sphere. Upperclass and noble women generally wrote from a privileged perspective, whereas middle- and lower-class women wrote of activism, challenging the social system and their gender roles. Although they were making some gains in terms of social power, women were still dependent on men financially (Dolan 2003).

CULTURE AND ATTITUDES TOWARD SEXUALITY

The preceding overview of European history provides the context for understanding women's roles and sexualities in present day. Culture refers to systems of knowledge that are shared by a large group of people; people shape cultures and are shaped by culture (European Institute for Gender Equality 2019a). Gender is relevant to culture because the socially constructed roles of gender are determined by culture, and these differ across time and place. Gender is a construction that is defined by the power relations between women and men and the norms and values regarding what is considered feminine and masculine. The collective beliefs about female and male roles may contribute to stereotypes that limit or enable opportunities for each sex to act within the cultural context.

The Nordic countries (Denmark, Finland, Iceland, Sweden, and Norway) have long held traditions that favor equality between individuals and social groups regardless of gender. People in Nordic countries are generally accepting of women's and adolescents' sexualities (Træen et al. 2018). However, in many Southern European countries, such as Italy, Greece, Croatia, Slovenia, and Spain, sexuality is strongly influenced by patriarchal traditions. In these countries, men are expected to be sexually motivated, dominant, assertive, and independent, while women are expected to be sexually passive, submissive, and dependent (Træen et al. 2018).

A common difference in sexual behavior and expression across European countries is the prevalence and frequency of masturbation. Men typically report that they are more likely to be engaging in masturbation than women. Masturbation prevalence among women has increased over time in European societies, yet it is often associated with feelings of guilt and shame (Baćak a and Štulhofer 2011; Hogarth and Ingham 2009). In the early 1990s, 42% of women in France between 18 and 69 reported having masturbated. Data collected from the general population in Great Britain in 1999 and 2001 indicate that the lifetime prevalence of masturbation among women between 16 and 44 was 71% (Baćak a and Štulhofer 2011; Gerressu et al. 2008). Two Dutch population-based surveys found an increase in masturbation frequency from 55% in 1991 to 75% in 2006 (Baćak a and Štulhofer 2011; Vanwesenbeeck, Bakker, and Gesell 2010). Women with strong religious beliefs are less likely to report masturbation, as are those who find it difficult to talk about sex and sexuality with their partners (Gerressu et al. 2008).

Attitudes regarding same-sex relationships differ based on region. A majority of people in Western Europe support same-sex marriage, with the highest support in Sweden (88%), Denmark (86%), and the Netherlands (86%). The main exception is Italy, whose citizens are strongly connected to the Roman Catholic Church and who has been less supportive than other European countries but began recognizing same-sex civil unions in 2016 (Lipka and Masci 2019). Central and Eastern European countries are more broadly opposed to same-sex marriage, with only 5% of Russians and 9% of Ukrainians in favor of them. The highest level of support from this region is the Czech Republic, where 65% support same-sex marriage (Lipka and Masci 2019). No country in Central or Eastern Europe allows same-sex couples to marry legally, but the Czech Republic, Croatia, Estonia, Hungary, and a few others allow civil unions for same-sex couples. Same-sex marriage is legal in 16 countries in Europe (e.g., the Netherlands, Germany, Portugal, Ireland, and France), and 12 countries acknowledge some form of civil union or partnership but not marriage (e.g., Hungary, Italy, Cyprus, Greece, and Croatia). Twenty-two countries still do not acknowledge same-sex unions of any kind (e.g., Poland, Russia, Turkey, Romania and Bulgaria; Lipka and Masci 2019).

RELIGION AND SEXUALITY

Throughout Europe, religion continues to influence societal norms and expectations such as attitudes toward birth control, abortion, same-sex marriage, and fertility. While much of Europe remains Christian, nonaffiliated religious people and those identifying as Muslim, Jewish, Hindu, and

Buddhist continue to grow in number (Pew Research Center 2015). The three most dominant Christian affiliations are Orthodoxy, Catholicism, and Protestantism. Religious affiliation and its influence on sexuality vary across different regions in Europe. In Central and Eastern Europe, most people oppose same-sex marriage, while a majority of Western Europe support it (Pew Research Center 2018). This is likely influenced by the strong beliefs and identity associated with being Christian, either Catholic or Orthodox, in Central and Eastern Europe, respectively. Western Europeans are less likely to affiliate with a religious denomination; they are therefore more supportive of legal abortions, compared to those in Central and Eastern Europe (Pew Research Center 2018). However, the country of Ireland, which is more religious than other countries in Western Europe, did not legalize abortion and same-sex marriage until 2019 (Ferguson 2019).

The strong Christian identity throughout Europe has also influenced the structure of marriage and partnerships. Depending on the specific religion, women have been expected to remain married, even in unhappy unions, because divorce is perceived as contrary to the institution and sacrament (Oxley 2017). Previously, the law had worked against women, seeing them as not existing except within the context of their marriage (Oxley 2017). Once the Married Women's Property Act passed in 1870, women were allowed to own property and have an income separate from their husband; later in the 20th century, women were given the right to divorce (Oxley 2017).

SEXUAL VIOLENCE

Like many other world regions, sexual violence in Europe is a major health concern, with serious short- and long-term effects (De Schrijver et al. 2018). Sexual violence affects people of all genders and ages. Regardless of its context, sexual violence is a violating and painful experience that encompasses a range of behaviors such as sexual harassment, sexual violence without penetration, and attempted and completed rape (De Schrijver et al. 2018). It can include victimization, perpetration, or the witnessing of the violent act and can occur between strangers and people in close relationships (De Schrijver et al. 2018).

Gender-based violence stems from gender inequality and refers to violence that is directed at people because of their gender (European Institute for Gender Equality 2019f). It is important to note that although women face violence and discrimination based on gender, some women experience multiple and interrelated forms of violence relating to their other statuses, including race, disability, age, social class, religion, and sexual orientation (European Institute for Gender Equality 2019d). The terms "gender-based violence" and "violence against women" are used interchangeably. The approximate cost of gender-based violence in a given year is 366 billion euros. This figure includes the cost of lost economic output, provision of services (health, legal, and social), and the personal (physical and emotional) impact on the victim (European Institute for Gender Equality 2021).

Most gender-based violence is perpetrated by men against women and can take multiple forms, including physical, sexual, and psychological. Physical violence refers to any act that causes physical harm as a result of unlawful physical force. Serious or minor assaults, deprivation of liberties, and manslaughter are all considered physical violence (European Institute for Gender Equality 2019d). One in three women aged 15 and older have experienced physical violence in Europe (European Institute for Gender Equality 2019f). Sexual violence refers to any sexual act performed on an individual without the person's consent, including rape and sexual assault (European Institute for Gender Equality 2019d). In Europe, 1 in 3 women have experienced sexual violence by the age of 15, 1 in 2 women have experienced sexual harassment, and 1 in 20 women have been raped (European Institute for Gender Equality 2019f). Lastly, psychological violence is defined as any act that causes psychological harm to an individual, which can take the form of coercion, defamation, verbal assault, and harassment (European Institute for Gender Equality 2019d). Forty-four percent of women in Europe have experienced psychological abuse by a current or former partner (European Institute for Gender Equality 2022).

Across the European Union, 25% of people say they know a woman among their friends or family who has been a victim of domestic violence, 21% say they know a woman in their neighborhood, and 11% say they know a case from where they work or study (European Commission 2010). The highest reports of knowing a woman in their friends or family network are from Lithuania (48%), Latvia (39%), Estonia (39%), Sweden (39%), Finland (38%), and the UK (38%), and the lowest reports were from Bulgaria (11%), Italy (16%), Germany (16%), the Czech Republic (17%), and Slovakia (17%; European Commission 2010). Since 1999, there has been a general rise in the number of people reporting they know a victim of domestic violence, although Finland, Ireland, and Portugal report no significant change. The largest increases are in Luxembourg (31%, up from

18%), Belgium (34%, up from 22%), and Sweden (39%, up from 30%; European Commission 2010).

Sexual abuse and domestic violence disproportionately affect women and girls relative to boys and men, across all social classes. In the European Union, 9 out of 10 victims of intimate partner violence are women, with 12% to 35% of women experiencing intimate partner violence in a lifetime (European Institute for Gender Equality 2019e). Thirty percent of women in the EU report having been in a relationship in which they experienced some form of physical or sexual violence from their partner (European Institute for Gender Equality 2019e). Similarly, about 22% of women have experienced violence by someone other than their intimate partner, and 1 in 3 women has been a victim of physical and sexual violence from a partner, someone other than their partner, or both (European Institute for Gender Equality 2019e). The prevalence of intimate partner violence (including sexual and physical) in the European region is estimated to be 19.3% in high-income countries and 25.6% in low- and middle-income countries, indicating that approximately 49 million women between the ages of 14 and 49 have been abused (WHO 2013). Among children under 18, the sexual abuse rate is 9.6% (13.4% for girls and 5.7% for boys), suggesting that approximately 18 million children are affected. Actual rates may be much higher given that offenses occurring within families often go unreported. In an analysis of solved cases of sexual abuse, researchers found that in 26.85% of cases involving girls and 37.6% of cases involving boys, the offender was related to the child (Kury, Obergfell-Fuchs, and Woessner 2004).

Human trafficking involves the recruitment, transportation, or harboring of persons through threat, force, coercion, abduction, fraud, or deception for the purpose of exploitation (Zimmerman et al. 2008). Women and girls are often lured by individuals whom they or their families know, and they are forced into sex work or are exploited while working as domestic helpers or in factory and agricultural professions. The trafficking of women and girls is increasingly being recognized in Europe. In a study including women from Belgium, Bulgaria, Czech Republic, Italy, Moldova, Ukraine, and the United Kingdom, more than half of the women reported pre-trafficking experiences of sexual violence, 12% experienced forced or coerced sexual experiences before the age of 15 years, and 26% noted more than one perpetrator, which commonly included either a father or a stepfather. Nearly all the women (95%) experienced sexual violence while in the trafficking situation (Zimmerman et al. 2008).

Cyber violence is a relatively new form of violence that includes cyber-stalking, nonconsensual pornography (or "revenge porn"), gender-based

Open Your Eyes to Human Trafficking ceremony in France. (Ifeelstock/ Dreamstime.com)

slurs and harassment, "slut shaming," unsolicited pornography, "sextortion," rape and death threats, and electronically enabled trafficking (European Institute for Gender Equality 2019b). Nonconsensual pornography or "revenge porn" involves the distribution of sexually graphic photos or videos online without the consent of the participants in the images (European Institute for Gender Equality, 2019b). Cyber harassment includes unwanted sexually explicit emails, texts, or messages, inappropriate or offensive advances on social networking sites, and threats of physical or sexual violence by email or text. It is estimated that 1 in 10 women have experienced a form of cyber violence (European Institute for Gender Equality 2019b). In 2015, it became a criminal offense in the UK to share private sexual photos or videos without the consent of the people in the images. The offense can lead to a maximum of two years in prison (Cyber Violence against Women and Girls 2017). In France, a law titled the "Digital Republic Law" was adopted in 2016 and carries a two-year prison sentence for anyone found guilty of revenge porn. Similarly, in Germany in 2014, the court made it illegal to store intimate photos of a former partner after they have asked for the photos to be deleted (Cyber Violence against Women and Girls 2017). As access to the internet continues to increase, it is critical that digital spaces be made safe and empowering for women and girls (European Institute for Gender Equality 2019b).

In Europe, supranational and national governance are key to the development of policies concerning violence against women; however, there is still work that needs to be done regarding policy. The fight against violence toward women began more than 40 years ago in the United Kingdom, with many countries following the UK's lead from the 1980s onward, especially in Northern Europe. The term "violence against women" was defined in 1993 by the UN World Conference on Human Rights as "any act of gender-based violence" that resulted in or is likely to result in harm to women, that occurs in the family or within the general community, and that is perpetrated or condoned by the state (Hester 2004). This definition would include domestic violence, rape, and trafficking. In a sense, the linking of the different types of violence against women serves to maintain structural gender inequalities. Conversely, in some countries, the term has come to largely represent only one form of violence against women; for example, in the United Kingdom, the term "violence against women" mainly refers to domestic violence (Hester 2004). A recent analysis of rape legislation in 31 European countries reflected that only eight had laws defining rape as sex without consent, whereas all the others defined rape according to the force, threat of force or coercion, or the victims' (in)ability to defend themselves (Błuś 2018). Change is occurring within each country. For example, in 2018, both Iceland and Sweden adopted new legislation defining rape according to lack of consent, and Spain, Denmark, and Portugal are working toward legislation using this definition as well (Błuś 2018). While changing the laws will not eliminate rape or sexual violence, it is a critical step in the process.

REPRODUCTIVE HEALTH AND MENSTRUATION

Menstruation continues to be a taboo and stigmatized subject across the EU. Given that life spans are increasing and there are fewer pregnancies than centuries ago, women today often experience many more menstrual periods than women of previous generations did (Szarewski, von Stenglin, and Rybowski 2012). Yet inequality persists regarding menstrual hygiene management, information about menstruation, sanitation infrastructures, and the availability and affordability of menstrual hygiene supplies (WHO 2018).

In some areas, such as the former Yugoslav Republic of Macedonia, many female students, specifically in rural areas, do not attend school for four to five days during menstruation. Although missing school is more common in rural areas, many girls in urban areas also miss two to three days during their menstrual period. Reasons for needing to miss days include inadequate conditions for managing menstrual hygiene in addition to the high prices of sanitation products (WHO 2018). In other areas of Europe, such as Scotland, steps are being taken to combat inequalities and provide support to young girls. The Scottish government provides free menstrual sanitation products to girls in schools, colleges, and universities. They also began an initiative to provide access to digital platforms that include information about menstrual periods as well as access to the menstrual hygiene products (WHO 2018).

Many women report that their menstrual cycle has a severe negative impact on their life, including their sexual life, social life, sports/exercise activities, and work (Szarewski, von Stenglin, and Rybowski 2012). Women commonly report wanting the flexibility to not only decide when their menstrual cycle begins but also to control menstruation based on their life demands or to postpone their menstrual cycle altogether (Szarewski, von Stenglin, and Rybowski 2012). Across all ages, women's preference is to have fewer periods, though older women are more likely than younger ones to express this desire (Fiala et al. 2017). Quality of life is the most common reason for wishing to reduce or alter the menstrual cycle.

Most European countries have universal or near-universal health-care coverage for a core set of services, such as consultations with doctors, tests and examinations, and hospital care. In some countries, these core services may not be universal. In Ireland, only 50% of the population is covered for general practitioner visits. In Greece, a law was passed in 2016 that provided universal health-care coverage for everyone in the population, which closed the gap for the 10% of the population that was previously uninsured (OECD/EU 2018). Cyprus, Bulgaria, and Romania still have at least 10% of their population not covered for health services. In Romania, only 89% of the population was covered in 2017. The uninsured mainly included people working in agriculture, those who were self-employed, and those who were unemployed and not registered for unemployment or social security benefits (OECD/EU 2018). In terms of women's health care and coverage specifically, little published research addresses concerns that are unique to women. However, women's health has been discussed briefly in terms of how it relates to infant health. Infant mortality rates are low in most EU countries, with the exception of Romania, Bulgaria, and the Slovak Republic, which still have infant mortality rates above 5 deaths per 1,000 live births (OECD/EU 2018). These rates are estimated to be higher because induced abortions after the detection of congenital abnormalities are illegal, whereas in other countries, abortions are possible in cases of severe and/or lethal anomalies (OECD/EU 2018). The lack of information regarding health-related concerns in accessibility, affordability, availability, and quality of care for women is likely an indicator of the continued inequality of women.

The Together for Yes campaign is a current example of how women transformed their experiences with the health-care system. It is a group comprised of 70 organizations, groups, and communities in Ireland that aim to remove the Eighth Amendment regarding abortion laws (Together for Yes n.d.). The codirectors of the campaign include Grainne Griffin, a board member of the Abortion Rights Campaign; Orla O'Connor, the director of the National Women's Council of Ireland; and Ailbhe Smyth, the former head of women's studies at the University College of Dublin who has initiated numerous women's rights campaigns (Together for Yes n.d.). Together for Yes represents people who believe Ireland is compassionate and who advocate for laws that support, respect, and protect the health of women in their greatest time of need (Together for Yes n.d.). The campaign was ultimately successful in repealing the Eighth Amendment in May 2018, which led to free, safe, and legal abortion access for almost every county in Ireland (Abortion Rights Campaign 2019). This was a huge milestone, but the Abortion Rights Campaign is still pushing for continued work in this domain (Abortion Rights Campaign 2019). The Abortion Rights Campaign promotes support for stigma-free access to legal, free, and safe abortion care in Ireland. The Campaign also advocates for greater access to abortion care and aims to educate the public and policy makers about the need to expand the right to legal abortion care. The Abortion Rights Campaign website offers current news releases and information about the criteria for legal abortion as well as other options and resources (Abortion Rights Campaign 2018).

MARRIAGE AND PARTNERSHIPS

Throughout Western Europe, young adults are getting married at lower rates than those of previous generations. Nearly 80% of women born from the 1930s to the 1960s are married, whereas only 50% of Gen X and millennial women are getting married (Coleman 2013). The ability for women to gain independence and self-sufficiency through the workplace, ownership of property, and access to birth control has enabled them to marry later in life, if they choose to marry at all. These advances allow women to enter partnerships, on average, in their late 20s and early 30s, as opposed to their early 20s in the 1950s through the '90s, because they are now able to support themselves and control reproduction (Coleman 2013).

In Europe, it is common practice for partners to live apart while together. This means that they remain in a relationship together indefinitely while not requiring marriage or cohabitation. While this practice was traditionally used during periods of war and among those who traveled for work, such as migrant laborers, it has now become a preference for many EU residents (Coleman 2013). Marriage is still considered the norm, but across Europe, 15% to 30% of couples are choosing to cohabitate rather than marry (Coleman 2013). This rise in cohabitation rates has been coupled with an increase in premarital sex. As premarital sex has become more common, so has the availability of birth control for women. Birth control methods include abortion, sterilization, the IUD, the pill, condoms, planned intercourse, and interrupting intercourse prior to ejaculation. Most people in Western Europe have access to and use condoms, hormonal methods, and/or sterilization, while in Central and Eastern Europe, birth control is less readily available and traditional contraception, such as withdrawal or the rhythm method, is used by approximately one-quarter of the population. The legalization of birth control, including abortion and contraceptives, has been difficult to attain in most European countries across time (Salles 2018). Presently, a majority of women use contraception; however, the EU has among the lowest fertility rates in the world (Population Reference Bureau 2001). These low rates are linked to the increased accessibility of birth control options as well as to women choosing to not get married or to marry later in life.

MEDIA AND SEXUALITY

The Council of Europe reports that the representation of women in media has become more diverse in recent years and that there is greater awareness about gender-sensitive approaches to content production (Sarikakis 2013). Initiatives such as the Everyday Sexism Project in the UK have attempted to address sexist and hate language. This project put pressure on Facebook to filter and ban images and groups that portrayed

Social media plays a significant role in shaping European gender roles. Compared to men, women have limited access to the creation of media products and to decision-making in the media and culture industries. The media has historically played a critical role in the promotion of gender equality, as it reflects and creates sociocultural patterns and norms. The influence of the media, particularly with the advent of social media, is becoming increasingly powerful in shaping public opinion and culture. However, the media continues to depict life from a male perspective, and many factors serve to strengthen and perpetuate gender stereotypes and attitudes (European Institute for Gender Equality 2019a).

violence against women (Sarikakis 2013). Despite these efforts, women continue to be disadvantaged by the media, as they are portrayed in overly sexualized terms in advertisements, computer games, movies, magazines, music, fashion, and social media (Council of Europe 2018).

This portrayal of women and especially young girls has contributed to gender inequalities and violence against women (European Women's Lobby 2012). Young girls are increasingly portrayed in sexualized terms, which involves imposing an adult sexuality on them before they are mentally, physically, and emotionally ready. These messages suggest that young girls are valued for their physical attractiveness alone. The sexualization of women has become so prominent that it often goes unnoticed but strongly impacts how girls view themselves. The representation of girls in the media has led to an increase in plastic surgery and eating disorders. One survey has found that 75% of European girls between 7 and 11 years old want to change some part of their physical appearance (Council of Europe 2018).

Dr. Linda Papadopoulos, a psychologist in the UK, found that youth between 8 and 18 years old identify the media as an important source of information on sexual issues (Papadopoulos 2010). A majority of girls believe they must present themselves as sexually desirable in order to attract men. Their views were influenced by articles with cover lines and photos encouraging girls and women to look and dress in ways that will make them attractive to men (Papadopoulos 2010). When girls in the UK were asked about their future profession, 62% wanted to be glamour models, and an astonishing 25% wanted to be lap dancers (Papadopoulos 2010). Papadopoulos theorized that the overuse of sexualized images of women in advertising influenced the views of her study participants. To provide evidence for this point, she noted that a recent study analyzing the content of 72 beer and non-beer ads that were randomly selected found that 75% of the beer ads and 50% of the non-beer ads featured women in objectified roles (Papadopoulos 2010; Rouner, Slater, and Domenech-Rodríguez 2003).

Papadopoulos also shed light on the alarming number of sexualized images of children. Children are commonly depicted as "sexy adults," whereas adult women are portrayed in childlike terms (Papadopoulos 2010). Papadopoulos notes that the Advertising Standards Authority (ASA) ruled on an incident where a model was portrayed in hypersexualized terms. There were six photos of the model gradually unzipping her top until her nipple was exposed. Although the model was 23 years old, the ASA noted that she was made to appear 16 years old (Papadopoulos 2010). Ringrose (2008) has similarly described the blurred lines between sexual immaturity and maturity with children being sexualized and women being infantilized. For example, the Playboy bunny logo has appeared on the pencil cases of children, while the magazine cover portrays models in pigtails, holding teddy bears (Ringrose 2008). Some European countries are taking steps to protect children from being targeted by advertisements. In Greece, toy advertisements have been banned between 7:00 a.m. and 10:00 p.m. In Sweden, all TV advertisements that are aimed at children under 12 have been banned, and in Norway, Finland, and Denmark, the sponsorship of children's programs is not allowed (Papadopoulos 2010).

With growing access to the internet and social media, the potential for exposure to sexualized marketing imagery and messages is becoming an increasing concern. In the UK, the internet is now the single biggest advertising platform, comprising 23.5% of the market (Papadopoulos 2010). Almost 99% of youth between the ages of 8 and 17 years have access to the internet. A quarter of young internet users between 8 and 11 years old have a social media profile such as those featured on Facebook, Instagram, and Snapchat. Ringrose (2008) conducted interviews with students aged 14 to 16 years who were attending a school in South London. Girls reported feeling pressured to display themselves in their undergarments or bikinis online, in order to signal their attractiveness (Ringrose 2008). Girl frequently reflected on the degree to which they should display cleavage in online photos, including from which angle the photos should be taken to appear sexy but not too "slutty" (Ringrose 2008). Boys often posted photos of themselves posing in dominant, hypermasculine positions. These pressures to appear in hyperfeminine and hypermasculine roles underscore the influence of heteronormativity.

The availability of the internet has provided easier access to pornography than ever before. Pornographic websites including Pornhub, YouPorn, and RedTube are in the top 65 most-viewed sites in the UK. Approximately 68 million requests for pornographic material are searched for each day. A 2008 YouGov survey reported that 58% of British youth between the ages of 14 and 17 years old have ever seen porn, while 71% of sexually active teens have viewed porn, and 42% of sexually active teens view porn regularly (YouGov 2008). In 2010, youth between the ages of 14 and 16 years were surveyed in a North London secondary school, and the results indicated that 81% consumed pornography at home (Covenant-Eyes 2015). The nature of pornographic content has expanded to include explicit "hard-core" and "gonzo" pornography. These forms of pornography depict sexual activity without a storyline or relationships, showing participants (especially women) being pushed to their physical limits (Papadopoulos 2010). Pornography increasingly normalizes sexually aggressive behaviors that blur the lines between consent, pleasure, and violence. Viewers of violent pornography are especially likely to perceive of women as sex objects (Papadopoulos 2010; Peter and Valkenburg 2007). Pornography also normalizes and increases pressure for the removal of women's pubic hair, which results in a prepubescent appearance. Prior to the mid- to late 20th century, the removal of women's pubic hair was relatively rare, but this practice is now considered mainstream (Papadopoulos 2010).

Video games are another influential form of media. They are the fastest-growing segment of the entertainment industry, with more than 300 million people playing them worldwide (Kimmel 2017). Video game characters tend to be presented in exaggerated, gender-stereotyped terms and with a notable lack of strong female characters. In a content analysis of video games, 60% of women were portrayed in a sexualized manner and 39% were portrayed with little clothing (Papadopoulos 2010). Violence against women in video games is trivialized. One example is a game called *Rape-Lay*, in which players take on the role of a rapist who stalks a mother before raping her and her daughters. This game was available for some time on Amazon's marketplace worldwide. People with aggressive, violent, and misogynistic tendencies are more drawn to violent games, but playing them also changes a person's physiology and encourages violence (Kimmel 2017).

One reason media content perpetuates stereotypes is that women are underrepresented in positions of power in this industry (Byerly 2011; Council of Europe 2018). In Eastern Europe, great disparities exist between men and women. In Nordic Europe (i.e., Denmark, Finland, Iceland, Norway, and Sweden), men are paid more than women at every occupational level (European Institute for Gender Equality 2019c). Fifty-seven percent of companies in this region have policies on gender equality, 49% have policies on sexual harassment, all adopt maternity leave policies and ensure that women return to the same job prior to their leave, and 12% offer childcare assistance (European Institute for Gender Equality 2019c). In Western Europe, women make up about 43% of the media workforce, but only 22% to 32% of middle, senior, and top management positions (European Institute for Gender Equality 2019c). In upper-level positions, men are paid significantly more than women. Nearly all companies have maternity leave policies and return women to the same jobs after their leaves, and about 53% offer some form of childcare assistance. Only 69% have specific policies on gender equality, and 47% have policies on sexual harassment (European Institute for Gender Equality 2019c).

One example of women revolutionizing their media roles is through an anonymous feminist punk band in Russia called Pussy Riot. This name was chosen in order to promote radical rebellion against cultural order (Langston 2012). The group is described as a militant, punk-feminist street band that serves to enrich cultural and political climates, including the promotion of gender and LGBT rights (Langston 2012). They allow members to join if they are interested in promoting their message, even if the members reside outside of Russia (Langston 2012). Group members wear neon balaclavas (ski masks) to maintain their anonymity and engage in illegal guerrilla performances, which has led to the arrest of three members. In 2019, the group scheduled a concert in Alabama following the state's passing of a law to prohibit abortions, even in cases of incest and rape (Campisi 2019; Associated Press 2019).

CONCLUSION

Throughout this chapter, women's roles in ancient and modern Europe have been discussed. Across these eras and in all the domains reviewed, women have experienced discrimination. European history has included practices such as witch hunts, prohibitions against sex, and laws that defined women as property. The fight for women's rights continues into the present day, especially pertaining to the objectification and sexualization of women's bodies, gender-based violence against women, and women's unequal employment opportunities. Women are still perceived in gender-stereotyped terms and viewed predominantly as caretakers. They are socialized in ways that hinder their professional opportunities and are pressured to present themselves as sexual and submissive beings. Although progress has occurred for European women in their abilities to express themselves and explore their sexualities, barriers remain. The following chapter will address women's sexualities in North Africa and the Middle East, a region where women's oppression and their fight for equality continues to face considerable barriers.

REFERENCES

Abortion Rights Campaign. 2018. "About ARC." December 14. Accessed June 22, 2022. https://www.abortionrightscampaign.ie/about-arc.

Abortion Rights Campaign. 2019. "The 8th Is Gone but the Fight Is Far from Won." May 24. Accessed June 10, 2019. https://www.abortionrightscampaign.ie/2019/05/24/the-8th-is-gone-but-the-fight-is-far-from-won.

Associated Press. 2019. "Russian Band Pussy Riot to Stage Planned Parenthood Benefit." *USA Today*, June 6. Accessed June 10, 2019. https://www.usatoday.com/story/life/music/2019/06/06/russian-band-pussy-riot-stage-planned-parenthood-benefit/1368898001.

Baćak a, Valerio, and Aleksandar Štulhofer. 2011. "Masturbation among Sexually Active Young Women in Croatia: Associations with Religiosity and Pornography Use." *International Journal of Sexual Health* 23 (4): 248–57. https://doi.org/10.1080/19317611.2011.611220.

Bailey, Michael D. 2006. "Origins of the Witch Hunts." In *Encyclopedia of Witchcraft: The Western Tradition*, edited by Richard M. Golden. Santa Barbara, CA: ABC-CLIO.

Błuś, Anna. 2018. "A Wave of Women Fighting Rape across Europe." Amnesty International. https://www.amnesty.org/en/latest/news/2018/11/a-wave-of-women-fighting-rape-across-europe.

Brenner, Alletta. 2009. "The Good and Bad of That Sex: Monstrosity and Womanhood in Early Modern England." *Intersections* 10 (2): 161–75. Accessed June 22, 2022. http://depts.washington.edu/chid/intersections_Spring_2009/Alletta_Brenner_Monstrosity_and_Womanhood_in_Early_Modern_England.pdf.

Brundage, James A. 1987. *Law, Sex, and Christian Society in Medieval Europe*. Chicago: University of Chicago Press.

Byerly, Carolyn M. 2011. "Global Report on the Status of Women in the News Media." International Women's Media Foundation. Accessed May 29, 2019. https://www.iwmf.org/wp-content/uploads/2018/06/IWMF-Global-Report.pdf.

Campisi, Jessica. 2019. "Pussy Riot to Raise Funds for Planned Parenthood with Alabama Concert." The Hill, June 6. Accessed June 10, 2019. https://thehill.com/blogs/blog-briefing-room/news/447269-pussy-riot-to-raise-funds-for-planned-parenthood-with-alabama.

Coleman, David. 2013. "Partnership in Europe; Its Variety, Trends and Dissolution." *Finnish Yearbook of Population Research* XLVIII: 5–49.

Council of Europe. 2018. "Women in Media." Accessed May 29, 2019. https://www.coe.int/en/web/genderequality/women-in-media.

CovenantEyes. 2015. "Porn Stats." Accessed June 22, 2019. https://www.bevillandassociates.com/wp-content/uploads/2015/05/2015-porn-stats-covenant-eyes-1.pdf.

De Schrijver, Lotte, Tom Vander Beken, Barbara Krahé, and Ines Keygnaert. 2018. "Prevalence of Sexual Violence in Migrants, Applicants for International Protection, and Refugees in Europe: A Critical Interpretive Synthesis of the Evidence." *International Journal of Environmental Research and Public Health* 15, no. 9 (November): 1979. https://doi.org/10.3390/ijerph15091979.

Dolan, Frances E. 2003. "Gender and Sexuality in Early Modern England." In *Gender, Power and Privilege in Early Modern Europe*, edited by Penny Richards and Jessica Munns, 7–21. Harlow, UK: Pearson Longman.

European Commission. 2010. *Domestic Violence against Women Report*. Brussels: Directorate-General for Justice. Accessed June 22, 2022. https://www.ojp.gov/ncjrs/virtual-library/abstracts/domestic-violence-against-women-report-2010.

European Institute for Gender Equality. 2022. "Almost 1 in 2 Women in the EU have Experienced Psychological Violence." July 14. for the 2015 Edition." Accessed May 30, 2019. https://eige.europa.eu/news/almost-1-2-women-eu-have-experienced-psychological-violence

European Institute for Gender Equality. 2019a. "Culture." February 24. Accessed May 31, 2019. https://eige.europa.eu/gender-mainstreaming/policy-areas/culture.

European Institute for Gender Equality. 2019b. "Cyber Violence against Women." March 7. Accessed May 30, 2019. https://eige.europa.eu /gender-based-violence/cyber-violence-against-women.

European Institute for Gender Equality. 2019c. "Education." February 24. Accessed May 29, 2019. https://eige.europa.eu/gender-main streaming/policy-areas/education.

European Institute for Gender Equality. 2019d. "Forms of Violence." March 7. Accessed May 30, 2019. https://eige.europa.eu/gender -based-violence/forms-of-violence.

European Institute for Gender Equality. 2019e. "Health." February 24. Accessed May 31, 2019. https://eige.europa.eu/gender-mains treaming/policy-areas/health.

European Institute for Gender Equality. 2019f. "What Is Gender-Based Violence?" February 27. Accessed May 30, 2019. https://eige .europa.eu/gender-based-violence/what-is-gender-based-violence.

European Institute for Gender Equality. 2021. "Estimating the Costs of Gender-Based Violence in the European Union." March 7. Accessed July 25. https://eige.europa.eu/gender-based-violence /costs-of-gender-based-violence-in-eu.

European Women's Lobby. 2012. "European Parliament Studies Sexuali-sation of Young Girls in Media." June 14. Accessed May 29, 2019. https://www.womenlobby.org/European-Parliament-studies -sexualisation-of-young-girls-in-media.

Ferguson, Amanda. 2019. "Northern Ireland Legalizes Abortion and Same-Sex Marriage." *Washington Post*. Accessed June 22, 2022. https://www.washingtonpost.com/world/europe/northern-ireland -is-legalizing-abortion-and-same-sex-marriage/2019/10/21 /238ccdc4-f1a9-11e9-bb7e-d2026ee0c199_story.html.

Fiala, Christian, Nathalie Chabbert-Buffet, Günther Häusler, Christian Jamin, Iñaki Lete, Paloma Lobo, Rossella E. Nappi, and Axelle Pintiaux. 2017. "Women's Preferences for Menstrual Bleeding Fre-quency in 12 European Countries: The Inconvenience Due to Women's Monthly Bleeding (ISY) Survey." *European Journal of Contraception & Reproductive Health Care* 22, no. 4 (August): 268.

Gerressu, Makeda, Catherine H. Mercer, Cynthia A. Graham, Kaye Wellings, and Anne M. Johnson. 2008. "Prevalence of Masturba-tion and Associated Factors in a British National Probability Sur-vey." *Archives of Sexual Behavior* 37 (2): 266–78. https://doi .org/10.1007/s10508-006-9123-6.

Harvey, Katherine. 2018. "The Salacious Middle Ages." *Aeon*. Accessed June 22, 2022. https://aeon.co/essays/getting-down-and-medieval -the-sex-lives-of-the-middle-ages.

Heckel, N. M. n.d. "Sex, Society, and Medieval Women." University of Rochester. Accessed May 1, 2019. https://www.library.rochester .edu/robbins/sex-society.

Hester, Marianne. 2004. "Future Trends and Developments." *Violence against Women* 10 (12): 1431–48. https://doi.org/10.1177 /1077801204270559.

Hogarth, Harriet, and Roger Ingham. 2009. "Masturbation among Young Women and Associations with Sexual Health: An Exploratory Study." *Journal of Sex Research* 46 (6): 558–67. https://doi.org /10.1080/00224490902878993.

Karras, Ruth Mazo. 2011. "The Regulation of Sexuality in the Late Middle Ages: England and France." *Speculum* 86: 1010–39. https://doi .org/10.1017/S0038713411002466.

Kimmel, Michael. 2017. *The Gendered Society*. New York: Oxford University Press.

Kury, Helmut, Joachim Obergfell-Fuchs, and Gunda Woessner. 2004. "The Extent of Family Violence in Europe." *Violence against Women* 10 (7): 749–69. https://doi.org/10.1177/1077801204265550.

Langston, Henry. 2012. "Meeting Pussy Riot." Vice, March 12. Accessed June 10, 2019. https://www.vice.com/en_us/article/kwnzgy/A-Russian -Pussy-Riot.

Lipka, Michael, and David Masci. 2019. "Where Europe Stands on Gay Marriage and Civil Unions." Pew Research Center, May 30. Accessed June 24, 2019. https://www.pewresearch.org/fact-tank/2019/05/30 /where-europe-stands-on-gay-marriage-and-civil-unions.

McNamara, Jo Ann, and Suzanne Wemple. 1973. "The Power of Women through the Family in Medieval Europe: 500–1100." *Feminist Studies* 1 (3–4): 126–41. http://www.jstor.org/stable/1566483.

OECD/EU. 2018. *Health at a Glance: Europe 2018*. Paris: OECD Publishing. https://doi.org/10.1787/health_glance_eur-2018-en.

Oxley, John. 2017. "Divorce and Women's Rights: A History." Accessed June 22, 2022. https://vardags.com/family-law/divorce-and-womens -rights-a-history.

Papadopoulos, Linda. 2010. *Sexualisation of Young People*. London: Crown copyright.

Peter, Jochen, and Patti M. Valkenburg. 2007. "Adolescents' Exposure to a Sexualized Media Environment and Their Notions of Women as

Sex Objects." *Sex Roles* 56 (5–6): 381–95. https://doi.org/10.1007
/s11199-006-9176-y.

Pew Research Center. 2015. "The Future of World Religions: Population
Growth Projections, 2010–2050." Accessed June 22, 2022. https://
www.pewforum.org/2015/04/02/europe.

Pew Research Center. 2018. "Eastern and Western Europeans Differ on
Importance of Religion, Views of Minorities, and Key Social
Issues." Accessed June 22, 2022. https://www.pewforum.org
/2018/10/29/eastern-and-western-europeans-differ-on-importance
-of-religion-views-of-minorities-and-key-social-issues.

Population Reference Bureau. 2001. "Most European Women Use Contraceptives." Accessed June 22, 2022. https://www.prb.org/most
europeanwomenusecontraceptives.

Richards, Jeffrey. 1994. *Sex, Dissidence and Damnation: Minority Groups
in the Middle Ages.* New York: Routledge.

Ringrose, Jessica. 2008. "Every Time She Bends Over She Pulls Up Her
Thong: Teen Girls Negotiating Discourses of Competitive, Hetero-
sexualized Aggression." *Girlhood Studies* 1, no. 1 (January).
https://doi.org/10.3167/ghs.2008.010104.

Rouner, Donna, Michael D. Slater, and Melanie Domenech-Rodríguez.
2003. "Adolescent Evaluation of Gender Role and Sexual Imagery in
Television Advertisements." *Journal of Broadcasting & Elecronic
Media* 47 (3): 435–54. https://doi.org/10.1207/s15506878jobem4703_7.

Salles, Anne. 2018. "Birth Control in Europe." *Encyclopédie pour une his-
toire nouvelle de l'Europe* [online]. Accessed June 22, 2022. http://
ehne.fr/en/node/1410.

Sánchez Romero, Margarita. 2015. "Sexuality: Ancient Europe." *The
International Encyclopedia of Human Sexuality.* Wiley. Accessed
June 22, 2022. https://login.proxy.lib.fsu.edu/login?url=https://
search.credoreference.com/content/entry/wileyhs/sexuality
_ancient_europe/0?institutionId=2057.

Sarikakis, Katharine. 2013. "Media and the Image of Women." *Council of
Europe*, November. https://edoc.coe.int/en/gender-equality/5994
-report-of-the-1st-conference-of-the-council-of-europe-network-of
-national-focal-points-on-gender-equality.html

Studd, John, and Annelise Schwenkhagen. 2009. "The Historical Response
to Female Sexuality." *Maturitas* 63: 107–11. https://doi.org/10.1016
/j.maturitas.2009.02.015.

Szarewski, Anne, Ariane von Stenglin, and Sarah Rybowski. 2012. "Wom-
en's Attitudes Towards Monthly Bleeding: Results of a Global

Population-Based Survey." *European Journal of Contraception and Reproductive Health Care*, 17(4): 270–83. https://doi.org/10.3109 /13625187.2012.684811.

Together for Yes. n.d. "Who We Are." Accessed June 10, 2019. https:// www.togetherforyes.ie/about-us/who-we-are.

Træen, Bente, Ana Alexandra Carvalheira, Gert Martin Hald, Theis Lange, and Ingela Lundin Kvalem. 2018. "Attitudes towards Sexuality in Older Men and Women across Europe: Similarities, Differences, and Associations with Their Sex Lives." *Sexuality & Culture* 23 (1): 1–25. https://doi.org/10.1007/s12119-018-9564-9.

United Nations Statistics. 1999. "Standard Country or Area Codes for Statistical Use." Accessed June 22, 2022. https://unstats.un.org/unsd /methodology/m49.

Vanwesenbeeck, Ine, Floor Bakker, and Susanne Gesell. 2010. "Sexual Health in the Netherlands: Main Results of a Population Survey among Dutch Adults." *International Journal of Sexual Health* 22 (2): 55–71. https://doi.org/10.1080/19317610903425571.

Welborn, Amy. 2017. "Women and the Protestant Reformation." *Catholic World Report*. Accessed June 22, 2022. https://www.catholicworld report.com/2017/10/28/women-and-the-protestant-reformation.

WHO (World Health Organization). 2013. *Global and Regional Estimates of Violence against Women: Prevalence and Health Effects of Intimate Partner Violence and Nonpartner Sexual Violence*. Geneva, Switzerland: World Health Organization. https://www.who.int /publications/i/item/9789241564625.

WHO (World Health Organization). 2018. "Tackling the Taboo of Menstrual Hygiene in the European Region." November 8. Accessed June 22, 2022. http://www.euro.who.int/en/health-topics/environment-and -health/pages/news/news/2018/11/tackling-the-taboo-of-menstrual -hygiene-in-the-european-region.

YouGov. 2008. "Sex Education Survey." Conducted for the *Sex Education Show*, channel 4. Accessed June 22, 2022. www.yougov.co.uk /extranets/ygarchives/content/pdf/   Channel%204_topline_sexed .pdf (site discontinued).

Zimmerman, Cathy, Mazeda Hossain, Katherine Yun, Vasil Gajdadziev, Natalia Guzun, Maria Tchomarova, Rosa Angela Ciarrocchi, et al. 2008. "The Health of Trafficked Women: A Survey of Women Entering Posttrafficking Services in Europe." *American Journal of Public Health* 98 (1): 55–59. https://doi.org/10.2105/ajph.2006 .108357.

FOUR

North Africa and the Middle East

Jessica Gomez

In many realms of today's study, countries of North Africa and the Middle East are commonly considered together in a grouping abbreviated as MENA (Middle East and North Africa). The acronym WANA (West Asia and North Africa) generally refers to the same region. With their significant similarities in culture, environment, and economics, considering these countries together makes sense for many fields of research. Some organizations argue exactly which African countries should be considered "North Africa" and which West Asian countries should be considered "Middle East" depending on the field of study, such as agricultural and environmental studies, economics, political science, or sociocultural studies. For the purposes of this chapter, we are considering MENA as including the following countries and territories: Afghanistan, Algeria, Armenia, Azerbaijan, Bahrain, Cyprus, Djibouti, Egypt, Eritrea, Ethiopia, Georgia, Iran, Iraq, Israel, Jordan, Kuwait, Lebanon, Libya, Malta, Mauritania, Morocco, Oman, Pakistan, Palestine (West Bank and Gaza), Qatar, Saudi Arabia, Somalia, Sudan, Syria, Tunisia, Turkey, United Arab Emirates (UAE), and Yemen. Together this region makes up approximately 6% of the global population (World Bank 2020). The International Work Group of Indigenous Affairs has identified four groups of Indigenous peoples of the Middle East: Jahalin Bedouin of West Bank, Marsh Dwellers (Arabs), Arab-Bedouins of the Negev Desert, and the Assyrians, who are Indigenous to the regions that are now Iraq, Iran, Turkey, and Syria (Mamo 2021).

Ivory sculpture of Syrian women (8th–9th BCE). (The Metropolitan Museum of Art, New York, Rogers Fund, 1962. www .metmuseum.org.)

Approximately 93% of the region identifies as Muslim, which is significantly higher than neighboring regions of sub-Saharan Africa, at 30%, and the Asian Pacific, at 24% (Desilver and Masci 2017). Other religions practiced in the region include Christianity, Judaism, Berberism, Yazidism, Druzism, and some forms of Arab paganism and African folk religions. Some migrant populations from Asian regions continue to practice their religions from their country of origin, such as Hinduism and Buddhism. Along with many religions, many languages can also be found in MENA. While the most widely used language is Arabic, more than 60 languages can be heard spoken throughout the region (Sawe 2019).

MENA has a primarily arid climate, with high temperatures and low rainfall. Most areas are what you would think of as a typical desert environment, although there is some variation around the coastal ocean areas. There are scarce agricultural and freshwater sources in the region, but there are large reserves of petroleum and natural gas, which are important natural economic assets. The region is prone to frequent extreme weather events and high levels of greenhouse gas emissions, with many experts expressing concern that parts of MENA could become uninhabitable by the year 2100 if emissions are not significantly reduced (Broom 2019; Gornall 2019; Pal and Eltahir 2016).

A BRIEF HISTORY OF WOMEN'S SEXUALITY IN THE MIDDLE EAST AND NORTH AFRICA

One MENA region with thorough documentation of early sexuality beliefs and behaviors is ancient Mesopotamia, which would be today's countries of Iraq, Iran, Kuwait, Syria, and Turkey. Marriages in the ancient world were often motivated by familial business arrangements rather than romantic love, and Mesopotamia was no exception to this trend (Mark 2014). While there are writings indicating that romantic love and sexual desire did often grow from these arranged marriages, a woman's sexuality was seen as having two primary functions: virginity as a feature of a bride's value and childbearing as an expected result of marital sexual interactions (Mark 2014). Despite this nonsensual view of female sexuality, sexual interactions in early poetry are portrayed as bonding activities that bring both physical pleasure and loving intimacy (Pryke 2018). However, as could be expected in a system of arranged marriages, these feelings of love and intimacy did not always develop, and partners often found themselves sexually dissatisfied or attracted to people outside of the marriage. In these cases, adultery was punishable by execution for both men and women, but men who were sexually dissatisfied with their wife (or whose wife could not become pregnant) had the option of taking additional wives or concubines.

As with many ancient religions, the ancient Mesopotamians saw their gods and deities as sexual beings. Their stories include positive elements of sexual desire, pleasure, and romantic love but also nefarious themes of dishonesty and trickery for sexual gain. This view of deities as sexual beings, along with a belief in their ability to impact both fertility and capacity for sexual pleasure, led to practices of sexual rites and rituals. While the exact details of these rites and the practice of temple prostitution (or sacred prostitution) are being actively debated among academic historians today, it is believed that some female temple workers and/or priestesses would interact sexually with men in the community as a form of ritual (Budin 2008; Lerner 1986).

In addition to temple prostitution, commercial prostitution was common in ancient Mesopotamia, often as an effect of poverty. Female family members would be given as payment for debt by their fathers or husbands or would turn to prostitution as a means of making enough money to prevent being taken into slavery (Lerner 1986). For some women, the potential connections made from prostitution and a willingness to enter the role of a concubine were a chance at escaping family poverty. Because of this societal pattern, prostitution became linked to "daughters of the poor" by around 2000 BCE (Lerner 1986, 247). It is thought that—this relationship between prostitution and poverty led to the monetary value of virginity—a "respectable" family who had a virginal daughter who had never been prostituted held an important financial asset and could ask for a higher bride-price. Early veiling laws in the Assyrian region (modern-day Iraq, Syria, and Turkey) tightly linked a woman's sexual role in society (concubine, "harlot," temple prostitute, slave, or wife) to her public appearance, clearly marking the "respectable" from the "disreputable" and creating highly visible class distinctions (Lerner 1986). In this way, a monogamous wife and a virginal daughter became key elements in cultural social order.

Moving beyond ancient Mesopotamia, discussions of women's sexuality in the historical Middle East must begin with an acknowledgment that most of our knowledge revolves around the history of Muslim culture (Peirce 2009). While we want to be cautious about not reducing every MENA country's history to a history of Islamic influence, there is a scholarly consensus that understanding Islam is critical in understanding sexuality in the region (Uhlmann 2005). At one point in time, there were pockets of Islamic culture that could be considered rather sex-positive. For example, in the 11th century, Al-Ghazzālī taught that women's pleasure and orgasm were an important element of a couple's sexual interaction, and others held a belief that a female partner's orgasm was necessary for conception (Peirce 2009; Ghazzālī and Farah 1984). However, a positive view of women's sexuality was not accepted by all. Many saw women as being unable to control their sexual urges, requiring the control of men to protect them from disgracing their family honor with their sexuality (Clancy-Smith 2004). It is important to note that a link between family honor and a female's virginity is prevalent across MENA history outside of Islam, whether examining subcultures or religions (Uhlmann 2005).

One topic of historical significance to Middle Eastern women's sexuality that is still subject to current debate is female genital mutilation (FGM), sometimes referred to as female circumcision or female genital cutting (FGC). Some scholars believe the practice originated in ancient Egypt, as mummies with indications of FGM have been found dating back to the fifth century BCE. Although we cannot be certain of the exact motives for FGM, it has been proposed that the ancient Egyptians believed the clitoris represented a masculine portion of a woman's body. By removing this tissue, she removed any element of masculinity from herself and was seen as fully embracing her womanhood (Boyle 2005). As the procedure has evolved into a sociocultural norm, the side effect of painful intercourse became more obvious, and the procedure grew into a method of discouraging premarital sex while removing sexual motives for marital infidelity among women (Lightfoot-Klein 1989). Historical records indicate that FGM was similarly used to exert behavioral and reproductive control over enslaved women. Specifically in Somalia and Egypt, there is evidence that slave girls would be subjected to FGM to prevent sexual activity, thus making them unable to conceive (28 Too Many 2013). The anatomical effects of FGM reduce, or even destroy, a woman's ability to feel sexual pleasure and creates scar tissue that would very obviously indicate if penetrative intercourse had occurred. In this way, the historical motives for FGM were not much different than they are today—the preservation of "purity" and virginity. FGM was seen as a guarantee of a woman's virginity upon marriage, which has historically been prioritized throughout MENA cultures (Ross et al. 2016).

CULTURE AND ATTITUDES TOWARD SEXUALITY

Most regions of MENA carry conservative attitudes toward sexuality. There is a pervasive attitude that the behavior of female family members can bring honor or dishonor to the family, with sexual misbehavior having the potential to produce irreparable damage. Bourdieu (2001) has proposed that a masculine-domination view of sexuality comprises three main pieces of logic: (1) sex as potentially dangerous, (2) inequal value of virginity based on gender, and (3) female objectification. Using this logic, we can summarize MENA sexual attitudes as arising from a place of caution and control. The objectification of the female body still occurs

---

In 1995, the Turkey national school system determined that "proof of unchastity" would justify expulsion. Female students under suspicion would be subjected to "virginity tests," sometimes motivated by actions as innocent as walking with a male classmate. These physical tests involved a vaginal exam to assess for an intact hymen. In 2001, Turkey's health minister issued a decree mandating that all nursing and midwife students be virgins and that physical exams would be administered to check this requirement (Lasco 2002). During this time, suicide rates among girls increased, with some professionals linking these suicides to the "virginity tests" (Ilkkaracan 2002).

Islamic women and children. (Tim Gurney/Dreamstime.com)

alongside a wide-scale cultural perception that its seductive nature has the potential to be dangerous, so numerous attempts are made to limit the expression and visibility of female sexuality. Both the family and community feel that it is their responsibility to manage a young woman's sexuality by regulating her behaviors and dress and ensuring she has remained a virgin until marriage. In fact, the virginity of a young woman until her wedding night is highly prioritized in most MENA countries.

One example of this phenomenon can be seen in the popularity of "virginity testing," which occurs in several MENA countries, including Afghanistan, Egypt, Iran, Iraq, Jordan, Libya, Morocco, Palestine, and Turkey (WHO 2018). These virginity tests have gone through phases of being banned and then reinstated throughout many MENA countries. Turkey, in this cyclical nature, removed the "proof of unchastity" statute from the education system in 2002. However, the education system was not the only perpetrator of forced virginity tests. Some government jobs would require a virginity exam, and the practice would often be part of arrest procedures for women accused of political activism or suspected of prosti-tution or "immodest behavior" (Lasco 2002). It is important to note that sexually immodest or suspicious behavior for a woman can include actions such as staying at a hotel, walking alone, having a male visitor, sitting on a park bench after dark, or having dinner with a group of female friends, which illustrates the severity of restrictions placed on a woman's social behaviors (Lasco 2002). If behaviors go beyond "suspicious" to the actual discovery of nonmarital sexual relations, the punishments can be strict. For example, in Tunisia and Morocco, nonmarital sex can lead to a prison sentence (Zanaz 2019). In other MENA countries, failing a virginity test can lead to fines, cancellation of marriage contracts, imprisonment, lash-ings, family banishment/disownment, or even death. From this, it becomes clear just how conservative sexual attitudes are in some regions of MENA.

Another element of female sexuality is the commodification of virginity as an important "feature" of marital desirability that a woman possesses. Given that a woman was traditionally considered property of her father until she was transferred to being property of her husband upon marriage, her virginity was seen as something that her father needed to protect to ensure the appropriate value of that property transfer. In some regions of MENA still today, a woman who is not a virgin is seen as damaged prop-erty, not desired by most. This ideology encouraged a disturbing legal loophole that became known as "marry-your-rapist laws." These laws allow men to avoid legal prosecution for sexual assault by marrying the woman whom he assaults, thus compensating her father for the goods that he has damaged. Marry-your-rapist laws will be explained in further detail later in this chapter during the discussion of sexual violence.

Given the focus on marriage and childbearing, it should come as no surprise that same-sex relationships among women are still illegal in many countries of the Middle East. According to Iranian law, a woman found in a lesbian relationship will receive 100 lashes and will be put to death at the fourth offense (Whitaker 2006). Even if a woman may face jail time rather than the death penalty in her country, many still fear the possibility of becoming the victim of an "honor killing" if her family discovers her orientation.

Despite these widespread conservative attitudes, there are some pockets of MENA where more permissive sexual attitudes exist. Dubai, the largest city in the United Arab Emirates, has a quickly growing sex tourism mar-ket and is considered to provide easy access to prostitutes in bars and hotels despite the UAE's official ban on prostitution. There is concern that a substantial number of these prostitutes represent women who have fallen victim to sex trafficking from both Western Europe and East Asia (Al Javed 2020; Butler 2010; UN Women 2017). Prostitution is also open and legal in some parts of Tunisia, but those caught engaging in prostitution outside of officially regulated areas can face prison sentences (El Feki 2019).

RELIGION AND SEXUALITY

Disentangling Middle Eastern culture from Islamic culture can often be difficult, as Islam is the significantly dominant religion in the area. Examining the belief systems of the various religions present in MENA would be too exhaustive to accomplish in this chapter, but there are many commonalities when it comes to their views on sexual behaviors. For example, Islam, Judaism, Baha'i, and Zoroastrianism all condemn sex before marriage and, even within marriage, discourage or even prohibit sex with a menstruating wife due to her being "unclean." There is a wide range of disparity in the actual enactment and enforcement of these prohibitions, dependent upon divisions, sects, denominations, and regional modifications of these religious teachings.

Islam has a long-standing history of encouraging men to enact control over women's sexuality. Modesty mandates (in the form of head coverings and veils), honor killing, and virginity checks are just a few examples of this. However, it is important to note that the patriarchal ideology of the Islamic Middle East is not directly rooted in the teachings of the Qur'an (Islam's holy text). The Qur'an teaches that men and women are mutual, are equals. Both men and women are recognized as sexual beings—both with sex drives, both capable of feeling sexual pleasure, both responsible for their sexual actions (Bouhdiba 1998). The disconnect arises in that historical Muslim culture took teachings about women's active sexual desires and turned them into a caution about the potential disruption to social order if the emotional, less-controlled nature of women acted in combination with their sexual drive without the protective regulation of rational, self-controlled men (Ilkkaracan 2002). These practices of men taking control over women's sexuality and physical appearance then became absorbed into MENA culture, creating a cultural practice that is often attributed to religious motivation without truly being founded in that religion's core teachings.

Forced marriage. (Riccardo Mayer/Shutterstock.com)

It is also important to note that the instances of forced marriages that have been documented among Muslims in MENA are in violation of the Qur'an. A young woman who has reached legal age is to be free to marry whom she desires, even without the consent of her father or other male relative. Furthermore, a young woman is not to be forced to marry by any male relative (Carroll 1998; Ilkkaracan 2002). Marriage is especially important for young adults in Muslim culture, as sexual interactions are to be confined to marriage. The bonds of marriage are not taken lightly in Islam, and in some countries that practice more extreme forms of Islam, a woman found guilty of adultery is eligible for the death penalty under Shari'ah (Islamic) law.

Despite stern prohibitions against premarital sex and adultery in Islam, current events indicate that these are much more strongly enforced for women than men. While women are still put to death under Shari'ah law for nonmarital sex, men are allowed a more lenient interpretation of expected behavior. In many cultures, we see double-standards of sexual mores enforced more strongly for women than for men—a pattern you will notice throughout this book. However, it is an unfortunate reality that some groups of Islamic extremists have moved past simply a double standard to a weaponization of sexual violence. Before moving forward with this discussion, it is important to note that this is specifically referring to actions taken by Islamic extremist groups, such as ISIS. This is not implying that the religion of Islam, as a whole, supports or perpetuates systematic rape. Some groups of these extremists have adopted belief systems that they perceive permit sexual violence against certain groups. One religious group that has been specifically targeted by weaponized rape and sexual slavery is the Yazidi.

The Yazidi religion has traditionally been conceptualized as "devil worship" by the Islamic religion due to their vast theological differences. Although a detailed discussion of the roots of this accusation would be beyond the scope of this chapter, it is important to understand that this accusation exists as a motive for the widespread sexual violence that Yazidi women have experienced at the hands of Islamic extremists. Islamic extremists began advocating for a revival of slavery through the capture of "unbelievers," along with the traditional belief that a slave owner would have sexual rights over his female slaves, even those still in childhood (Callimachi 2015). Due to the Yazidi's own conservative beliefs about sexual purity, these acts of sexual violence have wide-reaching, ripple effects for the women within their communities.

The Yazidi practice endogamy, meaning that they hold to a caste system and only marry within their castes. These castes are not based upon wealth but rather upon religious duties. Some castes also contain subgroups, among which intermarriages are also prohibited. The Yazidi see these marriage restrictions as important for maintaining the purity of the lines and preventing political problems within their groups (ServantGroup International 2017). Adults who marry outside of Yazidi are unable to raise their children in the faith, and any form of sexual interaction with a non-Yazidi results in banishment (Graham-Harrison 2017). Of particular significance to the current weaponization of sexual violence is that this restriction also applies to rape. This means that a young woman who is sexually assaulted by a non-Yazidi experiences not only the trauma of her assault but also the trauma of losing her family and community. In recent years, there has been some leniency allowed in this practice, as the kidnapping and sexual slavery of Yazidi women have become a devastating component of the regional wars. Women who have been taken and sold into sexual slavery now have options of engaging in purification rituals to rejoin their community (Graham-Harrison 2017).

Another religion that has traditionally practiced purification rituals is Judaism. Judaism requires that sexual desire be expressed at appropriate times in appropriate manners, including that the motivation be one of mutual desire and love between a husband and wife but that this timing cannot be while the wife is menstruating (AICE 2021). Following menstruation, a woman must participate in a purification ritual to be considered "clean" and to engage sexually with her husband.

It is important to note that Judaism does not conceptualize sexuality as shameful for women but rather as a physical desire akin to hunger and thirst (AICE 2021). Women are to be treated respectfully by their husbands during sexual interactions; forcing a wife to have sex is strictly prohibited. In fact, a wife's right to frequent, satisfying sex is called *onah* and is seen as one of her three basic rights in marriage, along with access to food and clothing. As sex is the right of the wife, the husband is seen as the partner with the obligation to provide his wife with regular sexual interactions and ensure that she experiences physical pleasure during these interactions (AICE 2021).

SEXUAL VIOLENCE

Discussing sexual violence in MENA has many layers, and accurate statistics can be difficult to find. Many women are hesitant to come forward in cases of sexual violence, as it is not unusual for a female victim to also be arrested for having sex outside of marriage after being the victim of sexual assault in some Arab countries (Ghazal 2019). Nonetheless, a 2018 study included six MENA countries in its list of the top 10 most dangerous countries for women worldwide, identifying Syria as ranked third specifically for risks of sexual abuse (Thomas Reuters Foundation 2018).

Earlier in the chapter, the concept of marry-your-rapist laws was introduced. It is important to consider these laws from the lens of the violated woman, as the victim has no choice in denying this marriage—it is an arrangement between her rapist and her father (Jolly and Raste 2006). This is because the rape is not seen as a crime against the woman or her body but as a form of dishonor against her family (UNFPA 2021). Thus it is the family that can agree to the marriage to release themselves from the shame of having an unmarried, nonvirgin daughter. Many of the young women in these situations feel trapped, not only due to their lack of consent to the marriage but also because of a lack of alternative options. Women are often seen as unmarriageable if they have been raped, and many heartbreaking

<table>
</table>

TOP 10 MOST DANGEROUS COUNTRIES	
FOR WOMEN WORLDWIDE	
1.	India
2.	Afghanistan
3.	Syria
4.	Somalia
5.	Saudi Arabia
6.	Pakistan
7.	Democratic Republic of Congo
8.	Yemen
9.	Nigeria
10.	United States

stories can be found of teenage girls and young women choosing to end their own lives rather than face the reality of marrying their rapists or the shame of living out their lives as impure or damaged (UNFPA 2021). These laws were common throughout MENA until the 1970s, when many challenges and repeals began. However, as recently as 2017, the practice has continued to be documented in several countries, including Afghanistan, Algeria, Bahrain, Eritrea, Iraq, Kuwait, Libya, Palestine, and Syria (Belhaj, Soliman, and Kalle 2021; Equality Now 2017). In recent years, repeals have often begun with an instance of another teenage girl committing suicide after being forced to marry her rapist; then the story gains media attention and draws international advocacy efforts. The very presence of these laws reinforces not only the view of women as property but also the commodification of a woman's virginity and sexuality as little more than a feature of that property.

Another form of violence against women that should be noted is that of honor crimes. While not "sexual violence" according to a strict definition, these acts are nonetheless marked by physical harm perpetuated against a woman as a result of her sexuality. Honor crimes are defined as violence against women (either physical lashings or execution) for "dishonorable" use of her sexuality, such as premarital sex, same-sex relations, adultery, or even being the victim of rape. Within the last 30 years, some estimates have stated that as many as 70% of murder cases of Palestinian women may have been the result of honor crimes (Ruggi 1998). While some countries have legal codes stating that these murders are not technically legal, the sentences are often very light. For example, in 2005, a Palestinian man murdered his daughter, Faten, after her attempted elopement and "compromising" relationship. Despite being convicted of his daughter's murder, he was sentenced to only six months in jail due to a legal loophole that gives special consideration to situations of "honor" crime (Uhlmann 2005).

Despite prioritizing the sexual purity of daughters until marriage, many young girls experience sexual assault. Laws related to marriage age in Egypt, Iraq, Lebanon, and Turkey are written in such a way that loopholes can be found for temporary child marriages. Temporary arrangements, referred to as "summer marriages" or "pleasure marriages," result from a girl's family taking payment from a traveler for a short-term marriage. The "marriage" is cancelled when the traveler returns home or at the end of an agreed-upon period of time, typically only a few weeks. Increasing poverty in the region has made this situation worse (Save the Children 2021). These temporary marriages make it difficult to track sex trafficking in the Middle East. Since the girls involved in "summer marriages" are often underage, do not consent to the arrangement, and have few (if any) rights in the arrangement, these situations would typically be considered a form of trafficking or forced prostitution. In other MENA countries, laws do exist against sex trafficking, but the enforcement of these laws is overly lax. For example, a report focusing on trafficking in Israel documented a decrease in both investigations and prosecutions related to trafficking, and Saudi Arabia was found to not investigate officials complicit in trafficking nor to sentence traffickers to appropriate prison terms (Breiner and Peleg 2021; U.S. Department of State 2021). In fact, six MENA countries (Afghanistan, Algeria, Eritrea, Iran, Sudan, Syria) are classified at the lowest level of trafficking protection efforts, meaning their governments do not comply with nor are significantly working toward even the minimum standards of the Trafficking Victims Protection Act (U.S. Department of State 2021).

Even in looking at behaviors that would not particularly make international news, there are still high prevalence rates of sexual assault and harassment in MENA. One United Nations study found that in Algeria, 66% of women have experienced sexual harassment, with this figure being as high as 99% in Egypt (Schultz 2014; Zanaz 2019). Furthermore, it has been estimated that nearly 40% of Turkish women will endure some form of sexual or physical violence perpetrated by their intimate partner (Hacettepe University 2015). High rates of intimate partner sexual violence in MENA countries are often the norm, given that marital rape is not technically illegal in many of these regions. In Sudan, for example, there have been cases of women being hospitalized for injuries following a marital sexual assault yet still not having the option to open a criminal case, with some labeling marital rape in Sudan "a common occurrence" (Amin 2018). Similarly, it is estimated that 10% of married women in Egypt experience marital rape, with these assaults technically being legally excusable (Samir 2021).

REPRODUCTIVE HEALTH AND MENSTRUATION

An introduction to FGM was provided earlier in the chapter. It is important to understand the drastic ramifications that this practice may have on a female's reproductive health. Over 80% of girls ages 15 and over have experienced FGM in Djibouti, Egypt, Eritrea, Ethiopia, Somalia, and Sudan. More than half of girls in Mauritania will be subjected to the procedure before their 14th birthday, most in infancy (UNICEF 2021). In many regions it is not only the opinions of men that perpetuate this practice but most females are also in favor of it continuing (UNICEF 2021). Many women see the practice as being a way to achieve higher social status as well as having the benefit of reducing their sexual desire (Ouldzeidoune et al. 2013). While it may seem puzzling to consider the reduction of female sexual desire to be a benefit, it is important to keep in mind that this is a region with a long-standing tradition of perceiving women's sexuality as being both dangerous and threatening. FGM is often considered to be a way of discouraging the temptation of premarital sex as well as encouraging sexual fidelity to a woman's husband after marriage. In some cultures, willingness to undergo FGM has even become requirement for marriage, with uncut genitalia being perceived as both unattractive and unhygienic (UNFPA 2020).

There are obvious health risks immediately surrounding the time of the procedure. Given that it is often performed in unsanitary conditions by members of the community rather than trained health practitioners, there are often high rates of infection and hemorrhage. Many women suffer from intense pain following the procedure, with the risk that ulcerations and keloids may form as the area begins to heal. The wounds from the procedure can easily become infected, and other infections of the urinary tract are common. If not treated, the infections and hemorrhages that may follow this procedure can lead to long-term complications or even risk the woman's life. Due to frequently unsanitary conditions and improper sterilization of the cutting instruments, there is also a risk of HIV or tetanus transmission during the procedure (UNFPA 2019, 2020).

Not only are there health complications immediately surrounding the procedure but there are also long-term health consequences. Women may face complications during childbirth due to the narrowing and obstruction of the vaginal canal and may experience long-term sexual dysfunction, urinary incontinence, and pain during sexual activities. It is not uncommon for a woman to have to be cut again before her wedding night, as the scar tissue can narrow the vaginal canal to the point that penetration would be impossible (UNFPA 2020). Even if enough scar tissue is cut away to allow for penetrative intercourse, many women must be cut again to facilitate childbirth. Women who have undergone FGM have significantly higher rates of death during childbirth and fetal death (UNFPA 2019).

The long-standing "purity" motives of FGM have been discussed in prior sections, but it is important to note that inaccurate beliefs regarding women's anatomy and reproductive health play a secondary role in maintaining this practice in some areas. Some pockets believe that FGM is necessary to protect both women's health and fetal health. FGM is thought to increase the chances of conception and to protect the baby by preventing physical contact with toxins from the clitoris during birth, which some believe could be fatal to the fetus/newborn (Ross et al. 2016). With modern medicine, we know that this is not an actual risk—there are no toxic tissues found within the clitoris, nor are there any toxic secretions from this anatomical region. Another inaccurate belief about female anatomy that motivates FGM is that there is a risk that the clitoris could continue growing if not cut, hanging lower and lower, possibly even reaching the ground (Nour 2008).

Additional inaccurate beliefs surround the relationship between the hymen and virginity. As discussed, "virginity tests" often focus on examining the hymen, and the hymen is expected to tear on the wedding night to indicate virginity by leaving blood. With the possibility of a torn hymen from other nonsexual activities, a history of sexual assault, or prior consensual sexual activity, women often fear that they will not bleed on their wedding night and face a serious dilemma. This has led to demand for a procedure known as "hymenoplasty" or hymen reconstruction, sometimes referred to as "virginity repair surgery." This procedure is technically forbidden by Shari'ah law, as it is seen as an encouragement of premarital sex and promiscuity (Holleis 2021). Despite being a quick procedure that involves only a few stitches around the inside of the vaginal wall, the risks of lasting pain are significant (Li 2020). Of additional concern is the perpetuation of the belief that a virgin must bleed at first intercourse, as this procedure does nearly guarantee bleeding at penetration due to the method of stitching up the vaginal tissue in a way that it is specifically intended to tear. Some providers even advertise "super hymenoplasty," which guarantees a greater quantity of blood to remove any doubt of the presence of the hymen and, therefore, status of virginity (Nevra 2010). While some have proposed banning hymenoplasty procedures, this could ultimately risk the lives of women who live in areas where honor killings still occur for premarital sex (Li 2020; Schweiger 2011).

These misconceptions about anatomy are partially allowed to continue due to a pervasive lack of sex education. As of the time of this writing, Tunisia was the only Arabic country with a sex education curriculum, which was not introduced until 2020 (Nabulsi 2021). Other countries have had programs at some point in the past but have since repealed them, as was the case when Lebanon began its curriculum in 1995 only to remove it due to public criticism (Nabulsi 2021). Activists have called for better education, going all the way down to the basics of the language used to discuss anatomy and physiology. For example, the Arabic word for hymen is "virginity membrane," and the literal translation of the term for masturbation is "secret habit" (Nabulsi 2021). Recent research supports the idea that women in the Middle East lack adequate knowledge about their sexual and reproductive health. One study focusing on Lebanese women found that less than 9% of participants had adequate knowledge about sexual health. Specifically related to contraception, only 13.5% could score higher than a 65% on a basic knowledge exam (Hamdanieh et al. 2021).

Many topics of reproductive health and menstruation in MENA revolve around religious protocols. Issues such as contraception, abortion, and "appropriate" behaviors during menstruation often trace back to the guidelines set forth by Islam and Judaism. For example, Judaism allows contraception as long as it is not a method that damages the sperm or prevents it from entering the woman's body. This means that while spermicides, condoms, and other barrier methods are forbidden, hormonal contraception and IUDs are permitted (BBC 2009). In contrast, the

The First Day of School. (Jean Baptiste Vanmour, c. 1720–c. 1737, *The First Day of School.* Rijksmuseum, Amsterdam)

majority of the Islamic divisions permit contraception if it is within the context of marriage, but some conservative Islamic authorities frown upon contraception (BBC 2009). With these supportive messages in place, despite their restrictions and caveats, MENA reports reasonable levels of contraceptive usage among married women, with many countries offering hormonal contraceptive pills and condoms for free or at very low prices due to government subsidies (United Nations Foundation 2018). Rates of contraception usage do vary significantly by marital status. For example, from 2014 to 2020, 40% to 42% of married women were using a contraceptive method (United Nations Foundation 2020). However, within this same time frame, only 26% to 28% of all women of reproductive age were using contraception (United Nations Foundation 2020). While it is possible that some of these women were following cultural norms and were not sexually active outside of marriage, thus reducing their need for contraception, it is also possible that cultural taboos were limiting their access to contraception. One study has estimated that only 3% of sexually active unmarried women in Arab countries use contraception, acknowledging that this statistic may be low due to stigma in admitting to premarital sex and contraceptive use in the region (Farzaneh et al. 2012).

One concern in the discussion of contraception among young women in MENA is the degree to which these women hold agency in making their own decisions about their reproductive health. Some studies have indicated that the opinions of a woman's husband and his family hold greater weight than a woman's own preferences in relation to family planning (Alomair et al. 2020). Women often feel pressured to continue having children for economic support and social/familial approval. Family pressure or a husband's disapproval of contraceptives can lead to a woman becoming pregnant when she does not desire to be, but she often has restricted options for pregnancy termination. Not only do religious beliefs limit the situations in which a woman may feel like she is able to terminate a pregnancy with a clean conscience, but strict laws in the region—often shaped at least in part by these religious beliefs—further limit options for safe and legal pregnancy termination.

Both Islam and Judaism allow for abortion in specific situations. The discussion of abortion in Judaism revolves around the physical well-being of the mother. While abortion is not taken lightly, if the life of the mother were in jeopardy due to the pregnancy, Jewish law would require an abortion. The logic behind this goes back to how Judaism conceptualizes "life." An unborn child is seen as "potential life"; as such, it has value and should not be ended without good cause. However, this "potential life" does not have greater value than the life of the mother and therefore should not be prioritized over her (AICE 2021). In Islam, there are three primary considerations when deciding if an abortion is permissible: (1) if the fetus received its soul, which is believed to occur at 120 days; (2) if there is a threat to the mother; (3) if the fetus has defects that would cause it to die shortly after birth. Most branches of Islam allow abortion prior to that 120-day mark if the mother's health is in danger or there are life-threatening fetal abnormalities (Al-Matary and Ali 2014). However, abortion after 120 days is strictly forbidden, with only very narrow exceptions of risk to the mother's life, similar to the ideology seen in Judaism. While these are the general religious beliefs in these regions, many countries enact abortion laws that introduce further prohibitions. It is estimated that approximately 24% of women in MENA live in areas where abortion is allowed only in cases of protecting a woman's mental or physical well-being, and 55% live in areas where abortion would only be allowed if a mother's life were in danger (Atay 2019). These restrictions drive many women to seek out unsafe,

It is estimated that unsafe abortions are the cause of at least 12% of maternal deaths in MENA, with prior statistics indicating that over 1,000 unsafe abortions occur daily in Iran alone (Global Health Council 2002; WHO 2011).

secret abortions. Throughout MENA, only Tunisia and Turkey permit elective abortion during the first trimester but still with several restrictions. Turkey only allows abortion up to 10 weeks, with the consent of a woman's husband, and any hospital or clinic is allowed to refuse to perform the procedure (Nawa 2020). Tunisia is slightly less restrictive, as it does not require a husband's approval, but termination is only permitted during the first trimester (Maffi and Affes 2019).

Cultural beliefs in MENA shape a woman's access not only to sex education, contraception, and abortion but even health-care needs as related to menstrual hygiene. There is a great deal of shame and stigma surrounding menstruation, primarily originating from religious beliefs. Women are often viewed as unclean during their periods and are prohibited from going to church, having sex with their husbands, and sometimes even caring for their children or attending social events. This sense of shame combined with pervasive period poverty, which is defined as a level of poverty that affects the ability to acquire menstrual hygiene products, leads to disastrous effects for young girls of this region. For example, in Afghanistan, most girls will miss an average of five days of school each month because of menstruation (Noori 2019). Many unmarried women in the region are afraid to use tampons or menstrual cups due to a belief that it may break the hymen, and inexpensive or makeshift sanitary pads are often made from contaminated or otherwise harmful materials (Scene Arabia 2019). Improper menstrual hygiene is leading to increased rates of gynecological infections, some of which can have lifelong consequences or even be life-threatening without proper medical care (Abaza 2021).

MEDIA AND SEXUALITY

MENA has a long-standing history of media censorship. In fact, a 35-year ban of movie theaters in Saudi Arabia was not lifted until 2018 (Petroff 2018). While few films are banned entirely, many are censored before being allowed to be distributed in the region. Scenes demonstrating even brief

Internet access. (http://www.istockphoto.com)

public displays of affection, such as a kiss, are often cut from movies, with sex and nudity being banned as a general rule. When an entire film is banned rather than censored, it is often given a generic explanation, such as "the theme of the film does not fit with our cultural values" (Murphy 2010). Given this censorship of mainstream Hollywood movies, it should come as no surprise that pornography is illegal throughout most of MENA; however, advances in technology allow many citizens to bypass internet blockers and view pornography. In fact, a 2015 data report by Google showed that MENA countries accounted for six (Pakistan, Egypt, Iran, Morocco, Saudi Arabia, and Turkey) of the top eight countries that search for pornography on the internet, with a Lebanese actress who commonly begins her films in hijab ranking among the most popular searches (Weisman 2015).

It is important to analyze media and sexuality beyond the scope of mainstream movies and television, as social media has become an important tool in discussing sexuality in a highly censored culture. Given that sex education is highly restricted and often nonexistent, in MENA countries, some women have taken the risk of providing digital sex education through less-restricted media platforms. For example, a sexual wellness Instagram page run in collaboration by women from Egypt, Lebanon, and Saudi Arabia gained over 50,000 followers in less than one year (Nabulsi 2021). Although social media outlets offer more freedom of speech than these women may be able to find through the school system or other public education options, the delivery of their message is still not guaranteed. Many MENA countries, including Saudi Arabia, utilize hackers as part of their legal system to remove social media content that is considered inappropriate (Hay 2015).

Despite such strict censorship laws, women are often portrayed negatively in the media in the Middle East, often with a sexual tone. One study found that nearly 80% of portrayals of women in mainstream media were negative, with much of this negativity focusing on sexual immorality or sexual objectification (Allam 2008). When abortion is portrayed on television, it is often with the tone of a woman failing her family (O'Neil 2013). However, there have been instances of mainstream entertainment media in MENA using its voice to cultivate change for women. In Lebanon, a television program titled *Let the Brave Speak Out* (or *Al-Chater Yehki*), reached a top rating featuring live debates on sexual issues, such as masturbation, sexual orientation, and incest (Foster 2000). Research has indicated that women in Turkey find soap operas that depict sexual empowerment, modern dress, and alcohol consumption to be important conversation starters (Yalkin and Veer 2018). An Egyptian miniseries titled *Newton's Cradle* recently portrayed the violence of marital rape, reopening the debate surrounding outdated laws that allow men to abuse their wives with no legal consequence (Bassel and Abdulaal 2021).

In summary, women in MENA often find themselves subject to male-dominated legal, social, and familial structures that hold many regulations over their sexuality. In many areas of their sexual health and engagement, they have little agency over their decision-making. Some women find their bodily autonomy compromised in multiple ways throughout their life span, with pervasive messages that their bodies are to be utilized for family honor above all else. It is with cautious optimism that we can point to a few positive changes that have been made in the past decade as small steps toward increased safety and autonomy for women. More countries are allowing marital rape to be seen as a crime, fewer countries are upholding "marry-your-rapist" loopholes, FGM and honor killings are being more heavily advocated against, and—at least on paper—child marriages are being more explicitly prohibited. However, as has been reviewed here, there is still much work to be done. The combination of conservative religion with generations of patriarchal cultural ideology has created long-standing practices and beliefs that are proving hard to eliminate, even when technically outlawed. True change will not occur until the value of women is recognized, their worth appreciated, and their autonomy validated.

REFERENCES

Abaza, Mariam. 2021. "Lack of Menstrual Products in Syria Threatens Women's Health." August 23. Accessed June 22, 2022. https://borgenproject.org/menstrual-products.

AICE (America-Israeli Cooperative Enterprise). 2021. "Issues in Jewish Ethics: 'Kosher' Sex." Accessed June 22, 2022. https://www.jewishvirtuallibrary.org/quot-kosher-quot-sex.

Al Javed, Hasan. 2020. "Dubai Sex Trafficking Victims Relate Tales of Duplicity and Horror." September 12. Accessed June 22, 2022. https://www.dhakatribune.com/bangladesh/2020/09/12/dubai-sex-victims-relate-tales-of-duplicity-and-horror.

Allam, Rasha. 2008. *Countering the Negative Image of Arab Women in the Arab Media: Toward a "Pan Arab Eye" Media Watch Project.* Washington, DC: Middle East Institute, 2008. Accessed June 22, 2022. files.ethz.ch/isn/57131/No_15_Countering_the_Negative_Image.pdf.

Al-Matary, Abdulrahman, and Jaffar Ali. 2014. "Controversies and Considerations Regarding the Termination of Pregnancy for Foetal Anomalies in Islam." *BMC Medica Ethics* 15 (10). https://doi.org/10.1186/1472-6939-15-10.

Alomair, Noura., Samah Alageel, Nathan Davies, and Julia V. Bailey. 2020. "Factors Influencing Sexual and Reproductive Health of Muslim Women: A Systematic Review." *Reproductive Health* 17 (33). https://doi.org/10.1186/s12978-020-0888-1.

Amin, Mohammed. 2018. "Where Marital Rape Is Legal: Sudanese Teen's Death Sentence Fuels Wider Fight." May 19. Accessed June 22, 2022. https://www.middleeasteye.net/news/where-marital-rape-legal-sudanese-teens-death-sentence-fuels-wider-fight.

Atay, Hazal. 2019. "Debate: When Abortion Is 'Haram,' Women Find Strategies to Claim Their Rights." May 17. Accessed June 22, 2022. https://theconversation.com/debate-when-abortion-is-haram-women-find-strategies-to-claim-their-rights-104177.

Bassel, Mona, and Mirna Abdulaal. 2021. "Calls for Marital Rape Criminalization in Egypt after Viral Instagram Video." June 22. Accessed June 22, 2022. https://egyptianstreets.com/2021/06/22

/calls-for-marital-rape-criminalization-in-egypt-after-viral
-instagram-video.

BBC. 2009. "Contraception." Accessed July 26, 2022. https://www.bbc.co
.uk/religion/religions/islam/islamethics/contraception.shtml.

Belhaj, Ferid, Ayat Soliman, and Mirjam Kalle. 2021. "MENA Must Take
Bold Action against Gender-Based Violence (GBV)." December 10.
Accessed June 22, 2022. https://blogs.worldbank.org/arabvoices
/mena-must-take-bold-action-against-gender-based-violence-gbv.

Bouhdiba, Abdelwahab. 1998. *Sexuality in Islam*. London: Saqi Books.

Bourdieu, Pierre. 2001. *Masculine Domination*. Translated by Richard
Nice. Redwood City, CA: Stanford University Press.

Boyle, Elizabeth Heger. 2005. *Female Genital Cutting: Cultural Conflict
in the Global Community*. Baltimore, MD: JHU Press.

Breiner, Josh, and Bar Peleg. 2021. "Israel Failing to Do Minimum to Fight
Human Trafficking, U.S. Says." July 2. Accessed June 22, 2022.
https://www.haaretz.com/israel-news/.premium-israel-failing
-to-do-minimum-to-fight-human-trafficking-u-s-claims-1.9963346.

Broom, Douglas. 2019. "How the Middle East Is Suffering on the Front
Lines of Climate Change." April 5. Accessed June 22, 2022. https://
www.weforum.org/agenda/2019/04/middle-east-front-lines
-climate-change-mena.

Budin, Stephanie. 2008. *The Myth of Sacred Prostitution in Antiquity*.
New York: Cambridge University Press.

Butler, William. 2010. "Why Dubai's Islamic Austerity Is a Sham—
Sex Is for Sale in Every Bar." May 15. Accessed June 22, 2022.
https://www.theguardian.com/world/2010/may/16/dubai-sex-tourism
-prostitution.

Callimachi, Rukmini. 2015. "ISIS Enshrines a Theology of Rape." *New
York Times*. August 13.

Carroll, Lucy. 1998. "Arranged Marriages: Law, Custom, and the Muslim
Girl in the UK." *Women Living under Muslim Law* 20. Accessed
June 22, 2022. https://www.wluml.org/2003/07/04/dossier-20.

Clancy-Smith, Julia Ann. 2004. "Exemplary Women and Sacred Journeys:
Women and Gender in Judaism, Christianity, and Islam from Late
Antiquity to the Eve of Modernity." In *Women's History in Global
Perspective Volume 1*, edited by B. G. Smith, 92–144. Champaign:
University of Illinois Press.

Desilver, Drew, and David Masci. 2017. "World's Muslim Population More
Widespread Than You Might Think." January 31. Accessed June
22, 2022. http://pewrsr.ch/116QRmk.

El Feki, Shereen. 2019. "The Last Legal Sex Workers in Tunisia." October 2. Accessed June 22, 2022. https://www.bbc.com/news/world -africa-49890471.

Equality Now. 2017. *The World's Shame: The Global Rape Epidemic.* New York: Equality Now.

Farzaneh, Roudi-Fahimi, Ahmed Abdul Monem, Lori Ashford, and Maha El-Adawy. 2012. *Women's Need for Family Planning in Arab Countries.* Washington, DC: Population Reference Bureau.

Foster, Angel M. 2000. *Sexuality in the Middle East: Conference Report.* Oxford: St Anthony's College Middle East Center.

Ghazal, Rym T. 2019. "Arab Countries Struggle with the Stigma Associated with Rape." January 1. Accessed June 22, 2022. https:// asiatimes.com/2019/01/arab-countries-struggle-with-the-stigma -associated-with-rape

Ghazzālī, and Madelain Farah. 1984. *Marriage and Sexuality in Islam: A Translation of al-Ghazālī's Book on the Etiquette of Marriage from the Iḥyā'.* Salt Lake City: University of Utah Press.

Global Health Council. 2002. *Promises to Keep: The Toll of Unintended Pregnancy on Women in the Developing World.* Washington, DC: Global Health Council.

Gornall, Jonathan. 2019. "With Climate Change, Life in the Gulf Could Become Impossible." April 24. Accessed June 22, 2022. https:// www.euractiv.com/section/climate-environment/opinion /with-climate-change-life-in-the-gulf-could-become-impossible.

Graham-Harrison, Emma. 2017. "'I Was Sold Seven Times': The Yazidi Women Welcomed Back into the Faith." July 1. Accessed June 22, 2022. https://www.theguardian.com/global-development/2017/jul /01/i-was-sold-seven-times-yazidi-women-welcomed-back-into-the -faith.

Hacettepe University. 2015. *Research on Domestic Violence against Women in Turkey.* Ankara, Turkey: Elma Teknik Basim Matbaacilik.

Hamdanieh, Maya, Louna Ftouni, Bara'a Al Jardali, Racha Ftouni, Chaymaa Rawas, Marina Ghotmi, Mohammad Hussein El Zein, Sara Ghazi, and Salah Malas. 2021. "Assessment of Sexual and Reproductive Health Knowledge and Awareness among Single Unmarried Women Living in Lebanon: A Cross-Sectional Study." *Reproductive Health* 18 (24). Accessed June 22, 2022. https://doi .org/10.1186/s12978-021-01079-x.

Hay, Mark. 2015. "Saudi Arabia's Morality Police and 'Ethical Hackers' Are Targeting Online Pornography." January 2. Accessed June 22,

2022.   https://www.vice.com/en/article/av4pj5/inside-the-world-of
-saudi-arabias-ethical-hackers.

Holleis, Jennifer. 2021. "Egypt: New Ruling on Hymen Repair Stirs Up
Controversy." September 10. Accessed June 22, 2022. https://www
.dw.com/en/egypt-new-ruling-on-hymen-repair-stirs-up-controversy
/a-59134641.

Ilkkaracan, Pinar. 2002. "Women, Sexuality, and Social Change in the
Middle East and the Maghreb." *Social Research* 69 (3): 753–79.
Accessed June 22, 2022. http://www.jstor.org/stable/40971572.

Jolly, Stellina, and M. S. Raste. 2006. "Rape and Marriage: Reflections on
the Past, Present and Future." *Journal of the Indian Law Institute*
48 (2): 277–84. Accessed June 22, 2022. http://www.jstor.org
/stable/43952037.

Lasco, Chante. 2002. "Virginity Testing in Turkey: A Violation of Wom-
en's Human Rights." *Human Rights Brief* 9 (3): 10–13.

Lerner, Gerda. 1986. "The Origin of Prostitution in Ancient Mesopotamia." *Signs* 11 (2): 236–54. Accessed June 22, 2022. http://www
.jstor.org/stable/3174047

Li, Yuexin. 2020. "Myths and Dilemma of the Controversial 'Virginity
Repair' Surgery." February 13. Accessed June 22, 2022. https://
theowp.org/reports/myths-and-dilemma-of-the-controversial
-virginity-repair-surgery.

Lightfoot-Klein, Hanny. 1989. *Prisoners of Ritual: An Odyssey into
Female Genital Circumcision in Africa*. Philadelphia: Haworth
Press, Inc.

Maffi, Irene, and Malika Affes. 2019. "The Right to Abortion in Tunisia
after the Revolution of 2011: Legal, Medica, and Social Arrangements as Seen through Seven Abortion Stories." *Human and
Health Rights Journal* 21 (2): 69–78.

Mamo, Dwayne, ed. 2021. *The Indigenous World 2021*. Copenhagen,
Denmark: International Work Group for Indigenous Affairs.

Murphy, Meagan. 2010. "Muslim Countries Vary Greatly on Censorship
of Hollywood Films." October 21. Accessed June 22, 2022. https://
www.foxnews.com/entertainment/muslim-countries-vary-greatly
-on-censorship-of-hollywood-films.

Nabulsi, Mira. 2021. "Arab Content Creators Use Social Media to Talk
about Sex, Sexuality, and Reproductive Health." August 9.
Accessed June 22, 2022. https://globalvoices.org/2021/08/09/arab
-content-creators-use-social-media-to-talk-about-sex-sexuality
-and-reproductive-health.

Nawa, Fariba. 2020. "Abortion Increasingly Hard to Access in Turkey." October 5. Accessed June 23, 2022. https://theworld.org/stories/2020-10-05/abortion-increasingly-hard-access-turkey.

Nevra, Jin. 2010. "Hymenoplasty, Hymen Repair Surgery." Accessed June 23, 2022. http://hymenoplastyistanbul.com/hymenoplasty_types _techniques.html.

Noori, Hikmat. 2019. "In Afghanistan, Replacing Shame with Understanding on the Topic of Menstruation." February 18. Accessed June 23, 2022. https://undark.org/2019/02/18/afghanistan-menstruation -taboo.

Nour, Nawal M. 2008. "Female Genital Cutting: A Persisting Practice." *Reviews in Obstetrics and Gynecology* 1 (3): 135.

O'Neil, Mary Lou. 2013. "Selfish, Vengeful, and Full of Spite: The Representations of Women Who Have Abortions on Turkish Television." *Feminist Media Studies* 13 (5): 810–18. https://doi.org/10.1080/146 80777.2013.838360.

Ouldzeidoune, Nacerdine, Joseph Keating, Jane Bertrand, and Janet Rice. 2013. "A Description of Female Genital Mutilation and Force-Feeding Practices in Mauritania: Implications for the Protection of Child Rights and Health." *PLoS One* 8 (4): e60594.

Pal, Jeremy S., and Elfatih A. B. Eltahir. 2016. "Future Temperature in Southwest Asia Projected to Exceed a Threshold for Human Adaptability." *Nature Climate Change* 6 (2): 197–200. https://doi .org/10.1038/nclimate2833.

Peirce, Leslie. 2009. "Writing Histories of Sexuality in the Middle East." *American Historical Review* 114 (5): 1325–39. Accessed June 23, 2022. http://www.jstor.org/stable/23303429.

Petroff, Alanna. 2018. "'Black Panther' Comes to Saudi Arabia as Movie Theater Ban Ends." April 18. Accessed June 23, 2022. https:// money.cnn.com/2018/04/18/media/saudi-arabia-movies-black -panther-amc/index.html.

Pryke, Louise. 2018. "In Ancient Mesopotamia, Sex among the Gods Shook Heaven and Earth." April 22. Accessed June 23, 2022. https://theconversation.com/in-ancient-mesopotamia-sex-among -the-gods-shook-heaven-and-earth-87858.

Ross, Cody T., Pontus Strimling, Karen Paige Ericksen, Patrik Lindenfors, and Monique Borgerhoff Mulder. 2016. "The Origins and Maintenance of Female Genital Modification across Africa." *Human Nature* 27 (2): 173–200. https://doi.org/10.1007/s12110-015-9244-5.

Ruggi, Suzanne. 1998. "Commodifying Honor in Female Sexuality: Honor Killings in Palestine." *Middle East Report* 206: 12–15. https://doi .org/10.2307/3012473.

Samir, Nehal. 2021. "Hiding in Plain Sight: Marital Rape Still Not Criminalized in Egypt." January 14. Accessed June 23, 2022. https:// dailynewsegypt.com/2021/01/14/hiding-in-plain-sight-marital -rape-still-not-criminalised-in-egypt.

Save the Children. 2021. "Girls Facing Higher Risk of 'Summer' Marriages in Middle East and North Africa." June 25. Accessed June 23, 2022. https://www.savethechildren.org.au/media/media-releases /girls-facing-higher-risk-of-summer-marriages.

Sawe, Benjamin Elisha. 2019. "What Languages Are Spoken in the Middle East?" January 22. Accessed June 23, 2022. https://www.world atlas.com/articles/what-languages-are-spoken-in-the-middle-east .html.

Scene Arabia. 2019. "Period Poverty: How an Organization in Lebanon Provides Sustainable Solutions for Syrian Refugees." August 17. Accessed June 23, 2022. https://scenearabia.com/Life/Period -Poverty-Syrian-Refugees-Organisation-Lebanon-Days-for-Girls -Sustainable-Solutions.

Schultz, Colin. 2014. "In Egypt, 99 of Women Have Been Sexually Harassed." June 13. Accessed June 23, 2022. https://www.smithsonianmag .com/smart-news/egypt-99-women-have-been-sexually-harassed -180951726.

Schweiger, Laura. 2011. "'Virginity Surgery' Is on the Rise across Europe." July 3. Accessed June 23, 2022. https://www.dw.com/en/virginity -surgery-is-on-the-rise-across-europe/a-14881879.

ServantGroup International. 2017. "Yeziki Castes, Culture, and the Elephant in the Room." May 2. Accessed June 23,2022. https:// servantgroup.org/yezidi-castes-culture.

Thomas Reuters Foundation. 2018. "Factbox: Which Are the World's 10 Most Dangerous Countries for Women?" June 25. Accessed June 23, 2022. https://www.reuters.com/article/us-women-dangerous -poll-factbox/factbox-which-are-the-worlds-10-most-dangerous -countries-for-women-idUSKBN1JM01Z.

28 Too Many. 2013. "What are the Origins and Reasons for FGM?" February 19. Accessed June 23, 2022. https://www.28toomany.org /blog/what-are-the-origins-and-reasons-for-fgm-blog-by-28-too -manys-research-coordinator.

Uhlmann, Allon J. 2005. "Introduction: Reflections on the Study of Sexuality in the Middle East and North Africa." *Social Analysis: The International Journal of Social and Cultural Practice* 49 (2): 3–15. http://www.jstor.org/stable/23178869.

UN Women. 2017. "In the Words of Luiza Karimova: 'We Were Sex Slaves.'" February 17. Accessed June 23, 2022. https://www .unwomen.org/en/news/stories/2017/2/in-the-words-of-luiza-we -were-sex-slaves.

UNFPA. 2019. "5 Ways Female Genital Mutilation Undermines the Health of Women and Girls." May 20. Accessed June 23, 2022. https:// www.unfpa.org/news/5-ways-female-genital-mutilation-undermines -health-women-and-girls.

UNFPA. 2020. "Female Genital Mutilation (FGM) Frequently Asked Questions." July 20. Accessed June 23, 2022. https://www.unfpa .org/resources/female-genital-mutilation-fgm-frequently-asked -questions.

UNFPA. 2021. "'You Have to Marry Your Rapist': Sexual Violence Survivor Victimized by Harmful Tradition in Ethiopia." August 17. Accessed June 23, 2022. https://reliefweb.int/report/ethiopia/you -have-marry-your-rapist-sexual-violence-survivor-victimized -harmful-tradition.

UNICEF. 2021. "Female Genital Mutilation (FGM)." August. Accessed June 23, 2022. https://data.unicef.org/topic/child-protection/female -genital-mutilation.

United Nations Foundation. 2018. "Contraceptive Prevalence on Rise in MENA Though at Varying Pace." April 30. Accessed June 23, 2022. https://www.familyplanning2020.org/news/contraceptive -prevalence-rise-mena-though-varying-pace.

United Nations Foundation. 2020. "FP2020 Data Dashboard." Accessed June 23, 2022. https://www.familyplanning2020.org/fr/data-dashboard.

U.S. Department of State. 2021. *Trafficking in Persons Report.* Washington, DC: Office to Monitor and Combat Trafficking in Persons.

Weisman, Carrie. 2015. "Why Porn Is Exploding in the Middle East." January 15. Accessed June 23, 2022. https://www.salon.com/2015 /01/15/why_porn_is_exploding_in_the_middle_east_partner.

Whitaker, Brian. 2006. "Behind the Veil: Lesbian Lives in the Middle East." July. Accessed June 23, 2022. https://al-bab.com/behind -veil-lesbian-lives-middle-east.

WHO (World Health Organization). 2011. *Unsafe Abortion: Global and Regional Estimates of the Incidence of Unsafe Abortion and Associated Mortality in 2008 and Trends during 1990–2008.* Geneva, Switzerland: WHO.

WHO (World Health Organization). 2018. *Eliminating Virginity Testing: An Interagency Statement.* Geneva, Switzerland: WHO.

World Bank. 2020. "Population Total—Middle East & North Africa." Accessed June 23, 2022. https://data.worldbank.org/indicator/SP.POP.TOTL?locations=ZQ-1W.

Yalkin, Cagri, and Ekant Veer. 2018. "Taboo on TV: Gender, Religion, and Sexual Taboos in Transnationally Marketed Turkish Soap Operas." *Journal of Marketing Management* 34 (13–14): 1149–71.

Zanaz, Hamid. 2019. "The Maghreb Needs a Sexual Revolution." *Arab Weekly*, October 6.

FIVE

Sub-Saharan Africa

Tiffany Fawn Jones

In 1810, a young Khoikhoi woman, Sara Baartman, was put on display in freak shows in Europe. Taken from her home in South Africa, she ended up being gawked at by European audiences in traveling exhibitions. She was promoted as a "phenomenon of nature" with a "natural morose disposition" and became renowned for her pronounced buttocks (Wellcome Collection c1810). Baartman, also known derogatorily as the "Hottentot Venus," became synonymous with European misguided views about Africans and African sexuality (Gilman 1985). Because there were questions about whether or not she freely chose to leave South Africa and participate in these shows abroad, she also became central to abolitionist debates about freedom and equality (Magubane 2001). She died a few years later, in 1815, without her family. It is unclear whether she died of pneumonia, smallpox, or alcoholism. Her body was used by a French comparative anatomist, Georges Cuvier, to advance his ideas of evolutionary biology and forward concepts of racial difference. He made a cast of her body and pickled jars of her brain and genitalia, which were put on display in the *Musée de l'Homme* (Museum of Man) in Paris, France, until 1974. In 2002, the South African government and Khoikhoi communities fought to have her remains repatriated to her birthplace. She was buried in a symbolic ceremony of reconciliation and restitution against a tragic colonial past (Crais and Scully 2011).

The story of Sara Baartman is indicative of the long, sordid, and complicated history of ideas about race and African female sexuality—ideas that still have ramifications in sub-Saharan Africa today. African bodies have been at the forefront of Western debates about normality, racial difference, sexuality, health, and power for hundreds of years (Vaughan 1991). Westerners often depict Africa as a uniform, unchanging continent, and the stereotypes that were created throughout its colonial past have echoes in current debates about African sexuality. There are many misrepresentations about African sexualities. Far from being uniform and static, the African continent is one of the most diverse, complex, and mutable continents in the world. It is made up of 54 official countries and has approximately 2,000 languages, more geographical diversity than any other continent, and many religions, including Indigenous religions, Christianity, Islam, Hinduism, Judaism, Buddhism, and others (Sawe 2018; Chepkemoi 2019; Olupona 2014). This means that to talk of a uniform "African" or an "African sexuality" is a misnomer. We need to recognize that in sub-Saharan Africa, views about sexuality are complex, ever-changing, and determined by local circumstances. Sexuality can mean more than reproduction; it also relates to ideas of love, intimacy, agency, health, expression, identity, and desire. Therefore, it is better to use the plural term African *sexualities*, which recognizes the complex and multifaceted contexts in which sexualities are practiced (Tamale 2011a, 2). Once we understand the multiplicity of African sexualities, we will also understand the diverse and complex nature of the many societies in sub-Saharan Africa.

BRIEF HISTORY OF WOMEN'S SEXUALITY IN AFRICA

Scholars debate the extent to which African women had agency over their bodies prior to colonization. They agree that women had some semblance of political and social authority, but their degree of power over their own lives is still unknown. Indigenous communities certainly recognized women's reproductive, social, and political power. Women held high positions in governing bodies; they were queens, chiefs, queen mothers, sisters, elders, and political advisors (Sudarkasa 1986, 91). Griots, other oral historians, and healers, many of whom were women, were the keepers of stories that dictated social norms and political mores. They were also the political counselors of those in power. But we also know that women were often constrained by strict social structures, and many of those indentured or enslaved in domestic servitude on the continent and in the Arab slave trade before the arrival of Europeans were women (Lewis 1990).

When European countries colonized much of the African continent from the 17th century through to the end of the 20th century, they each undermined women's roles and specifically attempted to erode the agency of the keepers of tradition and political advisors. Colonialists disputed the authority of healers, griots, and spiritual advisors. The notion of the "evil witchdoctor" was deemed a threat against European ideas of "civilization." In colonial Tanzania, for example, anyone who practiced sorcery with intent to injury could be jailed for up to seven years (Machangu 2015). In the Cape Colony in South Africa, the British government passed the Witchcraft Suppression Act of 1895 that made divination illegal (Jolles and Jolles 1998). Under the guise of promoting development and enlightenment, European colonialists, missionaries, and traders undermined local African agency and imposed European definitions of gender and sexual norms. They justified and framed their actions within the context of European heterosexual patriarchy. The colonialist was deemed a "trustee" or "patriarch" of the colony, and in turn, each colonial power sought to shape the lives and minds of their populations.

In order to control their subjects, it became important to classify them. Europeans often became engrossed with defining, categorizing, and shaping African groups. Classification charts and census surveys became popular in the 19th century (Kertzer and Arel 2002). Colonialists were very concerned with ordering nature and humans, and they believed in segregation among races. Indeed, the defining and delineation of static "races" and "tribes" became vitally important in the process of colonial control. Sometimes they even constructed tribes and makeshift chiefs to suit their political objectives. Because Europeans brought with them gendered notions of power, however, they made men the overseers of these tribes, regardless of previous tradition, and made women their subjects. They negated the existing power structures, such as female leaders and community groups to which women belonged, and disregarded any political standing that women may have held.

Missionaries, doctors, and colonial officials also explicitly set out to define and control the reproductive and sexual actions of Africans. Leaning on European religious teachings and often poorly researched and racist scientific writings, colonists argued that Africans were inherently sexually underdeveloped and closer to animals than Europeans were (Epprecht 2008, 2013). Pseudoscience, like eugenics and ethnopsychiatry, emerged as a means to explain behavior that did not fit the European norm. Colonial practitioners argued that Africans were more "primitive" and therefore closer to nature and, in turn, less developed in their sexual behavior than Europeans were. These ideas were propagated in popular exhibitions and shows such as those in which Sara Baartman was presented. As Marc Epprecht (2013) explains, "In colonial times, Africans' supposed stunted or brutish sexuality was thought to oppress and degrade women, to engender laziness and stultify intellectual growth in men, to threaten public health and safety, and to impoverish culture and the arts (there being no love or higher emotions, just lust, superstition, and steely transactions)" (63). Europeans therefore framed their views in terms of uplifting and protecting Africans, particularly African women, from their underdeveloped, primeval selves.

In many colonies throughout the continent, these ideas of enlightening Africans manifested themselves in interesting ways. For example, clothing became a key struggle in discussions of civilization. As Sylvia Tamale (2011b) points out, missionaries and other religious figures encouraged Africans to

> reject their previous beliefs and values and to adopt the "civilised ways" of the whites. With these new developments came the emphasis on covering and hiding body parts. Indeed, one of the most effective methods of controlling African women's sexuality has been through the regulation of their dress codes. (16)

Women were encouraged to cover their breasts and wrap their bodies with cloth. Men were urged to wear cloaks and vests, and dress became an important indicator of social hierarchy. Clothing was a means of disciplining and controlling the African body. In Kenya, for example, the British disdained any semblance of nudity but never fully approved of the complete adoption of Western dress. Instead, they wanted Africans to wear clothing that they deemed appropriate for Africans' lower status in the colony (Hay 2004, 68). Many times, young African men who worked or were educated in Western institutions preferred to wear Western-style clothing, much to the chagrin of colonial officials, missionaries, and their elders. At the same time, however, the African men who chose to wear Western-style jackets and trousers discouraged their wives and daughters from wearing anything but traditional attire. Women's adoption of Western-style clothing was an affront to their traditional power. Indeed, Gusii men begged colonial officials to help them stop African women from wearing westernized clothing. They believed that women who wore Western dress were promiscuous and were shrugging off patriarchal control (Hay 2004, 67–77).

Similar views dominated in West African areas where Muslim dress became a means through which to regulate women's bodies. In Niger, for example, women wore the veil as a sign of piety and morality (Masquelier 2009). Islamic preachers wanted women to willingly wear the hijab at an early age so they would internalize it as an inevitable part of their identity and cultural role. Colonial officials never fully encouraged the wearing of the veil, as they saw this practice as indicative of the inferiority of Africans and Islam. For African men, however, the veil became symbolic of a resistance to Western imperialism (Masquelier 2009, 214–15). As we see in these very different examples, the struggle over clothing highlighted complex notions of civilization and caused women's bodies to become symbolic sites of political struggle.

The debates over clothing were only one part of the Europeans' obsession with controlling the bodies of their subjects. Colonialists were particularly interested in understanding the family lives and sexual conduct of those they ruled. As Frederick Cooper and Ann Stoler (1989) point out,

> At different times, colonial regimes had to come to grips with how people—colonizers and colonized alike—reproduced themselves (in families that lived together, as part of migration, through enslavement, through temporary sexual relations), where they did so (in villages, controlled housing projects, or squatter settlements), with whom (through race and class-specific unions or miscegenation), under whose eyes (the prying company manager or the medical professional), and with what degree of success. (613)

Colonizers attempted to shape sexual relations by separating families temporarily, by enforcing the geographical movement of individuals, and by implementing specific health policies influenced by racist and sometimes eugenic thoughts that supposedly protected Europeans and to a limited extent, Africans (Vaughan 1991; Dubow 1995). African sexuality was discussed, theorized, and often deemed a "problem." Throughout much of the continent, Europeans debated ways in which they could control the reproductive practices of Africans. Even as late as the mid-20th century in South Africa, for example, when the strict racist system of apartheid was implemented, the first two acts passed by the new white nationalist government were the Prohibition of Mixed Marriages Act of 1949 and the Immorality Amendment Act of 1950, which dictated who individuals could marry and with whom they could have sexual relations, respectively. Other policies of segregation, such as the Group Areas Act and the migratory labor system that was set up with all-male hostels, reinforced the heteropatriarchal power structures of the white-led government. Glen Elder (2003) calls this the "procreational geography of apartheid" (5). Like in much of colonial Africa, albeit more strongly enforced, the white-led South African government set up a geographical system that separated Black men and women for extended periods. They deemed urban areas as male and rural areas as female, and they defined gender roles, with men as laborers and women as mothers.

Anyone moving outside of this prescribed system was deemed "wayward." Many of the women who pushed the boundaries of what was considered acceptable were ostracized, regarded as wicked, or seen as mavericks (Hodgson and McCurdy 1996). This does not mean that everyone adhered to these definitions. African women regularly stepped outside the strict boundaries of social and political control set up by the Europeans and the men in their communities. Both Europeans and Africans crossed the makeshift lines of separation, and new "mixed" populations arose, such as the *metis*, Cape coloureds, and other groups. Nonnormative sexuality also continued, and Europeans failed to fully restrain the activities of their subjects. But the procreational geography did become entrenched in many of the economic and social structures of several sub-Saharan countries and, even after decolonization, continued somewhat unabated.

CULTURE, RELIGION, AND ATTITUDES TOWARD SEXUALITY

In sub-Saharan Africa, a complex, often oppositional debate has existed between scientific and religious approaches to sexuality. Religious individuals have promoted abstinence, while scientific practitioners advocate for education and offering effective protection and medical care. The religious abstinence-only perspective has been supported by powerful politicians and serves to promote heteropatriarchal power structures (Campbell, Skovdal, and Gibbs 2011, 1211). Today, religion and science are perceived by many as incompatible, but for most of human history, they were considered as complementary to each other (Ferngren 2002, x–xi). Religion in sub-Saharan Africa, for example, has always played an important role in the lives of individuals. It has also been integral to controlling and policing sexuality—whether it is Indigenous religions, which regulate sexual practices and social norms, or Christianity and Islam, which reinforce heteropatriarchal ideals. Science has also played an important role in defining gender and social norms. Sometimes religious leaders are scientists, such as African healers who are often both spiritual and medical advisors. Missionary doctors tend to operate in the same manner. This blending of religion and science remains an everyday occurrence in many people's lives and helps frame key debates about health, reproduction, and sexuality for sub-Saharan Africans today.

Religious ideals have greatly influenced views regarding LGBTQ+ individuals. For the most part, there is widespread denial of nonheterosexual forms of sexuality, and homophobic rhetoric spouted by African leaders has had serious ramifications for those who do not fit within the confines of the heterosexual norm. Violence against the LGBTQ+ communities has risen dramatically in many of these countries (Kindzeka and Wright 2016). When Uganda reintroduced its Anti-Homosexuality Bill in 2013 and rumors emerged about its reinstatement in 2019, attacks against the gay community rose dramatically. And even in progressive South Africa, where gay rights are assured, there has been a backlash against gay men and women. On a daily basis, LGBTQ+ individuals face harassment, discrimination, and violence and are denied necessary services. While the exact rates of violence are not entirely clear, between 2000 and 2019, South African police estimate that there have been 40 lesbian women raped by men who believed they were "correcting" women's sexual orientations (Naidoo 2018). One of the most prominent examples is the 2008 "corrective rape" and stabbing of Eudy Simelane. She was a member of South Africa's national soccer team and an open lesbian and LGBTQ+ activist. She was gang raped, assaulted, and stabbed over 25 times after leaving a tavern near her home in KwaThema, near Johannesburg. She died at the age of 31 (Daniels 2018). The men partaking in these types of violent acts argue that women, particularly women who dress or act in a more masculine manner, are threatening to their masculine power and therefore deserving of such treatment. As individuals struggle for economic livelihood in an increasingly competitive and divisive economic climate, these types of attacks will likely increase. There is a direct correlation between access to economic power, ideas about patriarchy, perceived political powerlessness, and sexual violence.

SEXUAL VIOLENCE

As is the case in most parts of the world, sexual violence is a major issue in sub-Saharan African. In areas where access to economic wealth is restricted, and in regions where women have a high rate of unemployment and rely on men for their livelihoods, the rates of sexual violence tend to be higher (Terry 2004, 470). The African continent has been a site of tremendous violence and atrocities against women. Many countries, such as South Africa, Botswana, Swaziland, Lesotho, and Zimbabwe, report a high incidence of sexual assault and rape, and in countries such as Egypt, Libya, and Uganda, women have been killed, ostracized, and imprisoned for having sex out of wedlock or being involved in same-sex relationships. Women's bodies continue to be the site of struggle over discussions of morality, control, and power, and the promotion of a heteropatriarchy has meant a continued dismissal of women's rights.

The issue of female genital mutilation/cutting (FGM/C) is a poignant example of how ideas of heteropatriarchy and morality can play out on the female body. While its origins are not known, its sole purpose is to control female sexuality and promote a harmful ideal of femininity. Some cultures claim that the procedure can ensure a girl's fidelity and modesty. Although incidents of FGM/C are declining, like issues of cosmetic surgery in the

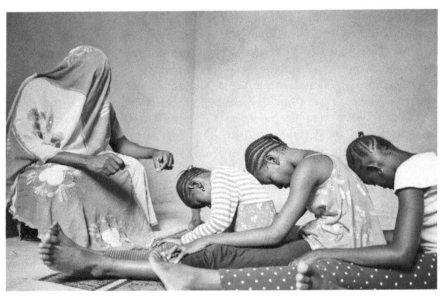

Female genital mutilation is practiced in a majority of African countries and involves cutting and removing parts of girls' genitals. The practice is used to exert power and control over women's bodies and causes numerous health problems for the girls. (Riccardo Mayer/Shutterstock.com)

Western world, where women partake in it despite risk, social pressures continue to play an important role in its continued practice. FGM/C is still prevalent in North and West African countries. In 2013, UNICEF reported that over 80% of girls between the ages of 15 and 49 in Somalia, Sudan, Egypt, Mali, Guinea, and Sierra Leone have undergone FGM/C (United Nations Children's Fund 2013). Usually performed against unsuspecting young girls, FGM/C can take various forms. The extreme case is infibulation, where the vaginal opening is narrowed by removing and repositioning the labia minora or labia majora, sometimes with stitching. There is also clitoridectomy, where the clitoris is partially or completely removed, but there can also be a cut without removing flesh, or a pricking, piercing, or scraping of the genital area. In all of these cases, there is no valid medical reason for undergoing the procedure, and women can experience severe complications. Women can end up with serious infections, have long-term urinary or menstrual problems, experience sexual difficulties, and have complications with childbirth. It can also bring on psychological problems such as depression, post-traumatic stress disorder, and low self-esteem (World Health Organization 2018). Yet, at the same time in these countries, women are expected to engage in sexual relations with their partners willingly. As Assitan Diallo points out, in Mali, for example, "There is a paradox in how society deals with female sexuality" (2004, 173). On the one hand, there are nuptial advisors who coach couples on how to enhance sexuality, but on the other, there are practitioners who engage in FGM/C as a means to reduce women's sexual pleasure (Diallo 2004, 173). Despite the fact that many countries have attempted to outlaw the practice, it has continued unabated. The fact that this practice involves very young women, many of whom have little to no ability to voice their opposition, is most concerning.

Young girls are also the victims of child marriages and human trafficking. Sub-Saharan Africa ranks second in the world behind South Asia for child marriages, with an estimated 115 million girls, or 18%, married before the age of 18 (United Nations Children's Fund 2018). In West and Central Africa, these rates are estimated to be higher at 41%. While there has been a decline in child marriage in South Asia and other places around the world, in West and Central Africa, the rates of child marriage are growing (United Nations Children's Fund 2018). Poverty, the perception that marriage will bring honor, adherence to religious laws, and lack of legislative enforcement contribute to the high rates of child marriage in the region. The impact of these marriages on girls' lives is tremendous. Girls who are forced to marry young often do not complete their education, experience higher rates of domestic violence, have children at a young age, and are socially isolated (United Nations Children's Fund 2017).

The profusion of child marriage is connected to the high rates of human trafficking. In 2016, 51% of those being trafficked were women. In addition, underage girls made up an additional 20%. The majority of those being trafficked originate from sub-Saharan Africa, and 29% were trafficked for sexually exploitative purposes (United Nations Office on Drugs and Crime 2016, 7–8). One of the main reasons why women are far more likely than men to be the target of human trafficking is that they are more vulnerable, both economically and socially (Ruiz Abril 2008). The commoditization of their bodies in terms of their reproductive and employment labor means that it is often deemed acceptable to sell or control them. Many women work in informal sectors and in homes, and their work can be more hidden and easily abused (Beegle et al. 2016, 13–14).

Sub-Saharan Africa also has high rates of conflict, where women and children become targets of militant groups seeking labor and sexual services and are easily targeted by those trying to make money from the exploitation of others (United Nations Office on Drugs and Crime 2016, 10). For example, in the 1994 Rwandan genocide, it was estimated that thousands of women were raped, sexually violated, held in sexual bondage, forced into "marriage," and abused. Many women became pregnant, and the Rwandan National Population Office estimated that between 2,000 and 5,000 children were born in the immediate year thereafter (Human Rights Watch/Africa 1996). During the Darfur genocide in the early 2000s, 1.4 million people were displaced, and women were repeatedly raped. Some women were abducted or raped when the Janjaweed militias attacked their villages. Others were raped when they left the refugee camps to look for wood. One Darfurian nongovernment organization tracked 9,300 rapes of women, but the total number of rapes was likely double (Gingerich and Leaning 2004). Similarly, in the Democratic Republic of Congo wars, tens of thousands of women, girls, men, and boys were raped or sexually abused. While the exact numbers are not known, Human Rights Watch (2014) detailed numerous sordid stories of women who were reportedly abducted, raped, and used as sex slaves for combatants. In one case in Shalio, 40 women were taken to a military camp nearby and kept as sex slaves, gang raped, and abused. Ten of the women escaped and managed to report the abuse to Human Rights Watch. One of the women's breasts and stomach had chunks of flesh cut out of them.

The Hotel des Mille Collines, where people took refuge during the Rwandan genocide in 1994. (Nmcavaney/Dreamstime.com)

Armed combatants use rape, human trafficking, and sexual assault as a means to demoralize their opponents, destroy communities, and assert domination (Heise et al. 1994, 1168). Far from being a sexual act, rape is about power and violence. It explicitly demoralizes women and those around them. In war, it is an overt attempt to completely disenfranchise women and terrorize and destroy their communities. In peaceful times, rape is often carried out to assert power, control women, and enforce heteropatriarchy. Gaining an accurate estimation of rape statistics in sub-Saharan countries is especially problematic, mainly because rape is often not reported or documented. When women feel that they have little to no agency over their bodies, they believe they have no right to deny sex. Moreover, when they are economically vulnerable, this makes them more likely to attach themselves to less desirable men and less likely to report rape by men upon whom they are dependent (Terry 2004, 471). As for those women who do report sexual violence, officials often do not take them seriously. Some women are blamed for the rape. This failure to take rape reporting seriously perpetuates a cycle wherein women are unlikely to want to report rape. Each country also has a different definition of what constitutes rape and sexual assault. Thus, clear statistics are difficult to obtain.

Yet some cursory statistics reveal that rape is prolific. South Africa, one of the wealthiest countries in the region, is slated as having the highest rape incidence in the world, with a 2010 estimate of 132.4 per 100,000 population, followed by Botswana with a rate of 92.9 (NationMaster n.d.). While it may be that more women report rape in South Africa and Botswana than in other countries, these numbers are disturbingly high. South Africa and Botswana have high female representation in their governments and are often at the forefront of women's rights initiatives. Yet the heteropatriarchal system set up during the colonial years and thereafter, the breakup of the family structure by the migratory labor system, a sustained culture of violence, the lack of criminal repercussions, and continued gender inequality perpetuate the cycle of sexual violence.

While most women remain silent victims in cases of sexual violence, there has been a recent rise in the number of women openly testifying against their abusers in public hearings (UN News 2017). Such cases can have considerable impact in highlighting the everyday rights of women. In 1998, four women who survived rape during the 1994 Rwandan genocide testified at the International Criminal Tribunal for Rwanda against Jean-Paul Akayesu, a mayor of Taba commune who had incited the violence and murder of Tutsis during the genocide. He was found guilty of genocide and crimes against humanity. In that case, rape became recognized as a means of perpetuating genocide, which was an important step forward in the way rape during wartimes would be prosecuted (UN News 2017). In Nigeria, after a woman was raped by five men in August 2011 and the video of her rape was uploaded to the internet, police did little to charge her attackers. The incident sparked an outcry on social media by women across the country. Women raised awareness about women's rights over their own bodies and organized "rape walks" in Abia and Lagos (Akinbobola 2021).

In 2018, in South Africa, Cheryl Zondi, a 22-year-old victim of famous Nigerian televangelist Timothy Omotoso, testified about the ongoing sexual assault she had experienced since the age of 13. Amid death threats, she took the stand to offer evidence for charges against him, which included trafficking, sexual assault, and racketeering. Just 12 years earlier, another woman, Fezekile Ntsukela Kuzwayo, had testified against the then African National Congress deputy president Jacob Zuma in a rape charge. She was vilified by his supporters and the public. But in her case, Zondi received great support from the South African public. Lyn Snodgrass (2018) argues that "the tide is turning" and women are now coming forward to speak out against a culture of rape. These types of public displays of solidarity for women have been inspired by the global #MeToo movement. Although not as popular in sub-Saharan Africa compared to North America, #MeToo has encouraged women to speak out and bring their perpetrators to justice.

Women are also forming supportive networks to ensure the rights of all women are protected. In South Africa, for example, Ndumie Funda, herself a survivor of "corrective rape," founded a nonprofit, community-based organization, the Luleki Sizwe Womyn's Project. The organization is dedicated to helping lesbian women heal from homophobic attacks. Named after Luleka Makiwane, a lesbian activist, and Nosizwe Nomsa Bizana, Fanta's former fiancée, both of whom were victims of "corrective rape" and died as a result of HIV, the organization works to offer medical care, legal justice, and a safe house for African lesbian women in the townships. Its ultimate goal is to raise awareness and confront misperceptions about queer women (Chauvin 2019). In the Democratic Republic of Congo, Martine Ndaya Nabothe, Dorcas Druja Mhushiya, Godelive Tshombo, and Audreille Dimwangala wa Katshumba set up the Fontaine d'Espoir pour Filles et Femmes (Center of Hope for Young Girls and Women) in the late 1990s. Based in Lubumbashi, the center defends the rights of women and girls, offers sexual health and independence seminars, provides shelter and clothing to women who need it, helps victims of sexual violence, and sponsors the studies of young girls who want to go to university.

REPRODUCTIVE HEALTH AND MENSTRUATION

Because of the lack of agency that women have over their bodies, their poor economic standing, and engrained heteropatriarchal ideals, women in sub-Saharan Africa have less access to education and health services and, in turn, are the most vulnerable to sexually transmitted diseases. Women often rely on individuals, families, communities, and self-care to deal with their sexual health issues (Hardon et al. 2019). When youth are well educated, they are less likely to engage in sexual behavior at an early age. They are also more likely to use contraception, avoid early child-rearing, and delay marriage, all of which coincide with increased agency over their bodies (Speizer et al. 2013). Because young women are, however, disenfranchised both politically and economically in most sub-Saharan African

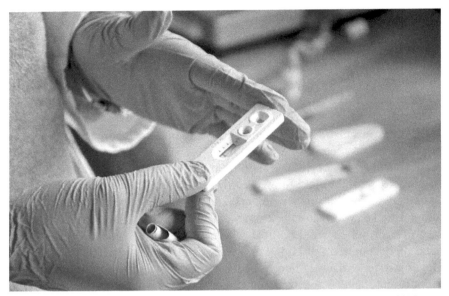

HIV rates in Africa are among the highest in the world. Here, an HIV test in Pomerini, Tanzania, is shown. (Francovolpato/Dreamstime.com)

countries, they are more likely to leave school at an early age and to get married and have children. This has serious ramifications in terms of gaining access to knowledge about their rights and ability to become economically self-reliant. If a woman fails to finish school, it is easier for her to be at risk for exploitation, abuse, and sustained poverty.

There is a direct connection between gender inequality, poverty, and high rates of sexually transmitted diseases. In 2018, for example, there were approximately 25.6 million adults and children in sub-Saharan Africa living with HIV (UNAIDS 2019b). There were 310,000 deaths related to AIDS the same year. While these numbers are from less than a decade ago and show a decline in the rates of contraction, the number of infected individuals is still extremely high. The region with the highest rates of infection is southern Africa, where a vast number of individuals migrate for work and thereby perpetuate gender imbalances. Young women aged 15 to 19 have double the infection rate of HIV that men have. This is not only because many young people are engaging with high-risk sex—that is, they are having sex outside of a committed relationship without condoms—but also because straight women are physiologically more susceptible to contracting the disease through the sex act than men are (UNAIDS 2019b).

When HIV/AIDS first became known in the late 1980s, initial approaches failed to recognize the social, political, and economic systems that were in place that helped facilitate its spread. Doctors, activists, theologians, and researchers became interested in understanding why individuals were contracting the disease at far higher rates than elsewhere in the world. The trends of infection in sub-Saharan Africa were also different in that gay and bisexual men predominated in the infection rates in the Western world, while in sub-Saharan Africa, women were the most commonly infected (Iliffe 2006, 65). The sheer numbers and rapid rate of infections in sub-Saharan Africa were alarming, and individuals were dying quickly without adequate access to health care. In 2001, UNAIDS estimated that 2.3 million people had died in sub-Saharan Africa and 3.4 million people had contracted HIV that year (UNAIDS 2001, 2). With high rates of death occurring in many regions, the issue of sexuality was brought from the private domain into the public. Throughout the 1990s and 2000s, donors were funding large projects to research African reproductive health and sexuality.

The biomedical approach, which included those promoted by doctors, psychiatrists, psychologists, physiologists, and epidemiologists, tended to dominate many of the research projects. As Sylvia Tamale (2011b) states, "With the global onslaught of HIV/AIDs and Africa as its epicentre, more researchers from the North flocked to the continent in a bid to find ways of curbing its spread, and in the process engendered a profound re-medicalisation of African sexualities" (17). Discussions of sexuality were placed in the hands of Western experts. These initial medical approaches for preventing HIV/AIDs missed the mark, however, probably because they failed to fully account for the complex meanings of sexuality in daily life (Nyanzi 2011, 47). All women should have the right to regulate their own fertility, remain free of disease, enjoy their sexual experiences, and choose their life partners. Far too often, however, Western medicine conceptualized sexuality according to disease and reproductive health. A sanitized version of female sexuality existed that failed to account for emotional aspects or social pressures.

The most effective approach to address the spread of HIV/AIDS has involved incorporating local community members and peer counselors (Khumalo-Sakutukwaet al. 2008; Genberg et al. 2016). Once local knowledge, politicians, healers, community organizations, educational institutions, peer counselors, and young people were incorporated as part

An example of a successful community-based program was initiated in Kagera Province in Tanzania in 1997. The HUMULIZA Project trained local teachers, caregivers, and nonprofit organizations to offer psychological support to AIDS orphans. It also initiated a group counseling program for orphans and youth aged 13–18 who were in turn encouraged to create their own organizations. The group was called "Vijana Simama Imara—VSI" (Youth Standing Upright Firmly). By 2004, there were 1,300 members of VSI, all overseen by the young members themselves. A secondary organization grew out of this program for the younger brothers and sisters of the children (Clacherty and Donald 2005). Another successful community-based program called loveLife emerged in 1999 in South Africa. It focused on increasing the awareness, activism, and education of young people and has thus far reached over 1.8 million people. Through peer counselors, sporting activities, local organizations, and families and schools, loveLife has shown great promise to help young people avoid risky behavior (Louw, Peltzer, and Ramlagan 2018; and loveLife).

of the solution, HIV infection rates began to decline. An example of a successful community-based program was initiated in Kagera Province in Tanzania in 1997. The HUMULIZA Project trained local teachers, caregivers, and nonprofit organizations to offer psychological support to AIDS orphans. It also initiated a group counseling program for orphans and youth aged 13 through 18 who were in turn encouraged to create their own organizations. The group was called *Vijana Simama Imara* (VSI; "Youth Standing Upright Firmly"). By 2004, there were 1,300 members of VSI, all overseen by the young members themselves. A secondary organization grew out of this program for the younger brothers and sisters of the children (Clacherty and Donald 2005). Another successful community-based program called loveLife emerged in 1999 in South Africa. It focused on increasing the awareness, activism, and education of young people and has thus far reached over 1.8 million people. Through peer counselors, sporting activities, local organizations, and families and schools, loveLife has shown great promise in helping young people avoid risky behavior (Louw, Peltzer, and Ramlagan 2018).

These community-based and grassroots approaches need to be supported, however, by larger, state-sanctioned initiatives. For too long, Africa's leaders failed to thwart the spread of the disease. In Uganda, when free antiretroviral drugs and education about the virus were offered, stigma against HIV declined, more people were willing to be tested, and the incidence of infection fell dramatically (Amolo Okero et al. 2003). On the other hand, governments in South Africa, Swaziland, and Lesotho failed to provide antiretroviral drugs and educational programs in the early years of HIV onset and currently have the highest rates of infection in the world (UNAIDS 2019a). Millions have died due to the lack of support. Southern Africa's migratory labor system, wherein large numbers of people move in and out of the region on a regular basis, makes it difficult to disseminate information and offer effective health care. The breaking up of traditional African family structures that occurred during colonialism, high levels of poverty, a heteropatriarchal power structure, and lack of education also play a part in the continuous spread of HIV. Thus it is vital that all countries in sub-Saharan Africa offer viable support to help quell the continued spread of HIV and other sexually transmitted diseases.

MARRIAGE AND PARTNERSHIPS

Traditional lineage practices have always dictated sub-Saharan African approaches to marriage and sexuality. Marriage is far more than simply an event between individuals; in most patrilineal and matrilineal sub-Saharan societies, it has also been a means to regulate property and lineage rights, control the transition of men and women from childhood to adulthood, establish rights to women's reproductive capabilities, and enable a social identity (Jeater 1993, 13). Marriage brought with it a sense of dignity and status in society (Jean-Baptiste 2014, 13). In many countries, such as Burkino Faso, Togo, Nigeria, South Africa, Chad, and Kenya, to name a few, it was common for men to have multiple wives, which was viewed as a sign of wealth. With the advent of colonialism and rapid urbanization, however, these traditional understandings of marriage, while still important, changed and, in some cases, were completely abandoned.

For example, in the Gwelo District of Southern Rhodesia in the 1920s, ideas of sexuality and morality transformed due to colonial influences. Diana Jeater (1993) argues that after the advent of colonial rule, "the sexual aspect of a person's life could be thought of separately from their membership of a family group. Women found that men would pay for sexual services, and men and women could become involved in sexual relationships which had no impact on their respective lineage-groups" (227). Moreover, by the mid-1920s, bridewealth, that is, the assurance paid by men to their bride's family, was no longer a means to establish the traditional lineage rights but instead became commoditized. It "no longer provide[d] appropriate rules to govern these new relationships between men and women" (Jeater 1993, 227). What ultimately emerged was a new, European-influenced notion of sexual morality, where African men were given new freedoms in their relationships but women were more restricted. African men, in cohort with missionaries and colonial officials, attempted to criminalize the sexual activities of women that took place outside of the traditional lineage structures. While men could have affairs and sexual relationships outside of marriage, women who committed adultery could be punished. In addition, the commoditization of bridewealth, that is, the payment of bridewealth now as cash instead of cows or other gifts, also ended up restricting women from the ability to acquire their own wealth. As one example, Harriet Ngubane (1987) argues that when bridewealth payments among the Zulu became cash instead of cows, the men in their families took the money, and women lost the ability to earn extra income from milking and rearing cows.

Today, bridewealth continues to fulfill important cultural and economic purposes and helps define one's status and identity. Some women still view bridewealth as a form of respect or an indication of their value. Others see it as a means of security and appreciation that may even help prevent divorce. If a man paid a considerable sum of money for his bride, the thought is that he would be less likely to stray or engage in activities that would risk that relationship (Rudwick and Posei 2014, 128–29). But many scholars looking at marriage practices in Africa today argue that current bridewealth transactions actually subvert women's autonomy. Because bridewealth payments are meant to "compensate a women's family for the loss of her reproductive and domestic labor," when he makes the payment, the man then "gains the right to the woman's reproductive services" (Horne, Dodoo, and Dodoo 2013, 504). While women may not fully want to give up their reproductive rights, social pressures to abide by their husband and

Although most societies in the world are patrilineal, a number of African cultures are matrilineal. In these societies, kinship is traced through the women's line, and property is inherited through the mother's rather than the father's side of the family. Research has demonstrated that in matrilineal cultures, political power is evenly shared between the sexes, and this egalitarian structure trickles down to impact functioning at the individual, family, and community levels. Children in matrilineal societies experience better health and attain higher education outcomes, and rates of domestic violence are much lower compared to patrilineal cultures.

A Pride celebration in South Africa, one of the few African countries that recognizes homosexual rights. (Timothy Hodgkinson/Dreamstime.com)

father's wishes and to have children often reinforce these beliefs (Ferim 2016). When women choose not to marry or have children, or they become involved in a relationship with another woman instead of a man, they are often ostracized and harassed for not fulfilling gender stereotypes.

Central to these debates about marriage and sexuality is a definition of marriage as being between a man and a woman, an idea effected and encouraged during colonial rule. While there has been important recognition of homosexual rights in some countries in sub-Saharan Africa— particularly South Africa, which allows gay marriage and recognizes the rights of the lesbian, gay, bisexual, transgender, and queer (LGBTQ+) communities in its constitution—for the most part, sub-Saharan African leaders are not supportive (Republic of South Africa 1996, chapter 2: 9.3). There has been a rise of scathing denials of homosexuality and assaults against gay men and women. Heads of state, such as Robert Mugabe, the former president of Zimbabwe, claimed that homosexuality was a colonial import and gays deserved no rights in the country. In 2000, the Namibian president, Sam Njoma, condemned homosexuals (Morgan and Reid 2003). In Uganda in 2009, an Anti-Homosexuality Bill was debated; it was then signed into law by President Museveni in 2014. It imposed a potential sentence from seven years to the death penalty for same-sex relations and a sentence of seven years to anyone aiding LGBTQ+ individuals. Same-sex sexual acts and marriages remain punishable with up to life imprisonment, but government officials have not been successful in reinstating the death penalty. In May 2021, the Parliament of Uganda passed a Sexual Offenses Bill which was meant to protect victims of sexual offense, but it again reinforced a ban on same-sex relations and painted all LGBTQ+ people as sexual offenders. Ugandan President Yoweri Museveni rejected the bill due to what he felt was redundant law and the debate still continues (Kamurungi and Wadero, 2021).

Homosexuality is still outlawed in 34 countries in Africa; and in Mauritania, Sudan, northern Nigeria, and southern Somalia, one could be given the death penalty for being gay (Carroll and ILGA 2016; Amnesty International USA n.d.). In Uganda and Zambia, people can be imprisoned for life for having a same-sex partner (Amnesty International n.d.). Many of these countries and their leaders argue that Africa is a "heterosexual continent" and homosexuality is a foreign import from the West. They ironically fail to recognize, as Sylvia Tamale (2013) points out, that "the homophobic laws that currently exist on the continent were a direct import from former European colonial powers" (252–53). Indeed, scholars have shown that precolonial and colonial African sexuality was far more complicated than these leaders would like to depict. Complex relationships, with individuals engaged in same-sex practices that they may not have defined as homosexual per se and may not have affected their ability to partake in heterosexual marriage and reproduction, certainly existed (Epprecht 2008, 6). The impact of the migrant labor system, wherein men and women were separated from each other, meant that same-sex practices prevailed, even if temporarily, and sex between men and men, and women and women, took place (Harries 1990, 1994; Epprecht 2004, 2008).

MEDIA AND SEXUALITY

An important recent change in discussions about sexuality in Africa is women's claims for sexual pleasure. Dr. Tlaleng Mofokeng, also known as "Dr. T" in South Africa, has written numerous columns and a book about what she calls "the pleasure revolution" (Samanga 2019). As a young medical doctor at a clinic in the outskirts of Johannesburg in 2010, during a period of intense focus on HIV/AIDs education, she "felt that the approach that was being used, stigmatized young people having sex and sex became something looked at as inherently diseased" (Mofokeng 2019, 1). She began using digital media platforms such as Twitter to reach youth on a grand scale, which greatly impacted her popularity. She became a regular guest of radio and television shows, wrote for magazines and online newspapers, initiated a podcast, and launched her own television show that broadcasts throughout the continent. She also works as an advocate for sexual rights and health reform and was recently elected as a commissioner on South Africa's Commission for Gender Equality (Mofokeng 2019, 1).

Similarly, in Ghana in 2009, Nana Darkoa Sekyiamah and Melaka Grant launched a blog called *Adventures from the Bedrooms of African Women* as means to destigmatize sex and empower women. They wanted to create a safe space where African women could "openly discuss a variety of sex and sexuality issues with the intention of learning from each other, having pleasurable and safer sex and encouraging continuous sex education for adults" (Sekyiamah and Grant 2009). Guest contributors today continue to write about their relationships, their sexual experiences, their fantasies, their struggles, and sexual health.

In Kenya in 2016, Karen Kaz Lucas created *The Spread*, a sex-positive podcast with the aim of "decolonizing sexuality." Episodes deal with contraceptives, pornography, open relationships, LGBTQ+ rights, sexual health, sexual pleasure, and legal issues. The podcast invites audiences to ask questions and openly discuss previously private issues (Lucas 2016). Lucas states that she is "trying to remind people that certain things we embrace as 'African' and defend when it comes to sex and sexuality, are elements that came to us through religion, westernized education, etc. The shame associated with sex and sexuality on the continent are remnants of Western teachings." In 2019, the podcast sponsored a day-long conference that attracted over 600 participants and dealt with issues of sexuality (Kimeria 2019).

In Senegal, a television show, *Maitresse d'un homme marié* (Mistress of a Married Man) launched in January 2019 and has been dubbed Senegal's *Sex and the City*. At the time of this writing, the pilot episode reached over 3.2 million viewers, and subsequent episodes attracted a dedicated 1.9 million viewers ("Mistress of a Married Man" 2019). In the show, five bold women assert their economic and sexual independence, address issues such as rape and domestic abuse, and explicitly challenge patriarchy. Written by Kalista Sy, a former television journalist who was frustrated with one-sided female characters written by men, the show has raised issues that have been predominantly kept in the private domain in the traditional, Muslim country (Turkewitz 2019). Despite some calls by religious leaders to ban the show, the soap has continued to be wildly popular throughout most of Francophone Africa (Seneweb News 2019).

These examples, where issues of sexuality and women's rights are discussed in the public domain, are important because they offer hope for generations of women who have been previously silenced and disenfranchised. The power of these popular shows toward shaping the minds of young audiences should not be underestimated. The women writers of the shows are cognizant of the importance of their work. Most have moved beyond the goal of simple entertainment and are using their platforms to support the revolution for women's rights.

CONCLUSION

By examining gender and sexualities in Africa, a lot can be learned about perceptions of choice, agency, and power throughout the continent. The analysis contributes to an understanding of how women and men in sub-Saharan Africa negotiate their positions in society, how legal issues change over time, how the economy and social factors of different countries and communities have included and excluded women, and how individuals navigate their worlds in the context of larger political processes. Although women lost much of their autonomy during the colonial years and have been victims of economic disenfranchisement, child marriages, rape, and other atrocities thereafter, they have continuously fought back to reclaim agency over their bodies. Women throughout sub-Saharan Africa have been challenging the status quo and demanding social justice. They are stepping forward today to assert their rights to sexual pleasure, sexual health, and agency over their bodies. They consistently demand control over their lives and are at the forefront of global initiatives to ensure their basic human rights.

Nonetheless, the continent still has a long way to go. While most African countries, with exception of Somalia, Sudan, and Tonga, have ratified the Convention of All Forms of Discrimination against Women—a convention initiated by the United Nations to promote the rights of women—and the African Union also declared 2010–2020 the decade for African women, women and young girls are, for the most part, still marginalized and repressed. The story of Sara Baartman, with which this chapter began, is not an anomaly—the way that Baartman was treated is not that far from today's atrocities that commoditize, exploit, and dehumanize women. The solution lies not only in having more African women speak out about their rights but also in having men become part of the solution. Sub-Saharan Africa needs to break from the unjust structures that arose during the colonial period and to enable women to be decision-makers in their own lives. Women need to be safe from all forms of sexual exploitation and violence, have access to quality health care, be involved in decision-making positions in their societies, have access to resources, and be offered comprehensive education. Once African women obtain full equality, only then will they be able to be fully in control of their sexuality.

REFERENCES

Akinbobola, Yemisi. 2021. "Social Media Stimulates Nigerian Debate on Sexual Violence." Africa Renewal. Accessed June 25, 2022. https://www.un.org/africarenewal/web-features/social-media-stimulates-nigerian-debate-sexual-violence.

Amnesty International. n.d. "LGBTI Rights." Accessed June 25, 2022. https://www.amnesty.org/en/what-we-do/discrimination/lgbt-rights.

Amnesty International USA. n.d. "Making Love a Crime: Criminalization of Same-Sex Conduct in Sub-Saharan Africa." Accessed June 25, 2022   https://www.amnestyusa.org/files/making_love_a_crime_-_facts__figures.pdf.

Amolo Okero, F., Esther Aceng, Elizabeth Madraa, Elizabeth Namagala, and Joseph Serutoke. 2003. *Scaling Up Antiretroviral Therapy: Experience in Uganda: Case Study.* Geneva, Switzerland: World Health Organization. Accessed June 25, 2022. https://apps.who.int/iris/handle/10665/42761.

Beegle, Kathleen, Luc Christiaensen, Andrew Dabalen, and Isis Gaddis. 2016. *Poverty in a Rising Africa.* Washington, DC: International Bank for Reconstruction and Development/World Bank. Accessed June 25, 2022. https://openknowledge.worldbank.org/handle/10986/22575.

Bhalla, Nita. 2019. "Uganda Plans Bill Imposing Death Penalty for Gay Sex." Thomson Reuters Foundation, October 10. Accessed June 25, 2022. https://www.reuters.com/article/us-uganda-lgbt-rights/uganda-plans-bill-imposing-death-penalty-for-gay-sex-idUSKBN1WP1GN.

Campbell, C., M. Skovdal, and A. Gibbs. 2011. "Creating Social Spaces to Tackle AIDS-Related Stigma: Reviewing the Role of Church Groups in Sub-Saharan Africa." *AIDS and Behavior* 15 (6): 1204–19.

Carroll, Aengus, and the International Lesbian, Gay, Bisexual, Trans and Intersex Association. 2016. *State-Sponsored Homophobia: A World Survey of Sexual Orientation Laws: Criminalisation, Protection and Recognition.* Geneva, Switzerland: ILGA. Accessed June 25, 2022. https://ilga.org/downloads/02_ILGA_State_Sponsored_Homophobia_2016_ENG_WEB_150516.pdf.

Chauvin, Kelsy. 2019. "Fighting for Lesbian Safety in South Africa: Women's Support Group Near Cape Town Counters 'Corrective Rape', Other the Crimes." *Gay City News* (June 27): 64–68.

Chepkemoi, Joyce. 2019. "How Many Countries Are in Africa?" January 7. Accessed June 25, 2022. https://www.worldatlas.com/articles/how-many-countries-are-in-africa.html.

Clacherty, Glynis, and David Donald. 2005. "Impact Evaluation of the VSI (Vijana Simama Imara) Organisation and the Rafiki Mdogo Group of the HUMULIZA Orphan Project, Nshamba, Tanzania." Accessed June 25, 2022. https://static1.squarespace.com/static/5519047ce4b0d9aaa8c82e69/t/5551c214e4b0027d29f9b315/1431421460030/VSI_impact_evaluation_draft.pdf.

Cooper, Frederick, and Ann L. Stoler. 1989. "Introduction—Tensions of Empire: Colonial Control and Visions of Rule." *American Ethnologist* 16 (4): 609–21.

Crais, Clifton, and Pamela Scully. 2011. *Sara Baartman and the Hottentot Venus: A Ghost Story and a Biography.* Princeton, NJ, and Oxford: Princeton University Press.

Daniels, Lou-Anne. 2018. "We Remember Eudy Simelane." *Independent Online*, August 9. Accessed June 25, 2022. https://www.iol.co.za/news/south-africa/gauteng/we-remember-eudy-simelane-16462128.

Diallo, Assitan. 2004. "Paradoxes of Female Sexuality in Mali: On the Practices of Magonmaka and Bolokoli-kela." In *Re-thinking Sexualities in Africa*, edited by Signe Arnfred, 173–89. Uppsala, Sweden: Nordiska Afrikainstitutet.

Dubow, Saul. 1995. *Scientific Racism in Modern South Africa.* Cambridge: Cambridge University Press.

Elder, Glen. 2003. *Hostels, Sexuality, and the Apartheid Legacy: Malevolent Geographies.* Athens: Ohio University Press.

Epprecht, Marc. 2004. *Hungochani: The History of a Dissident Sexuality in Southern Africa.* Montreal, Canada: McGill-Queen's University Press.

Epprecht, Marc. 2008. *Heterosexual Africa? The History of an Idea from the Age of Exploration to the Age of AIDS.* Athens: Ohio University Press.

Epprecht, Marc. 2013. "The Making of 'African Sexuality': Early Sources, Current Debates." In *Sexual Diversity in Africa: Politics, Theory and Citizenship*, edited by S. N. Nyeck and Marc Epprecht, 54–66. Montreal, Canada: McGill-Queen's University Press.

Ferim, Valery. 2016. "The Nexus between African Traditional Practices and Homophobic Violence towards Lesbians in the Eastern Cape Province of South Africa." *Gender & Behaviour* 14 (2): 7410–19.

Ferngren, Gary B. 2002. "Introduction." In *Science & Religion: A Historical Introduction* edited by Gary B. Ferngren, ix–xiv. Baltimore: Johns Hopkins University Press.

Genberg, Becky L., Sylvia Shangani, Kelly Sabatino, Beth Rachlis, Juddy Wachira, Paula Braitstein, and Don Operario. 2016. "Improving Engagement in the HIV Care Cascade: A Systematic Review of Interventions Involving People Living with HIV/AIDS as Peers." *AIDS and Behavior* 20 (10): 2452–63.

Gilman, Sander. 1985. "Black Bodies, White Bodies: Towards an Iconography of Female Sexuality in Late Nineteenth-Century Art, Medicine and Literature." *Critical Inquiry* 12 (1): 204–42.

Gingerich, Tara, and Jennifer Leaning. 2004. *The Use of Rape as a Weapon of War in the Conflict in Darfur, Sudan.* Boston: U.S. Agency for International Development/OTI.

Hardon, Anita, Christopher Pell, Efenita Taqueban, and Manjulaa Narasimhan. 2019. "Sexual and Reproductive Self Care among Women and Girls: Insights from Ethnographic Studies." *British Medical Journal* 365,no. 1333 (April 1). Accessed June 25, 2022. https://www.bmj.com/content/365/bmj.l1333.

Harries, Patrick. 1990. "La Symbolique du Sexe: L'Identité Culturelle au Début de L'exploitation des Mines D'Or du Witwatersrand (The Symbolism of Sex: Cultural Identity in the Early Witwatersrand Gold Mines)." *Cahiers d'Études Africaines* 30 (120): 451–74.

Harries, Patrick. 1994. *Work, Culture, and Identity: Migrant Laborers in Mozambique and South Africa, c. 1860–1910*. Portsmouth, NH: Pearson Education Ltd.

Hay, Margaret Jean. 2004. "Changes in Clothing and Struggles over Identity in Colonial Western Kenya." In *Fashioning Africa: Power and the Politics of Dress*, edited by Jean Allman, 67–83. Bloomington and Indianapolis: Indiana University Press.

Heise, Lori L., Alanagh Raikes, Charlotte H. Watts, and Anthony B. Zwi. 1994. "Violence against Women: A Neglected Public Health Issue in Less Developed Countries." *Social Science and Medicine* 39 (9): 1165–79.

Hodgson, Dorothy L., and Sheryl McCurdy. 1996. "Wayward Wives, Misfit Mothers, and Disobedient Daughters: 'Wicked' Reconfiguration of Gender in Africa." *Canadian Journal of African Studies* 30 (1): 1–9.

Horne, Christine, F., Nii-Amoo Dodoo, and Naa Dodua Dodoo. 2013. "The Shadow of Indebtedness: Bridewealth and Norms Constraining Female Reproductive Autonomy." *American Sociological Review* 78 (3): 503–20.

Human Rights Watch. 2014. "Democratic Republic of Congo: Ending Impunity for Sexual Violence." June 10. Accessed June 25, 2022. https://www.hrw.org/news/2014/06/10/democratic-republic-congo-ending-impunity-sexual-violence.

Human Rights Watch/Africa, Human Rights Watch Women's Rights Project. 1996. "Shattered Lives: Sexual Violence during the Rwandan Genocide and its Aftermath." Accessed June 25, 2022. https://www.hrw.org/reports/1996/Rwanda.htm.

Iliffe, John. 2006. *The African AIDs Epidemic: A History*. Athens: Ohio University Press.

Jean-Baptiste, Rachel. 2014. *Conjugal Rights: Marriage, Sexuality, and Urban Life in Colonial Libreville, Gabon*. Athens: Ohio University Press.

Jeater, Diana. 1993. *Marriage, Perversion and Power: The Construction of Moral Discourse in Southern Rhodesia*. Oxford: Oxford University Press.

Jolles, Stephen, and Frank Jolles. 1998. "Correspondence: African Traditional Medicine—Potential Route for Viral Transmission?" *The Lancet* 352, no. 9121 (July 4). Accessed November 1, 2019. https://www.thelancet.com/journals/lancet/article/PIIS0140-6736(05)79558-1/fulltext.

Kamurungi, Elizabeth and Arthur Arnold Wadero. 2021. "Museveni Rejects Sexual Offences and Succession Bills." Accessed July 18, 2022. https://www.monitor.co.ug/uganda/news/national/museveni -rejects-sexual-offences-and-succession-bills-3515430.

Kertzer, David I., and Dominique Arel. 2002. "Censuses, Identity Formation, and the Struggle for Political Power." In *Census and Identity: The Politics of Race, Ethnicity, and Language in National Censuses*, 1–42. Cambridge: Cambridge University Press.

Khumalo-Sakutukwa, Gertrude, Stephen F. Morin, Katherine Fritz, Edwin D. Charlebois, Heidi van Rooyen, Alfred Chingono, Precious Modiba et al. 2008. "Project Accept (HPTN 043): A Community-Based Intervention to Reduce HIV Incidence in Populations at Risk for HIV in Sub-Saharan Africa and Thailand." *Journal of Acquired Immune Deficiency Syndrome* 49 (4): 422–31.

Kimeria, Ciku. 2019. "'The Spread' Is the Sex-Positive Kenyan Podcast Offering a Safe Space for Women and LGBTQIA+ Issues." Okayafrica, June 25. Accessed June 25, 2022. https://www.okayafrica .com/the-spread-is-the-sex-positive-kenyan-podcast-offering-a -safe-space-for-women-and-lgbtqia-issues.

Kindzeka, Moki, and Loveday Wright. 2016. "Anti-Gay Sentiment on Rise in Africa." DW, June 17. Accessed June 25, 2022. https://p .dw.com/p/1J8rE.

Lewis, Bernard. 1990. *Race and Slavery in the Middle East*: *An Historical Inquiry*. New York: Oxford University Press.

Louw, Julia S., Karl Peltzer, and Shandir Ramlagan. 2018. "Self-Esteem, Sexual-Risk Behaviour and loveLife: Exposure among South African Young Women." *Journal of Psychology* 9 (1–2): 9–17.

Lucas, Karen. 2016. "The Spread." Accessed June 25, 2022. https://sound-cloud.com/karenkazlucas.

Machangu, H. M. 2015. "Vulnerability of Elderly Women to Witchcraft Accusations among the Fipa of Sumbawanga, 1961–2010." *Journal of International Women's Studies* 16 (2): 274–84.

Magubane, Zine. 2001. "Which Bodies Matter? Feminism, Poststructuralism, Race, and the Curious Odessey of the 'Hottentot Venus.'" *Gender & Society* 15 (6): 816–34.

Masquelier, Adeline. 2009. *Women and Islamic Revival in a West African Town*. Bloomington and Indianapolis: Indiana University Press.

"Mistress of a Married Man." 2019. YouTube, January 25. Accessed June 25, 2022. https://www.youtube.com/watch?v=BrKBkMCN4qE.

Mofokeng, Tlaleng. 2019. *Dr T: A Guide to Sexual Health and Pleasure*. Johannesburg: Pan Macmillan.

Morgan, Ruth, and Graeme Reid. 2003. "'I've Got Two Men and One Woman': Ancestors, Sexuality and Identity among Same-Sex Identified Women Traditional Healers in South Africa." *Culture, Health & Sexuality* 5 (5): 375–91.

Naidoo, Kammila. 2018. "Sexual Violence and 'Corrective Rape' in South Africa." *Global Dialogue* 8, no. 1 (April 1). Accessed June 25, 2022. http://globaldialogue.isa-sociology.org/sexual-violence-and -corrective-rape-in-south-africa.

NationMaster. n.d. "Rape Rate: Countries Compared." Accessed June 25, 2022. https://www.nationmaster.com/country-info/stats/Crime /Rape-rate#-amount.

Ngubane, Harriet. 1987. "The Consequences for Women of Marriage Payments in a Society with Patrilineal Descent." In *Transformations of African Marriage*, edited by D. Parkin and D. Nyamwaya, 172–82. Manchester: Manchester University Press.

Nyanzi, Stella. 2011. "From Minuscule Biomedical Models to Sexuality's Depths." In *African Sexualities: A Reader*, edited by Sylvia Tamale, 47–49. Cape Town: Pambazuka Press.

Olupona, Jacob K. 2014. "15 Facts on African Religions." Oxford University Press, May 16. Accessed June 25, 2022. https://blog.oup .com/2014/05/15-facts-on-african-religions.

Republic of South Africa. 1996. Constitution of the Republic of South Africa, chapter 2: Bill of Rights. Accessed Jul 27, 2022. https:// www.gov.za/documents/constitution/chapter-2-bill-rights#:~:text =of%20the%20law.-,2.,unfair%20discrimination%20may%20 be%20taken.

Rudwick, Stephanie, and Dorrit Posei. 2014. "Contemporary Functions of iLobola (Bridewealth) in Urban South African Zulu Society." *Journal of Contemporary African Studies* 32 (1): 118–36.

Ruiz Abril, M. E. 2008. *Girls' Vulnerability Assessment. Background Report for the Preparation of the Adolescent Girls and Young Women's Economic Empowerment*. Washington, DC: World Bank.

Samanga, Rufaro. 2019. "In Conversation: South Africa's Favorite Sex Doctor Launches a Pleasure Revolution." Okayafrica, October 10. Accessed June 25, 2022. https://www.okayafrica.com/dr-t -sex-pleasure-revolution-new-book.

Sawe, Benjamin Elisha. 2018. "How Many Languages Are Spoken in Africa?" October 11. Accessed June 25,2022. https://www.worldatlas .com/articles/how-many-languages-are-spoken-in-africa.html.

Sekyiamah, Nana Dorkoa, and Malaka Grant. 2009. "Adventures from the Bedrooms of African Women." Accessed June 25, 2022. https:// africasacountry.com/2020/05/the-bedroom-adventures-of-african -women.

Seneweb News. 2019. "Maîtresse d'un homme marié: Mame Mactar Guèye porte plainte contre Marodi TV et. . . ." March 20. Accessed June 25, 2022. https://www.seneweb.com/news/Audio/laquo -maitresse-d-rsquo-un-homme-marie-r_n_277027.html.

Snodgrass, Lyn. 2018. "Survivors of Sexual Violence Are Finally Finding Their Voices." The Conversation, November 14. Accessed June 25, 2022. https://theconversation.com/survivors-of-sexual-violence -in-south-africa-are-finally-finding-their-voices-106458.

Speizer, Ilene S., Jean Christophe Fotso, Joshua T. Davis, Abdulmumin Saad, and Jane Otal. 2013. "Timing and Circumstances of First Sex among Female and Male Youth from Select Urban Areas of Nigeria, Kenya and Senegal." *Journal of Adolescent Health* 53 (5): 609–16.

Sudarkasa, Niara. 1986. "'The Status of Women' in Indigenous African Societies." *Feminist Studies* 12 (1): 91–103.

Tamale, Sylvia. 2011a. "Introduction." In *African Sexualities: A Reader*, 1–8. Cape Town: Pambazuka/Fahamu.

Tamale, Sylvia. 2011b. "Researching and Theorising Sexualities in Africa." In *African Sexualities: A Reader*, 11–36. Cape Town, South Africa: Pambazuka/Fahamu.

Tamale, Sylvia. 2013. "The Politics of Sexual Diversity: An Afterword." In *Sexual Diversity in Africa: Politics Theory and Citizenship*, edited by S. N. Nyeck and Marc Epprecht, 250–53. Montreal, Canada: McGill-Queen's University Press.

Terry, Geraldine. 2004. "Poverty Reduction and Violence against Women: Exploring Links, Assessing Impact." *Development in Practice* 14 (4): 469–80.

Turkewitz, Julie. 2019. "Bold Women. Scandalized Viewers. It's 'Sex and the City,' Senegal Style." *New York Times*, August 22. Accessed June 25, 2022. https://www.nytimes.com/2019/08/22/world/africa /senegal-mistress-of-a-married-man.html.

UNAIDS. 2001. *AIDS Epidemic Update*. Geneva, Switzerland: UNAIDS. December. Accessed June 25, 2022. http://data.unaids.org/publications /irc-pub06/epiupdate01_en.pdf.

UNAIDS. 2019a. "Aidsinfo." Accessed June 25, 2022. https://aidsinfo .unaids.org.

UNAIDS. 2019b. "Global HIV & AIDS Statistics: 2019 Fact Sheet." Accessed June 25, 2022. https://www.unaids.org/en/resources/fact -sheet.

United Nations Children's Fund. 2013. *Female Genital Mutilation/Cutting: A Statistical Overview and Exploration of the Dynamics of Change*. New York: UNICEF.

United Nations Children's Fund. 2017. *Is Every Child Counted? Status of Data for Children in the SDGs*. New York: UNICEF. Accessed June 25, 2022. https://data.unicef.org/resources/every-child -counted-status-data-children-sdgs.

United Nations Children's Fund. 2018. *Child Marriage: Latest Trends and Future Prospects*. New York: UNICEF. Accessed June 25, 2022. https://data.unicef.org/wp-content/uploads/2018/07/Child-Marriage -Data-Brief.pdf.

United Nations Office on Drugs and Crime. 2016. *Global Report on Trafficking in Persons*. New York: United Nations.

UN News. 2017. "PODCAST: The Power of Bearing Witness: How Rape Became an 'Act of Genocide.'" Africa Renewal. Accessed June 25, 2022. https://www.un.org/africarenewal/web-features/podcast -power-bearing-witness-%E2%80%93-how-rape-became -%E2%80%98act-genocide%E2%80%99.

Vaughan, Megan. 1991. *Curing Their Ills: Colonial Power and African Illness*. Stanford, CA: Stanford University Press.

Wellcome Collection. c1810. "Poster advertising exhibition of the Hottentot Venus." https://wellcomecollection.org/works/svbbasrz.

World Health Organization. 2018. "Female Genital Mutilation." January 31. Accessed June 25, 2022. https://www.who.int/news-room/fact -sheets/detail/female-genital-mutilation.

SIX

Central and East Asia

Francesca Otero-Vargas and Qiong Wu

INTRODUCTION

This chapter discusses and explores the role of women from Central and East Asia. Attention is paid to both their history and how their roles, beliefs, and practices have changed over time. For the purpose of this chapter, Central and East Asia are considered to consist of Armenia, Azerbaijan, China, Georgia, Japan, Kazakhstan, Kyrgyzstan, Mongolia, North Korea, Russia, South Korea, Tajikistan, Taiwan, Turkmenistan, Uzbekistan, and the region of Hong Kong. Both Central and East Asia will be discussed conjointly. Central and East Asia cover a vast amount of land and are composed of different cultural and historical backgrounds. As such, there has been little published on these regions that is consistent and comprehensive. Both Central and East Asia have rich historical backgrounds that influence the way women view themselves, how they are treated, and how they are perceived by others in society. This chapter will first review historical cultural beliefs and attitudes toward sexuality while considering the roles of war, religion, and politics. Next, it addresses more current attitudes toward sexuality, highlighting how the media has influenced current practices in terms of dating and sex education.

BRIEF HISTORY OF CENTRAL AND EAST ASIA

Central and East Asia consist of countries and regions with considerable diversity in the historic societal roles that women assume. Throughout both regions, however, women have taken important roles within the respective cultures. Before the 16th century, many people in Central Asia lived a nomadic existence, traveling from place to place. "Pastoral nomadism," a form of agriculture based on the herding of domesticated animals practiced on a large scale, was the economic basis of some of the greatest Central Asian empires (Allworth et al. 2017). At its height, Central Asian nomad society was highly specialized and sophisticated; the nomadic people had the ability to construct war materials that were superior for the time period, and they domesticated horses, which was useful for both war and farming (Allworth et al. 2017). During this time, women took broad roles in society. Women in nomadic society participated in training and raising children, crafting, and housework. They also handled other domestic issues beyond both riding and owning horses and pitching and taking down tents. For example, a report from United Nations Educational, Scientific and Cultural Organization (UNESCO n.d.) showed that women were often responsible for selling or buying the family's livestock. The report documented that these women were also able to attend community meetings, ride freely, and take part in different cultural and sporting festivals. Their voice and opinions were considered important and regarded with respect. The nomadic people of Central Asia played an essential role in the history of the region through their trade and influence along the Silk Roads. Through the use of the Silk Roads, women from Central Asia were able to transfer and influence the broader culture. The UNESCO report indicated that women from Central Asia passed down different traditional crafts, knowledge on how to make certain fabrics and patterns, performing arts, and stories, through oral traditions and expressions. There were nomadic communities living along the Silk Road in what are now the countries of Kazakhstan, Kyrgyzstan, Afghanistan, Tajikistan, Turkmenistan, and Uzbekistan. Some nomadic communities are still present in this area today (Allworth et al. 2017).

The nomadic way of life eventually became unsustainable, as they were not able to defend their land from others who desired their land and had more advanced weaponry. The nomadic way of life was threatened by tensions with surrounding territories, such as Great Britain, Russia, and China, starting in the 19th century (Rossabi n.d.). Both Russia and China took steps to invade Central Asia beginning in the 17th century. By the 19th century, Central Asia had been completely conquered by Russia (Rossabi n.d.). After the Russian Revolution of 1917, Soviet rule replaced that of the Russian tsars. Kazakhstan, Uzbekistan, Turkmenistan,

Kyrgyzstan, and Tajikistan were all under Soviet Rule until 1991, when the Soviet Union collapsed (Allworth et al. 2017). The Central Asian cultural, religious, and lifestyle differences of the time reflect women's prominent roles that they had greater power and responsibility than in other regions in Asia.

East Asia consists of China, Japan, Mongolia, North Korea, South Korea, Taiwan, and the region of Hong Kong. These countries traditionally maintained a lifestyle based in farming and agriculture wherein women held more conventional roles in the home, such as housekeepers and caring for children. East Asia was primarily influenced by Confucianism, which played a considerable role in shaping the Chinese family system and determining women's place in that system (Ebrey n.d.). For example, in Chinese culture, the parenting philosophy embodies the Confucian values of respect for authority, devotion to parents, emotional restraint, and the importance of education; there is an emphasis placed on family hierarchy and harmony (Huang and Grove 2012). Moreover, during the period from 202 BCE to 220 CE, the family system was considered patrilineal, patrilocal, and patriarchal. Polygamous marriages were acceptable: men were able to have several wives and concubines (i.e., women who live with a man but have lower status than his wives in polygamous societies; Ebrey n.d.).

However, in Japan, sexuality developed slightly differently than in mainland Asia. Aristocratic culture dominated Japanese society in the Nara, Heian, and Muromachi eras. Inevitably, this society resulted in warlords battling each other until the Tokugawa shogunate was established in 1603. Military commanders and a variety of militaristic groups maintained control of much of the Japanese culture in subsequent eras as a result of this turmoil and eventual integration in Japanese society. Therefore, sexuality in Japan developed in a two-layered system (Noonan 1997). Specifically, strict ethical morality and behavioral rules were imposed on the families of the samurai class, including both soldiers and their commanding officers. This class of people was influenced by the principles of Confucianism mentioned above. Moreover, both romantic love and immoral behavior of any kind that conflicted with the moral code enforced on this class of Japanese people were strictly prohibited. Severe penalties, up to capital punishment, were instituted and could be bestowed upon any offending persons who were discovered (Noonan 1997).

In contrast with the samurai community and upper-class commoners, lower- and middle-class commoners did not subscribe to the same strict ethical code. In fact, romantic love was freely allowed and encouraged

Onoe Tamizo as a Samurai Woman. (The Metropolitan Museum of Art, New York. Purchase, Joseph Pulitzer Bequest, 1918. www .metmuseum.org)

among the commoners. Children conceived "illegitimately" according to the strict Confucian rules were often accepted without community prejudices that would be experienced in upper-class society (Noonan 1997). While not all women adhered to the values and ideas of Confucius, the messages Confucius shared continue to influence modern East Asian cultures. It was not until after World War II that countries in East Asia started to experience the influence of Western culture (Taylor 2014). More details about important historical events and how they have affected modern sexuality will be discussed within this chapter.

PAST CULTURE AND ATTITUDES TOWARD SEXUALITY

Women in War

Times of war, religious influences, and political agendas are vital to understanding the culture of sexuality in Central and East Asia. Throughout Central and East Asian history,

Victims of enslavement during Japan's militaristic period (1932–1945) became known as "comfort women" and lived in "comfort stations" under conditions of sexual slavery for Japanese military (Lynch 2019). It is estimated that over 400,000 Asian women and girls were trafficked and turned into military sex slaves (i.e., comfort women; Pun 2015). These practices continued until the end of the militaristic period in 1945, which was the end of World War II. Afterward, the Japanese government refused to acknowledge the enslavement of comfort women until 1991, when they finally admitted publicly that comfort stations existed during the war (Lynch 2019).

women have played many roles, sometimes for mere survival. Perhaps the most significant and known impact of war on women is Japan's militaristic period, between 1932 and 1945, which affected many areas in the region. During this time, the Japanese military invaded China, Korea, Indonesia, Malaysia, the Philippines, and several other countries. What may be less known about this period of invasion is that women in these countries were essentially enslaved along the way. Women who were victims of enslavement became known as "comfort women," a term for women who were forced to provide sexual services to the Japanese Imperial Army and generally lived under conditions of sexual slavery (Lynch 2019). These women were kept in "comfort stations," places that the Japanese military claimed were meant to enhance morale of the soldiers. Comfort stations were highly regulated to protect the soldiers; however, the enslaved women were not treated with the same concern. Women were often deprived of food, water, and other basic necessities. It is estimated that over 400,000 Asian women and girls were trafficked and turned into military sex slaves (i.e., comfort women; Pun 2015). These practices continued until 1945, which marked the end of World War II and the end of the militaristic period. However, many women did not survive the conditions of the comfort stations.

Many comfort women tragically took their own lives or were executed. Those who did survive still suffered the trauma of mental and physical conditions, including sterility, sexually transmitted diseases, and mental illness (Lynch 2019). Many survivors of comfort stations were rejected by their families and communities when the war ended, leaving them nowhere to turn. Following the end of World War II, the Japanese government refused to acknowledge the enslavement of comfort women. In 1991, they finally admitted publicly that comfort stations existed during the war (Lynch 2019). Even after this public acknowledgement, the Japanese government attempted to minimize these events by hiding and altering the existence of comfort women.

To date, one of the most appalling influences of war in terms of women's roles in this region has been the existence of comfort women, which has historical roots, possibly reflecting how women were traditionally viewed in this region. Before the emergence of comfort women, beginning in the 17th century, there were geisha women to cater to and entertain Japanese men in the "pleasure districts" of Japan (Dalby 2008). Geisha is perhaps the most misrepresented role of women in Japanese history, as they are often portrayed as prostitutes. Geisha women were different from comfort women, as their work was not physically sexual in nature. Some geisha women maintained sexual relationships with their clients, but this was considered to be different from prostitution. The role of the geisha was seen as a more traditional profession; however, for many young girls, it was a form of indentured labor (Dalby 2008). While some girls volunteered for geisha training, many were sold by their parents at an early age to a geisha house (*okiya*), as many Japanese families were struggling with poverty (Layton 2005). These young girls would train in hopes of eventually becoming geisha and being able to earn enough money to repay their parents' debts and for the okiya cost of their training. Young girls would often begin as maids in the teahouses between the ages of 10 and 12. This was done not only for the adolescents to learn by observing the older geishas work but also because suffering was considered necessary to build strong character (Greenwood 2013). In Japanese, the word "geisha" translates to "person of art"; these women were meant to represent the ideal woman, one who had many skills and could be the perfect hostess (Layton 2005). Such skills included singing, dancing, playing musical instruments, and doing hair and makeup, in order to then perform at parties and flatter guests.

An apprentice geisha would continue to receive this training until the age of 16, when she would be officially introduced at the teahouses as *maiko*. As they were considered more decorative than performative by the teahouse patrons, the costume of maikos was far more elaborate than that of older geishas. As maikos, the teenagers learned through observation and were not expected to interact with paying clients. At the age of 20, maikos would officially graduate and be addressed as geishas for the remainder of their career. At this time, a geisha's virginity would be sold to the highest bidder or whomever the okiya selected as the winning patron. Often the geisha would have little choice about which patron was chosen; however, she could influence the decision in subtle ways, such as providing extra warmth and attention to the men she found most desirable

SONGSTRESS ACCOMPANIED BY MUSICIANS

Four geisha women. (Library of Congress, Prints & Photographs Division, LC-USZ62-25326)

and/or projecting a colder and distant persona to the men she desired least. Although this influence would not always result in the geisha's desired outcome, it did provide the women with some power and control over their lives (Greenwood 2013). Geishas were particularly desirable during this time period, because they enacted multiple roles that included that of the attentive female at business gatherings, which was important because Japanese wives were mostly excluded from public life (Layton 2005). If a geisha chose to marry, she would have to retire from the profession. While there are still women in the profession today, they are far fewer than when the profession was at its height. During the 1940s, when the United States occupied Japan, entertainment by geishas was outlawed. Since then, the numbers have continued to decrease. Currently, there are less than 1,000 trained geishas still performing, which makes the entertainment even more exclusive and expensive than it was in the past (Layton 2005).

Modern-day geishas operate in much the same way as the geisha who began in the 1750s. Traditional white makeup with red lips, complex hairstyles, and intricate kimonos still dominate the image of the modern geisha. However, several differences and updates to the quality of life for these women also apply. Young children are no longer sold to the okiya as a way to pay off the debts of the parents. Instead, a geisha volunteers at the age of 14 or 15, after the adolescent has finished her primary education but before she enters high school. Young girls are no longer required to serve as maids to build character and are instead reportedly pampered by the house mothers due to the dwindling numbers of interested youths (Greenwood 2013). Also, the virginity of a geisha is no longer sold to the highest bidder; first intercourse now occurs with mutual desire and consent. Some geishas are also taken as "second wives" by men in Japan and serve as mistresses, with an apartment and living allowance provided by the patron, or *danna* (Greenwood 2013). Most importantly, modern geishas are allowed to leave the role and lifestyle at any point, without harmful repercussions. But while the role of geisha women has differed from that of the comfort women in some ways, many have still experienced violence from the men they were meant to please.

Women's sexuality has also been exploited through recent wars, when sex was used as a way to gain information in espionage operations. During the Cold War, for example, several witnesses reported that the KGB recruited attractive women from rural areas, promising a luxurious lifestyle in exchange for "services" to their country (Mijalković 2014). The women underwent training to diminish shyness and inhibitions, which included watching pornographic material and learning seduction techniques and manners of pleasing both men and women (Mijalković 2014). In order to gain the trust of the person who possessed the desired intelligence, the female operative would become involved in the target's daily life. The operative's goal was to demonstrate her willingness to place the target's happiness and priorities above her own well-being. The woman was trained to let the target speak openly and honestly, to not express judgment, and to show interest in his thoughts and perspectives. The operatives were instructed to use sex and seduction techniques to further gain the trust of their targets. This term was later coined "sex-pionage," meaning that sex was being used for espionage purposes (Mijalković 2014).

Women and Religion

As previously discussed, there was a strict interpretation of Confucius's views on the role of women, particularly in East Asia. These views also focused on sexual behaviors that were centered around strict morals. According to Confucius's principles, sex was only sanctioned for reproductive purposes within the context of marriage. Sex was not to be used

According to Confucius's principles, sex was only sanctioned for reproductive purposes within the context of marriage. Sex was not to be used for pleasure outside the marital relationship. Under the yin-yang doctrine of Confucianism, women were considered the "yin," representing passiveness, while the men were the strong and active "yang" (Higgins et al. 2002). Masturbation was considered a "loss of precious energy" (Higgins et al. 2002). In fact, up to 36.4% of Chinese men and 58.3% of Chinese women still believe that "masturbation is harmful" (Higgins et al. 2002).

for pleasure outside the marital relationship (Higgins et al. 2002). From this perspective, premarital relationships, extramarital affairs, same-sex activities, and masturbation were forbidden. In fact, masturbation was considered under the yin-yang doctrine of Confucianism to be a "loss of precious energy" (Higgins et al. 2002). In fact, up to 36.4% of Chinese men and 58.3% of Chinese women still believe that "masturbation is harmful" (Higgins et al. 2002). Under the yin-yang doctrine, women were considered the "yin," representing passiveness, while the men were the strong and active "yang" (Higgins et al. 2002).

Buddhism has also influenced the history of sexuality but was more prominent in Japan (Junko and Glassman 1993). Buddhist practices became more prevalent in Japan in the sixth century, and Buddhism was eventually accepted as the state religion (Ōgoshi 1993). However, Japanese Buddhism was different from the Buddhist philosophy and practices associated with India. Japanese Buddhism supported the patriarchal system present in Japan by teaching women that they were sinful because of their sexual power (Ōgoshi 1993). Women were expected to obey men, which placed them at the bottom of the societal hierarchy. Women were also kept from entering Buddhist temples and were acknowledged solely based on their relationships to men: daughter, wife, mother (Ōgoshi 1993; Junko and Glassman 1993). In modern society, Asian women are advocating for institutional reform, as women's roles in society are shifting.

In other parts of Central and East Asia, the Soviet Union was established by the Bolsheviks in 1922. At the time of the revolution in 1917, the Russian Orthodox Church was officially integrated into the authoritarian state (Dragadze 1993). This was a significant factor that contributed to the national attitude toward religion and lengths the government went to in order to control it. As a result, the USSR became the first state with an objective of atheism, and the Soviet Union sponsored a widespread program to convert the population to atheism. The communist regime in power at the time targeted religions based on the interests of the state. Most organized religions were never legally prohibited; however, religious symbols were taken, believers were socially harassed, and atheism was pushed through propaganda in schools (Dragadze 1993). In 1925, the government drastically increased the levels of persecution. Social stigma was imposed on believers through official government channels and the media. Teachers and government officials were heavily discouraged from exhibiting nonsecular beliefs, and citizens who did not conform were ostracized (Dragadze 1993). Believers were free to worship in their private residences and respective religious buildings, but public displays of religion were prohibited (Dragadze 1993). Religious institutions were additionally banned from expressing their perspectives in mass media of any kind. Eventually, it was determined that the state had failed to convert the majority of the population to atheism, and the program was disbanded. After World War II and the fall of communism, religion flourished once again. In this region today, a variety of beliefs are represented, including Christianity—Catholicism, Orthodox, and Protestant denominations—as well as Islam and small amounts of Buddhism and Shamanism (Dragadze 1993).

Women and Politics

Following the establishment of the People's Republic of China in 1949, more women began to join the workforce. As fewer women remained stay-at-home housekeepers and caregivers, they were exposed to more possibilities for potential spouses (Hare, Yang, and Englander 2008). As a result of this trend, the Marriage Law of 1950 was also established, which was intended to address issues of inequality among husbands and wives. This legislation prohibited concubinage, polygamy, bigamy, child betrothal, and interference with the remarriage of widows (Engel 1984; Hare-Mustin 1982). It was intended to combat many of the practices that were common in the previous feudal society, in which Chinese women were taught to be loyal to their husbands and remarriage was discouraged (Ng et al. 2014). However, even after revisions to the Marriage Law in 1980 to make it more family oriented, China has continued to face many challenges due to the treatment of women. For example, there are continued practices of bride-price payments and dowries in some rural areas (Engel 1984; Hare-Mustin 1982).

There were also laws introduced in Central Asia that were aimed at enfranchising women. In 1919, the right to vote for all adult citizens, or universal suffrage, was implemented in Azerbaijan. This legislation made

Azerbaijan the first Muslim-majority country to allow women the right to vote (UNESCO 2019). In 1948, women in South Korea also gained important rights. Women were given the right to vote, drive, and own and inherit property and assets (World Trade Press 2010). Yet marital rape in South Korea was not outlawed until 2013. In many ways, the culture was still behind on enacting vital legislation to promote the protection and safety of women (World Trade Press 2010). This has been the case for much of Central and East Asia and has affected the prevalence of gender-based violence and discrimination both in history and in the present day.

Conversely, in post-Soviet Russia, women began to enjoy a higher profile at the national level. The most noteworthy display of women's newfound political success in Russia has been the Women of Russia party (Paxton, Hughes, and Barnes 2020). After winning several seats in the 1993 parliamentary election, this party became active in a number of issues. The Women of Russia maintained a platform that addressed social concerns, including the protection of children and women. Unfortunately, in the 1995 election, this party did not reach the required threshold for representation in the new state, and they have since been unable to regain the level of power experienced in 1993 (Paxton, Hughes, and Barnes 2020). Women such as Ella Pamfilova, of the Republican Party, Socialist Workers' Party chief Lyudmila Vartazarova, and Valeriya Novodvorskaya, leader of the Democratic Union, have been successful in establishing themselves politically. Pamfilova, specifically, gained notoriety as an advocate for women and the elderly. Unfortunately, women have not occupied many influential positions in the national executive branch of Russia's government. The minister of social protection, a cabinet position in the national government of Russia, has become a gendered position, with women occupying the seat more often than not since 1992 (Paxton, Hughes, and Barnes 2020). Of the more than 120 countries in the world, women are the heads of government in only 12, as of 2020. Politics is an important arena for women to hold power, because their decision-making affects daily life across a variety of domains.

GENDER-BASED VIOLENCE AND DISCRIMINATION: PAST AND PRESENT

Throughout Central and East Asia, violence against women is one of the deadliest and most prominent forms of violence, causing many fatalities (Rodriguez, Shakil, and Morel 2018). Yet throughout history, government

The "Three Obediences" seen in traditional Confucian culture in China are built on doctrine linking gender inequality and distribution of power and resources, specifically for women (Zuo et al. 2018). Women are considered subordinate to men at all three stages of life: daughters to fathers, wives to their husbands, and widows to their sons. According to this doctrine, women were meant to be modest and submissive in temperament, and chastity was required until marriage (Zuo et al. 2018). Consequently, women are treated differently, and expectations of them enforce the dominance of men.

and policy makers have often overlooked these situations and statistics. In these regions, there are many historical customs that are still practiced today that view women as property, stemming from patriarchal traditions and harmful practices against women (Rodriguez, Shakil, and Morel 2018). For example, the "Three Obediences" seen in traditional Confucian culture in China are built on doctrine linking gender inequality and distribution of power and resources, specifically for women (Zuo et al. 2018). Women are considered subordinate to men at all three stages of life: daughters to fathers, wives to their husbands, and widows to their sons. Consequently, women were treated differently and were supposed to meet expectations that were not imposed on men. Confucian culture emphasized that women should not be allowed to attend school but instead should become educated at home on domestic skills. According to this doctrine, women were meant to be modest and submissive in temperament, and chastity was required until marriage (Zuo et al. 2018). These ideas around gender roles and expectations can be dangerous, as there is extensive research that shows men with more traditional gender role ideologies are more inclined to justify and engage in sexual coercion and violence toward women (Zuo et al. 2018).

While most countries in Asia currently have laws against domestic violence, that was not always the case. Even now, the laws are poorly implemented and may exclude unmarried intimate partners. Furthermore, most of these laws do not address other forms of violence, such as rape (including marital rape) or sexual abuse (UNFPA 2015b). Girls in many parts of Central and East Asia are subjected to practices such as early and forced child marriage, bride kidnapping, virginity tests, gender-based discrimination, and human trafficking, among other forms of abuse and violence. "Gender-based violence against women and girls is multi-dimensional, deeply rooted in inequitable societal norms, and persists throughout the life cycle"

(Rodriguez, Shakil, and Morel 2018, 1). Gender-based violence engulfs all aspects of society and prevents women from fully participating. It is a deep-rooted bias against girls that starts before birth and continues through the life cycle, affecting women's physical health, education, socioeconomic status, family life, and mental health (Rodriguez, Shakil, and Morel 2018).

While certain regions in East and Central Asia are actively trying to adopt more antidiscrimination legislation, gender stereotypes remain engrained in society and can lead to many challenges for women. For example, Kazakhstan was the first Central Asian country to implement a national entity to promote gender equality, through the National Commission on Women, Family, and Demographic Policy. Still, there is imbalance by gender in wages and in access to employment and career-based opportunities. In 2016, women in Kazakhstan earned on average 31.4 less than men (UNFPA 2015a). This lack of opportunity and equity puts women in more vulnerable positions than their male counterparts and contributes to the amount of gender-based violence still present in these regions. A survey by United Nations Women found that 17 of women (ages 18–75) who had ever been in a partnership had experienced physical or sexual violence. Twenty-one also experienced psychological abuse (UNFPA 2015a). In Kyrgyzstan, the figures only increase. Worldwide, 6 out of 10 women experience physical or sexual violence in their lifetime. The figures in Kyrgyzstan are similar (UNFPA 2015a). This includes domestic violence, trafficking, as well as other forms of physical or sexual abuse. Violence against both women and young girls is also prominent in Central Asia. It is often suggested that the revival of some cultural and social practices, often mistakenly interpreted as part of religious customs, are partly responsible for the increase in the restriction of women's rights in order to control their lives. Consequently, violence toward women ensues, as a result of their restricted rights (UNFPA 2015a).

There are many other global factors that can also affect women and their positions. In Tajikistan, for example, poverty and the socioeconomic status of the country largely affects women and girls. Tajikistan is one of the world's 30 poorest countries, and women suffer disproportionately from this poverty when compared to their male counterparts (UNFPA 2015b). At the highest risk of poverty are those living in households headed by women, by those with many children, or by people who have not had the privilege of receiving a formal education (predominantly women). The American Psychological Association suggests that poverty is systemically linked to conditions such as substandard housing or homelessness, inadequate nutrition, food insecurity, improper or nonexistent childcare, limited or lack of access to health care, unsafe neighborhoods, and underresourced schools or the inability to enroll children, specifically when it comes to the enrollment of young girls. These conditions are therefore more likely to expose women and children to violence.

Living in poverty can also have harmful psychological effects that may include increased feelings of anxiety, depression, marital distress, and low self-esteem (American Psychological Association n.d.). People in Tajikistan are aware of this situation; however, there is a culture of silence that persists and keeps women feeling discouraged and trapped. A culture that silences women, coupled with the lack of punishment for perpetrators in Tajikistan, stops victims of violence or discrimination from using their voices. It was reported that 20 of married women in this country have experienced some type of emotional, physical, or sexual violence by their husbands, yet only one in five victims files a report (UNFPA 2015a). Women in Georgia are also in this predicament, as women who choose to live on their own are also at a higher risk of poverty, social exclusion, and isolation. As with many other countries in the region, Georgia has gender perceptions that place men in a dominant position in many areas of social, economic, and political life (UNFPA 2015a). Georgia has tried to combat this with state policy and gender legislation. Unlike Uzbekistan, which still lacks laws on domestic violence and legislation on gender equality, Georgia recognizes this as a public concern and has been working since its independence in 1991 to remedy some of the issues (Solod 2019; UNFPA 2015a). These practices may be based on historical beliefs and tradition, but they are ever-present in modern society. It was not until 2017 that Uzbekistan allowed women to leave the country freely on their own recognizance (Solod 2019). Prior to 2017, women needed the permission of their parents or husband to leave the country. Additionally in Uzbekistan, domestic and gender-based violence are not seen as sufficient grounds for divorce in the eyes of the court. If a woman wants to divorce, there are high fees and social implications tied to that decision that are not applied to men (Solod 2019). This is similar to Armenia, where divorcing a husband, even for gender-based violence or domestic aggression, can cause women to be shamed by society and their families (Shirinian 2010). Lack of equal pay, social expectations, and gender-based discrimination are, then, barriers to safety and opportunity.

There is an immense need to increase awareness of gender-based violence and discrimination, both regionally and globally. Furthermore, policy makers and law enforcement must take on a more active role in promoting, implementing, and preserving change. Gender equality is not solely the problem of women but the problem of the society as a whole. Experts on this topic believe that society must empower women and girls or they will suffer, because equality and equity are relational (Third Committee 2011). This means increasing access to accurate and unbiased information for everyone. The more informed all people are about issues of sexuality, relationships, and how they affect the social and political factors, the better able they will be to make their own decisions. These decisions can determine women's roles and how they participate in the system and the rhetoric.

Sex Slavery and Human Trafficking

In addition to gender-based violence and discrimination that women in Central and East Asia face, women from this region also have a history of being taken against their will and traded for profit, as were the comfort women in Japan. Sex slavery and human trafficking have been happening for many years. As of 2016, an estimated 24.9 million men, women, and children were living in modern slavery in Asia and the Pacific Islands. According to the Global Slavery Index report (2018), North Korea and China have one of the highest rates of people living in modern slavery. China and North Korea remain Tier 3 countries, according to the 2019 Trafficking in Persons Report by the U.S. Department of State. Being a Tier 3 country means that the government does not fully comply with the Trafficking Victims Protection Act (TVPA) minimum standards and are not making significant efforts to do so. In contrast to China and Korea, Japan, South Korea, and Taiwan are recognized as Tier 1 countries with governments that fully comply with the TVPA's minimum standards (U.S. Department of State 2019).

It is difficult to obtain comprehensive and accurate information on human trafficking, because there are many people who are not able to report their experiences. Human trafficking often occurs between countries and regions within Central Asia. For example, Kazakhstan has a large number of human trafficking cases, as it acts as both the country of origin and the destination due to its prosperity (Dost 2017). In Kazakhstan, about 400 human trafficking cases are registered per year. There were 924 confirmed trafficking cases in Uzbekistan in 2015, 784 of which involved persons taken out of the country Dost 2017). Women and children trafficked from Uzbekistan are typically forced into prostitution throughout the Middle East, Eurasia, and Asia (Dost 2017).

There are two main types of human trafficking in Central Asia: forced slave labor and forced sex work. Women and children are most often subjected to sex slavery. Central Asian men are more commonly trafficked for labor purposes. Financial difficulties and unstable income in their home countries drive people to migrate, and these are most often the people who become enslaved. Men between the ages of 18 and 34 who do not have a university or specialized education and reside in the remote areas of Central Asian countries are increasingly vulnerable (Dost 2017). This type of necessary migration can also affect the women and children in the family. Women in these situations are essentially informally divorced from their migrant husbands and must provide for their families, leaving them more vulnerable to trafficking (Cooney 2016). According to the United Nations Office on Drugs and Crime (2016), there are more victims of forced labor compared to the number of victims of sexual exploitation in Central Asia. Data identified that 63% of the victims were men, 31% women, 4% male children, and 2% female children. However, these findings vary by country. In 2014, Kazakhstan and Uzbekistan had higher numbers of forced labor victims, while Tajikistan had more cases of people trafficked for prostitution (United Nations Office on Drugs and Crime 2016).

There are programs that have been set up to help combat human trafficking. One example is the Victim Case Management System (VCMS) through Liberty Shared. The purpose of VCMS is to work to prevent human trafficking through legal advocacy, technology interventions, and strategic collaborations with nongovernmental organizations (NGOs) and corporations in Asia and globally (U.S. Department of State 2019).

CULTURE AND ATTITUDES TOWARD SEXUALITY

Not all countries in Asia hold the same beliefs, attitudes, or policies with regard to sexuality, reproductive health, and menstruation. For example, in China, there is a history of family planning being highly regulated. The central government of China initiated the one-child policy in the late 1970s and early 1980s (Pletcher 2019). China's one-child policy was put in place to combat China's rapidly growing population, which at the time of the program's induction was roughly 900 million. The policy is controversial for many reasons, including the methods the government used to enforce it. Some families were offered financial perks for their compliance, while

Chinese diagnostic doll. (Ivory Chinese diagnostic doll. Wellcome Collection. Attribution 4.0 International [CC BY 4.0])

other women were provided contraceptives. These were not always optional, and many women were forced into involuntary sterilization or to have an abortion against their will (Pletcher 2019). Furthermore, it was more common for female fetuses to be aborted, as male children are more desirable in Asian cultures. The one-child policy was in place until 2016. However, it had long-lasting effects on China's population and culture. Even today, the birth of a female child is seen as a misfortune by some families; women are still in an inferior position (Breiner 1992).

As a result, there are currently fewer women available for marriage, causing problems for the culture. In China, getting married is considered to be the most significant event in a person's life (Amanpour and Harper 2018b). In Shanghai, parents will often participate in "marriage markets" in hopes of expediting the marriage process (Amanpour and Harper 2018b). Parents gather at these types of markets to advertise their children's best qualities, such as their job, income, and education level. This type of market originated in Shanghai but is now spreading throughout China. In about 80% of cases, the young people being advertised have no idea their parents are doing this (Amanpour and Harper 2018b). The pressure to get married is high for both men and women in China; however, it is particularly steep for women, who may be referred to as "left over" if they have not married by the age of 26 or 27 (Custer 2019).

For this reason, many young Chinese people may not feel as though they are able to "play the field" by casually dating or having more casual sexual experiences (Custer 2019). A study that compared attitudes to marriage and sexual behaviors between university students in the United Kingdom and China found that China maintains a more conservative sexual culture. This shows that traditional morality and attitudes prevail, especially among women (Higgins et al. 2002). More recently, there has been an increase in foreign marriages, especially among Chinese women. In 2010, about 40,000 Chinese women participated in a foreign marriage, compared to less than 12,000 men (Jeffreys and Pan 2013).

In Japan, arranged marriages and love matches are still common. A traditional arranged marriage is when the parents of the two partners come to an agreement about the marriage of their children. Often this was done for socioeconomic advantages (Watanabe and Hijino 2020). As love is not the primary focus of marriage in this culture, arranged marriages make more sense in terms of gaining more power, money, and status by building the family unit. In Japan, many couples do not say "I love you" in the way that Western cultures do. Instead, linguistically, "thank you" can mean more than "I love you" (Amanpour and Freeman 2018a). A love match is different from an arranged marriage in that the couple is choosing to get married. Often, even in love matches, a family friend, relative, or mentor will still act as the go-between (*nakodo*) for the couple (Hurst and Masamoto n.d.).

In Japan, cultural and business norms actually discourage women from getting married if their career and success at work are important to them (Beauchamp 2015). This is causing marriage to be on the decline in Japan. Also, the number of people having sex is declining in Japan. Forty percent of the male population in Japan are virgins (Amanpour and Freeman 2018a). This highlights the loss of "skinship," body touch and affection such as kissing, that is occurring in the Japanese culture. Japan, like many Asian cultures, can be described as more of a noncontact culture; however, this lack of physical affection, including sex, can cause a loss in confidence for women. One study found that "in comparison with men and women from 'Western' regions," respondents living in East Asian countries were "more sexually conservative, more male-orientated, and less sexually active" (Beauchamp 2015). In fact, "Japan is the only country in the world where a higher age of people report being dissatisfied with their sex lives than satisfied" (Beauchamp 2015). Much of this is being attributed to long working hours, causing couples to have less time together. This all affects Japan's birth rate, which is falling as fewer people get married and have sex.

In Hong Kong, the culture of marriage is shifting. While marriage was previously centered around similar traditional duties and expectations, women and men are not looking to marry based on personal happiness and romantic satisfaction (Sullivan 2005). This provides women with the opportunity to have a greater voice and more opportunities within the marriage. For example, women are now able to get a divorce from their husbands if the marriage is not working, which was previously not the case. As these shifts in the dynamics of marriage have become more commonplace, Hong Kong has more single individuals now than ever before (Sullivan 2005).

Dating Culture

There are several common patterns when it comes to dating in Asian cultures. These patterns are consistent with the research and align with many of the cultural values already discussed. As mentioned, dating in Asian cultures—whether it is engaged in or not engaged in—is typically based on practical reasons. Usually, dating does not take place until both parties are established. This means they have finished some type of schooling and the persons' job, lifestyle, and long-term prospects are taken into account (AsianDate Ladies 2019). As with marriage arrangements, it is not uncommon for family members and friends to set up dates. Moreover, the decisions on whom to date or the suitability of a partner is subject to both familial and friend approval (Custer 2019). This can make dating more difficult for both Asian men and women. Additional pressure is put on women when dating, as most Asian men say that they would prefer to marry a woman who has not had premarital sex (AsianDate Ladies 2019). In general, sex before marriage in Asian countries is not a common practice; however, physical intimacy can come much later in a dating relationship when compared to many Western cultures.

Reproductive Health and Menstruation

As with dating culture and sex education—the latter is addressed in the following section—there is regional variation in the knowledge and information women have with regard to reproductive health and menstruation. In Asia and the Pacific Islands, the little information that does exist on these topics shows that most adolescents (aged 10–14 years) do not have a comprehensive understanding of reproduction, puberty, and menstruation (UNFPA 2015b). The data also highlight that information that is being shared is not necessarily reliable, and there are many misconceptions about what reproduction, puberty, and menstruation are (UNFPA 2015b). For example, tampons are regarded by many women in East Asian countries as being sexual because they have been associated with hymen destruction in a culture where virginity and "purity" are greatly valued (Van Brunnersum 2019). Consequently, in mainland China, despite tampons being widely available, only 2% of women reported using them compared to approximately 70% of European women (Tai 2019).

Lack of sexual and reproductive knowledge, along with the stigma often associated with reproductive health and menstruation, can result in poor sexual and reproductive health outcomes. These outcomes can include, but are not limited to, unintended pregnancy, sexually transmitted infections, toxic shock syndrome, and urinary tract infections. Additionally, women are often stigmatized as "impure" when menstruating and are sent messages from the culture that there is shame associated with the occurrence of this very natural and physiological process. This message is historical, as many religious texts refer to the "impurity" of menstruation (Guterman, Mehta, and Gibbs 2007). For example, in Taiwan, Buddhists deem women who are menstruating to be "polluted" and call the menstrual blood "dirt" or "poison" (Guterman, Mehta, and Gibbs 2007).

While the past two decades have seen an increase in investments made to educate women about sexual and reproductive health globally and throughout Asia and the Pacific Islands, there is more work to be done (UNFPA 2015b). More Asian women ages 15 to 49 are utilizing modern contraceptives, about 61.8% (World Health Organization 2018). However, it is estimated that of woman ages 15 to 19, 50% lack access to modern contraception (UNFPA 2015b). Modern methods of contraception include any form of contraception that is not represented by the traditional withdrawal or calendar/rhythm methods (World Health Organization 2018). For example, the pill, the minipill, implants, contraceptive injections, contraception patches, and intrauterine devices are all included in modern methods of contraception.

While the topics of reproductive health and menstruation may still be taboo to some people in Asian culture, there are woman who are hoping to change this perspective. Female-led products are being developed throughout Asia in hopes of promoting change, helping women gain access to more knowledge, and supporting them to feel more comfortable in their bodies. One such product is the Eve Cup, which is an eco-friendly menstruation cup developed by Gina Park in South Korea (Tai 2019). This is just one example of how Asian women are taking their health and their education into their own hands.

Sex Education

Each culture faces unique challenges around sex education. The topic is highly debated, as people have conflicting ideas about the focus and what information should be included. For example, there is a lack of consensus as to who should provide sex education (e.g., teachers, doctors, parents) and whether sex education promotes increased sexual activity among youth. However, comprehensive research shows the presence of quality and encompassing sex education in schools actually helps prepare students for adulthood by giving them information around contraceptive use, sexually transmitted diseases, and pregnancy. Findings show sex education may even empower youth in their sexuality by discussing gender and human rights (Hulshof 2016). Therefore, avoiding teaching younger people about sex can be harmful, as it may put them at a greater risk of participating in risky sexual behavior. Yet many Asian cultures still limit sex education. In China, for example, educators do not wish to take any steps that would be seen to encourage sexual permissiveness. A survey of university students found that about 70% of students reported their knowledge was mostly from books and magazines, and only about 7% mentioned the role of sex education at school (Higgins et al. 2002).

This lack of formal sex education has dominant effects on women in Asian cultures. According to a report completed in 2016, "there are 13 million abortions in China every year" (Burki 2016). These statistics indicate that there is a lack of education for young people when it comes to contraceptive use, family planning, and information around the process of sexual intercourse (Burki 2016). Given these points and Asia's traditionally patriarchal culture, it follows that women are at greater risk when engaging in sexual activities. One study found that female university students in China, who held more traditional attitudes around gender and gender roles, were at a higher risk of being the victim of nonconsensual sex (Zuo et al. 2018). Separately, it was shown that most female university students were less prepared and less assertive in refusing unwanted sexual advances, which in turn appeared to increase the risk of sexual assault (Zuo et al. 2018).

The reluctance to formalize sex education extends beyond China. In Japan, there was a sizable historic movement against sex education as recently as 2002. The case was about a sex education book that was being used in schools, which some people believed was too graphic and inappropriate. The books ended up being removed from the schools by Parliament. Consequently, the case prompted the Ministry of Education in Japan to suggest that parental consent be required before students could be offered sex education in school (Hirose 2013). This is similar to how sex education is handled in Armenia, where parental consent is also required (Morrison 2019). Furthermore, religion and religious culture play a role in sex education and policy. In Georgia, the idea of establishing sex education in the schools is largely put down by the Orthodox Church (Morrison 2019). In contrast, Korea has implemented mandatory sex education as a part of its education curriculum (Shin, Park, and Cha 2011). By mandating sex education, Korean students who participate in sex education have reduced cases of sexually transmitted diseases and unplanned pregnancies (Shin, Park, and Cha 2011).

Values, ideas, and norms around sex are changing as adolescents become more aware of other cultures. Education and exposure to knowledge are all interconnected in the sociopolitical system. Yet parents, teachers, and health-care workers are often reluctant, due to more traditional cultural norms, to provide the information necessary for adolescents to make informed decisions, with agency, about their bodies, especially when it comes to adolescent girls (United Nations Economic and Social Commission for Asia and the Pacific 2018). Comprehensive, age-appropriate, and culturally relevant sex education has many benefits to both young women and young men. This type of education has been shown to increase self-esteem among adolescents, promote more gender-equitable relationships, delay onset of sexual intimacy, increase contraception use, lower rates of sexually transmitted diseases, decrease unintended pregnancies, and decrease the likelihood of being in a violent relationship (United Nations Economic and Social Commission for Asia and the Pacific 2018). However, many Central and East Asian countries have not yet employed these types of programs. Consequently, adolescents are turning more toward their peers and the media to gather such knowledge.

MODERN MEDIA AND SEXUALITY

The internet can be used to help connect people in the physical world. Nowadays people carry a plethora of information and ways to connect in their pockets. For example, more and more people are turning to dating apps and other online websites to learn more about sex, find sexual partners, and explore different sexual fetishes, preferences, and so forth (Jeffreys and Yu 2015).

Today, Chinese people still hold more conservative beliefs; however, the culture is shifting from one of communism into one of capitalism (Amanpour and Harper 2018b). Women and men in China are able to explore their sexuality and break their silence particularly through the use of the internet. For example, the profession of camming has become hugely popular in China. Webcam hosts in China are typically women who broadcast, livestream, and share their talents, ideas, and, on occasion, their bodies with their viewers (VICE Intl. n.d.). Camming, a part of the sex industry in China, is a platform where women can make millions (VICE Intl. n.d.). While the internet has become a huge platform for expression, censorship still exists. For example, in China, people are not allowed to show any exposed body parts such as nipples or genitals on the internet (Amanpour and Harper 2018b). The internet has also been used for the benefit of other marginalized populations. Members of the LGBTQ+ community have been able to explore their identities and find a community within cultures that discriminate against them.

Social Media and Advocacy Campaigns

Women and girls are seeking and finding a greater sense of community online. Through social media, there have been movements growing to counter violence against women and girls in Central and East Asia, where the issue is extensively prominent and mostly unaddressed. Many of these movements have been circulating on online platforms and advertised as social media and advocacy campaigns. For example, the United Nations have supported the voices and stories of many survivors and activists through campaigns such as #MeToo, #TimesUp, #Niunamenos, #NotOneMore, #BalanceTonPorc, and others (UN Women 2019). Most recently in 2019, the UNiTE campaign focused on "Orange the World: Generation Equality Stands against Rape!" which was a 16-day campaign focused on activism against gender-based violence. "While the names, times, and contexts may differ, women and girls universally experience rape, sexual violence, and abuse, in times of peace or war" (UN Women 2019). These voices have echoed in Asian countries such as South Korea, China, and Japan (Mistreanu 2019; Strother 2019).

Countries are continuing to develop plans and programs aimed at addressing gender-based violence and are creating plans for women, children, and families. In Kyrgyzstan, advancements have been made in a positive direction, including passing laws on preventing family violence and forbidding underage religious marriages (United Nations Development Programme 2018). Moreover, women are taking more control of their voices and stories. Women in Uzbekistan are increasingly engaging in these campaigns and starting conversations with other women using online media, such as blogs, to increase their visibility (United Nations Development Programme 2018). For example, "Speak Out!" is one online discussion group helping women in Uzbekistan gain resources and learn terms, and it provides support to women who have experienced any type of gender-based violence (Solod 2019).

The LGBTQ+ Community in Central and East Asia

No discussion of modern media and sexuality in Central and East Asia would be complete without the inclusion of those women who are members of the LGBTQ+ community, among whom there are those who may not identify with the gender binary common to Western cultures. The laws and policies regarding same-sex relationships, marriages, sexual activity, sex reassignment surgery, and discrimination based on sex differ throughout Central and East Asia. As of 2019, Taiwan was the only place in Asia to pass gay marriage legislation, which legalized same-sex marriage (Hollingsworth 2019). Other places in Asia, such as China and South Korea, do not explicitly have laws preventing same-sex consensual activity but lack laws that aim to protect members of the LGBTQ+ community. While same-sex activity is not illegal in China, same-sex marriage and partnership have not been legalized (Choy 2019).

In North Korea and Japan, same-sex marriage and activity are not recognized, and in North Korea they are strictly prohibited. Some municipalities in Japan recognize same-sex couples' rights, although many still refuse to acknowledge same-sex marriage as a legal union (Choy 2019). Japan's current social stigma and conservative values contradict the nation's own past regarding attitudes toward homosexuality, which are exemplified in ancient text. Writers such as Natsume Soseki and Yukio Mishima often approach non-heteronormative sexuality with both curiosity and speculation. Mishima wrote the scandalous 1949 novel *Kamen no Kokuhaku*, "Confessions of a Mask," which he described as exploring homosexual desire or *nanshoku* from a perspective unlike previously published works (Reichert 2002). Even further back in Japan's history, the Edo Period included compositions with themes of homoerotic desire. In 1776, "Kikka no Chigiri" or "Chrysanthemum Tryst," by Ueda Akinari, contained symbolism in the title of the piece—the chrysanthemum blossom—that represented homosexual intercourse (Reichert 2002). In the text of this piece, a samurai makes a promise to a Confucian scholar that he will return by the time of the Chrysanthemum Festival to visit. However, the samurai finds himself trapped in a distant place and is unable to fulfill his promise to the scholar, who had once nursed him back to health. The piece ends with the samurai killing himself so his ghost can meet the Confucian scholar and keep the promised appointment. Given the pointed symbolism behind the title of this piece, many scholars assume the two protagonists were in fact lovers and the samurai would rather take his own life than not see his lover again (Reichert 2002).

In a study using a Chinese student sample, researchers found that 78.6% of men and 66.4% of women disapproved of the statement "homosexuality should be allowed" (Higgins et al. 2002). The Chinese culture has a long history of negative attitudes and intolerance for those who are members of the LGBTQ+ community. Kyrgyzstan had its first gay pride march, aimed at promoting women's rights and equality, in March 2019. Many acknowledge this as the first march of its kind in Central Asia. It was highly controversial and passionately criticized by more socially conservative lawmakers, leaving marchers to face threats of violence and counterprotests (Baumgartner 2019). Legislation also varies around gender identity and expression. Kyrgyzstan, Tajikistan, Georgia, Kazakhstan, Russia, China, Hong Kong, Japan, Mongolia, South Korea, and Taiwan all have laws concerning gender identity and expression; however, the laws and what they cover vary by country. People trying to legally change their gender must comply with stringent guidelines that deprive them of other civil liberties (Choy 2019). For example, to gain legal gender recognition, multiple countries in Central Asia still require sterilization of trans persons and require a mental health diagnosis before adapting identity documents (TGEU 2019). These countries include Armenia, Azerbaijan, and Georgia (Stack 2017). The process and procedures are discriminatory and can take many forms. For example, some countries mandate the surgical removal of genitalia and reproductive organs, while others call for procedures that produce "irreversible infertility" but are not clear on what those procedures are (Stack 2017). However, in April 2017, the European Court of Human Rights ruled that requiring sterilization in legal gender recognition violates human rights law, which applied to Armenia, Azerbaijan, and Georgia (TGEU 2019).

LGBTQ+ people face limited support in Central and East Asia. While the situation varies by country and region, the rights of sexual minorities generally remain limited and challenging to access. Georgia is one of the few countries in Central Asia that has laws directly addressing the discrimination of LGBTQ+ people (Roth 2018). Nevertheless, the laws intended to protect LGBTQ+ people may not have the intended effect, as people in Georgia are still targeted. LGBTQ+ people have been abused, beaten, shamed, and are still considered to be engaging in a way of life that deviates from societal norms (McGuinness 2013; Swieca 2013).

The prejudicial statements and discriminatory behaviors faced by members of the LGBTQ+ community do not prevent them from advocating for themselves and speaking out. LGBTQ+ members have been increasingly active through social media posts and campaigns meant to inform and create more visibility in these populations (Yang 2019). The internet and modern media have allowed people to share content that is far reaching and to build social networks with people in their communities and across the world. Moreover, "the acquisition and dissemination of information regarding LGBT rights has helped the formation of a collective identity of Chinese sexual minorities" (Yang 2019, 664). In this way, social media can be used as a forum to bring people together and foster community for people who may not be able to find it in their immediate environment. This can be empowering and can provide a structure from which to create future policy.

CONCLUSION

Within this chapter, the complexities of women's role in history and in modern Central and East Asia have been discussed. Throughout history, it is clear that women played important roles in society and contributed significantly to the culture of their regions. Women and girls in Central and East Asia are continuing to live in societies where traditional, more patriarchal norms and gender roles prevail; however, more attention is being given to equality, equity, and safety in the legislation and in the modern-day media. It is important to remember that all women and girls will have unique experiences depending on where in Central and East Asia they live, their socioeconomic status, education level, family of origin, and other contextual factors. This chapter is meant to provide information that may help people from outside of these communities gain a better understanding of what it means to be a woman and how sexuality is viewed in these areas. While there have been steps toward increased freedoms and safety for women and girls, obstacles still remain—even more so for those who are members of the LGBTQ+ community. The following chapter will discuss women's sexuality in South and Southeast Asia.

REFERENCES

Allworth, Edward, David Roger Smith, Denis Sinor, and Gavin R. G. Hambly. 2017. "History of Central Asia." *Encyclopedia Britannica*, November 16. Accessed January 14, 2020. https://www.britannica.com/topic/history-of-Central-Asia.

Amanpour, Christiane, and Sally Freeman, dir. 2018a. *Sex & Love around the World*. Episode 1, "Tokyo." March 27.

Amanpour, Christiane, and Abigail Harper, dir. 2018b. *Sex & Love around the World*. Episode 6, "Shanghai." April 21.

American Psychological Association. n.d. "Effects of Poverty, Hunger and Homelessness on Children and Youth." Accessed January 9, 2020. https://www.apa.org/pi/families/poverty.

AsianDate Ladies. 2019. "Must-Know Differences in Asian Dating Culture." October 11. Accessed January 14, 2020. https://asiandateladies.com/5-must-know-cultural-differences-before-dating-asian-women.

Baumgartner, Pete. 2019. "Rainbow Rage: Kyrgyz Rail against LGBT Community after Central Asia's 'First' Gay-Pride March." *Radio Free Europe Radio Liberty*. Accessed January 10, 2020. https://www.rferl.org/a/rainbow-rage-kyrgyz-rail-against-lgbt-after-central-asia-s-first-gay-pride-march/29825158.html.

Beauchamp, Zack. 2015. "6 Maps and Charts That Explain Sex around the World." Vox, May 26. Accessed January 14, 2020. https://www.vox.com/2014/5/7/5662608/in-different-area-codes.

Breiner, Sander J. 1992. "Sexuality in Traditional China: Its Relationship to Child Abuse." *Child Psychiatry & Human Development* 23 (2): 53–67. https://doi.org/10.1007/bf00709750.

Burki, Talha. 2016. "Sex Education in China Leaves Young Vulnerable to Infection." *Lancet Infectious Diseases*, no. 1. https://doi.org/10.1016/S1473-3099(15)00494-6.

Choy, Gigi. 2019. "Gay Rights, LGBTQ and Same-Sex Marriage in Asia." *South China Morning Post*, March 12. Accessed January 14, 2020. https://www.scmp.com/week-asia/explained/article/3001296/explained-gay-rights-lgbtq-and-same-sex-marriage-asia.

Cooney, Jessica. 2016. "Human Trafficking and Migration in Central Asia: Two Tales of Ordeal." U.S. Agency for International Development, September 30. Accessed December 15, 2019. https://medium.com/usaid-2030/human-trafficking-and-migration-in-central-asia-two-tales-of-ordeal-acf9a87454d0.

Custer, Charles. 2019. "Dating in China . . . Helicopter Parents in Tow." ThoughtCo, August 16. Accessed January 14, 2020. https://www.thoughtco.com/dating-in-china-whats-different-687348.

Dalby, Liza. 2008. *Geisha*. Updated with a new preface. Berkeley: University of California Press.

Dost, Zaynab. 2017. "Fighting Human Trafficking in Central Asia: Problems and Challenges." *Central Asian Bureau for Analytical Reporting*. January 26. Accessed January 10, 2020. https://cabar.asia/en/zaynab-dost-fighting-human-trafficking-in-central-asia-problems-and-challenges.

Dragadze, Tamara. 1993. "The Domestication of Religion under Soviet Communism." *Socialism: Ideals, Ideologies, and Local Practice* 31: 141.

Ebrey, Patricia. n.d. "Women in Traditional China." Asia Society. Accessed December 20, 2019. https://asiasociety.org/education/women-traditional-china.

Engel, John W. 1984. "Marriage in the People's Republic of China: Analysis of a New Law." *Journal of Marriage and the Family* 46 (4): 955–61. https://doi.org/10.2307/352547.

Global Slavery Index. 2018. "Asia and the Pacific." Accessed January 14, 2020. https://www.globalslaveryindex.org/2018/findings/regional-analysis/asia-and-the-pacific.

Greenwood, Jocelyn. 2013. "Geisha: A History of an Empowered Group." *Footnotes* 6: 97–106.

Guterman, Mark A., Payal Mehta, and Margaret S. Gibbs. 2007. "Menstrual Taboos among Major Religions." *Internet Journal of World Health and Societal Politics* 5, no. 2 (December 31). Accessed April 30, 2020. https://www.ispub.com/IJWH/5/2/8213.

Hare, Denise, Li Yang, and Daniel Englander. 2008. "Land Management in Rural China and Its Gender Implications." *Feminist Economics* 13, nos. 3–4: 35–61. https://doi.org/10.1080/13545700701445298.

Hare-Mustin, Rachel, T. 1982. "China's Marriage Law: A Model for Family Responsibilities and Relationships." *Family Process* 21 (4): 477 . Accessed June 26. 2022. https://onlinelibrary.wiley.com/doi /abs/10.1111/j.1545-5300.1982.00477.x.

Higgins, Louise T., Mo Zheng, Yali Liu, and Chun Hui Sun. 2002. "Attitudes to Marriage and Sexual Behaviors: A Survey of Gender and Culture Differences in China and United Kingdom." *Sex Roles* 46, nos. 3–4: 75–89. https://doi.org/10.1023/a:1016565426011.

Hirose, Hiroko. 2013. "Consequences of A Recent Campaign of Criticism against School Sex Education in Japan." *Sex Education* 13 (6): i.

Hollingsworth, Julia. 2019. "Taiwan Legalizes Same-Sex Marriage in Historic First for Asia." CNN, May 17. Accessed April 30, 2020. https://www.cnn.com/2019/05/17/asia/taiwan-same-sex-marriage -intl/index.html.

Huang, Grace Hui-Chen, and Mary Grove. 2012. "Confucianism and Chinese Families: Values and Practices in Education." *International Journal of Humanities and Social Science* 2, no. 3 (February): 10–14. https://doi.org/10.1007/978-3-319-16390-1_3.

Hulshof, Karin. 2016. "Let's Talk about Sex: Why We Need Sexuality Education in Asia-Pacific." UNICEF East Asia & Pacific, September 1. Accessed December 20, 2019. https://blogs.unicef.org/east -asia-pacific/lets-talk-sex-need-sexuality-education-asia-pacific.

Hurst, G. Cameron, and Kitajima Masamoto. n.d. "Daily Life and Social Customs." *Encyclopedia Britannica.* Accessed December 19, 2019. https://www.britannica.com/place/Japan/Daily-life-and -social-customs#ref23318.

Jeffreys, Elaine, and Wang Pan. 2013. "The Rise of Chinese-Foreign Marriage in Mainland China, 1979-2010." *China Information* 27 (3): 347–69. http://doi.org/10.1177/0920203X13492791.

Jeffreys, Elaine, and Haiqing Yu. 2015. *Sex in China.* Cambridge: Polity.

Junko, Minamoto, and Hank Glassman. 1993. "Buddhism and the Historical Construction of Sexuality in Japan." *U.S.-Japan Women's Journal. English Supplement*, no. 5: 87–115. Accessed January 14, 2020. https://www.jstor.org/stable/42772062.

Layton, Julia. 2005. "How Geisha Work." HowStuffWorks, December 8. Accessed December 20, 2019. https://people.howstuffworks.com /geisha.htm.

Lynch, Ami. 2019. "Comfort Women." *Encyclopedia Britannica*, June 6. Accessed December 20, 2019. https://www.britannica.com/topic /comfort-women.

McGuinness, Damien. 2013. "Thousands Protest in Georgia over Gay Rights Rally." BBC News, May 17. Accessed December 20, 2019. https://www.bbc.com/news/world-europe-22571216.

Mijalković, Saša. 2014. "'Sex-Espionage' as a Method of Intelligence and Security Agencies." *Bezbednost Beograd* 56 (1): 5–22.

Mistreanu, Simina. 2019. "China's #MeToo Activists Have Transformed a Generation." Foreign Policy, January 10. Accessed April 30, 2020. https://foreignpolicy.com/2019/01/10/chinas-metoo-activists-have -transformed-a-generation.

Morrison, Thea. 2019. "Armenian PM Speaks about Necessity of Sex Education for Children." Georgia Today on the Web, May 9. Accessed December 20, 2019. http://georgiatoday.ge/news/15564/Armenian -PM-Speaks-about-Necessity-of-Sex-Education-for-Children.

Ng, Petrus, Angela Tsun, Daniel K. W. Young, and Wing-Chung Ho. 2014. "Coping with Bereavement of Widows in the Chinese Cultural Context of Hong Kong." *International Social Work* 59, no. 1 (March 24): 115–28. https://doi.org/10.1177/0020872813509395.

Noonan, R. J. 1997. *The International Encyclopedia of Sexuality*. Vol. 1. Edited by Robert T. Francoeur. New York: Continuum.

Ōgoshi, Aiko. 1993. "Women and Sexism in Japanese Buddhism: A Reexamination of Shinran's View of Women." *Japan Christian Review* 59: 19–25.

Paxton, Pamela Marie, Melanie M. Hughes, and Tiffany Barnes. 2020. *Women, Politics, and Power: A Global Perspective*. Lanham, MD: Rowman & Littlefield.

Pletcher, Kenneth. 2019. "One-Child Policy." *Encyclopedia Britannica*, November 7. Accessed December 20, 2019. https://www.britannica .com/topic/one-child-policy.

Pun, Raymond. 2015. "Modern-Day Slavery: Stories about Human Sex Trafficking and Comfort Women." New York Public Library, October 27 . Accessed December 20, 2019. https://www.nypl.org/blog/2013/04/30 /modern-day-slavery-human-trafficking-comfort-women.

Reichert, Jim. 2002. "Male Homosexuality in Modern Japan: Cultural Myths and Social Realities." *The Journal of Japanese Studies* 28 (1): 157–61. https://doi.org/10.2307/4126781.

Rodriguez, Barbara, Sofia Shakil, and Adrian Morel. 2018. "Four Things to Know about Gender-Based Violence in Asia." Asia Foundation, March 14. Accessed December 20, 2019. https://asiafoundation .org/2018/03/14/four-things-know-gender-based-violence-asia.

Rossabi, Morris. n.d. "Central Asia: A Historical Overview." Asia Society. Accessed December 20, 2019. https://asiasociety.org/central -asia-historical-overview.

Roth, Kenneth. 2018. "World Report 2018: Rights Trends in Georgia." Human Rights Watch, January 18. Accessed December 20, 2019. https://www.hrw.org/world-report/2018/country-chapters/georgia.

Shin, Kyung Rim, Hyojung Park, and Chiyoung Cha. 2011. "Sex Education during the School-Aged Years Influences Sexual Attitudes and Sexual Health in College: A Comparative Study from Korea." *Nursing & Health Sciences* 13 (3): 328–34.

Shirinian, Sanan. 2010. "Domestic Violence against Women in Armenia." United Human Rights Council, May 26. Accessed December 20, 2019. http://www.unitedhumanrights.org/2010/05/domestic-violence -against-women-in-armenia.

Solod, Darina. 2019. "In Uzbekistan, Women's Rights Are Changing—but Not Fast Enough." Open Democracy, July 4. Accessed December 20, 2019. https://www.opendemocracy.net/en/odr/uzbekistan -gender-ineaulity-violence-en.

Stack, Liam. 2017. "European Court Strikes Down Required Sterilization for Transgender People." *New York Times*, April 12. Accessed December 20, 2019. https://www.nytimes.com/2017/04/12/world /europe/european-court-strikes-down-required-sterilization-for -transgender-people.html.

Strother, Jason. 2019. "South Korea's #MeToo Movement Challenges Workplace Sexual Harassment." VOA News, November 11. Accessed December 20, 2019. https://www.voanews.com/east-asia -pacific/south-koreas-metoo-movement-challenges-workplace -sexual-harassment.

Sullivan, Patricia L. 2005. "Culture, Divorce, and Family Mediation in Hong Kong." *Family Court Review* 43, no. 1 (January): 109–23.

Swieca, Arianne. 2013. "LGBT Rights and the Long Road to Democracy in Georgia." Foreign Policy, May 17. Accessed December 20, 2019. https://foreignpolicy.com/2013/05/17/lgbt-rights-and-the-long -road-to-democracy-in-georgia.

Tai, Crystal. 2019. "Period Drama: How Asian Women Broke the Men-struation Taboo." *South China Morning Post*, April 14. Accessed January 14, 2020. https://www.scmp.com/week-asia/society/article/3005765/menstrual-misconceptions-how-asian-attitudes-towards-periods-are.

Taylor, Alan. 2014. "Japan in the 1950s." *The Atlantic*, March 12. Accessed December 20, 2019. https://www.theatlantic.com/photo/2014/03/japan-in-the-1950s/100697.

TGEU. 2019. "Trans Rights Europe & Central Asia Map & Index 2019." October 1. Accessed January 14, 2020. https://tgeu.org/trans-rights-europe-central-asia-map-index-2019.

Third Committee. 2011. "With Equal Rights, Empowerment, Women Can Be 'Agents of Change' for Sustained Socio-Economic Develop-ment, Security around World, Third Committee Told." United Nations, October 11. Accessed December 20, 2019. https://www.un.org/press/en/2011/gashc4009.doc.htm.

UNESCO (United Nations Educational, Scientific and Cultural Organiza-tion). 2019. "Women's Rights: Between East and West, the Case of Azerbaijan." July 6. Accessed January 9, 2020. https://en.unesco.org/news/womens-rights-between-east-and-west-case-azerbaijan.

UNESCO (United Nations Educational, Scientific and Cultural Organiza-tion). n.d. "Did You Know? The Role of Women in Central Asian Nomadic Society." Accessed January 14, 2020. https://en.unesco.org/silkroad/content/did-you-know-role-women-central-asian-nomadic-society.

UNFPA (United Nations Population Fund). 2015a. "Combatting Violence against Women and Girls in Eastern Europe and Central Asia." *United Nations Population Fund, Regional Issue Brief*, no. 6, 1–15. Accessed May 11, 2020. https://eeca.unfpa.org/sites/default/files/pub-pdf/21770%20Brief_web.pdf.

UNFPA (United Nations Population Fund). 2015b. *Sexual and Reproduc-tive Health of Young People in Asia and the Pacific: A Review of Issues, Policies, and Programmes*. Bangkok: UNFPA.

United Nations Development Programme. 2018. "#HearMeToo: Activists in Central Asia Break Ground in Fight against Violence." Accessed January 9, 2020. https://www.eurasia.undp.org/content/rbec/en/home/stories/hearmetoo-activists-in-central-asia-break-ground-in-fight-agains.html.

United Nations Economic and Social Commission for Asia and the Pacific. 2018. "Advancing Gender Equality and Universal Access to Sexual and Reproductive Health and Reproductive Rights." Accessed May 11, 2020. https://www.un.org/development/desa/pd/sites/www.un.org.development.desa.pd/files/escap_appc_2018_3.pdf.

United Nations Office on Drugs and Crime. 2016. "Global Report on Trafficking in Persons 2016." Accessed July 28, 2022. https://www.unodc.org/unodc/en/data-and-analysis/glotip_2016.html.

UN Women. 2019. "16 Days of Activism against Gender-Based Violence: What We Do." Accessed May 11, 2020. https://www.unwomen.org/en/what-we-do/ending-violence-against-women/take-action/16-days-of-activism.

U.S. Department of State Publication Office of the Under Secretary for Civilian Security, Democracy, and Human Rights. 2019. "Trafficking in Persons Report." Last modified June, 2019. Accessed January 9, 2020. https://www.state.gov/wp-content/uploads/2019/06/2019-Trafficking-in-Persons-Report.pdf.

Van Brunnersum, Melissa Sou-Jie. 2019. "Virginity and Menstruation Myths behind Asia's Tampon Taboo." DW, October 15. Accessed December 20, 2019. https://www.dw.com/en/virginity-and-menstruation-myths-behind-asias-tampon-taboo/a-50841434.

VICE Intl. n.d. "China's Webcam Industry Is a Modern-Day Gold Rush." VICE Digital. Accessed June 26, 2022. https://video.vice.com/en_us/video/chinas-webcam-industry-is-a-modern-day-gold-rush/5900bcba7e9e5f93224e38bb.

Watanabe, Akira, and Shigeki Hijino. 2020. "Daily Life and Social Customs." *Encyclopedia Britannica*. Accessed January 9, 2020. https://www.britannica.com/place/Japan/Daily-life-and-social-customs.

World Health Organization. 2018. "Family Planning/Contraception." Last modified February 8, 2018. Accessed January 9, 2020. https://www.who.int/news-room/fact-sheets/detail/family-planning-contraception.

World Trade Press. 2010. *South Korea Women in Culture, Business & Travel: A Profile of Korean Women in the Fabric of Society*. Petaluma, CA: World Trade Press.

Yang, Yifan. 2019. "Bargaining with the State: The Empowerment of Chinese Sexual Minorities/LGBT in the Social Media Era." *Journal of Contemporary China*, no. 118, 662. https://doi.org/10.1080/1067 0564.2018.1557943.

Zuo, X., C. Lou, E. Gao, Q. Lian, and I. H. Shah. 2018. "Gender Role Attitudes, Awareness and Experiences of Non-Consensual Sex among University Students in Shanghai, China." *Reproductive Health* 15 (49). https://doi.org/10.1186/s12978-018-0491-x.

SEVEN

South Asia and Southeast Asia

Kathleen Nadeau and Sangita Rayamajhi

INTRODUCTION

South Asia is the southern region of Asia and comprises eight countries, namely, Afghanistan, Bangladesh, Bhutan, India, Maldives, Nepal, Pakistan, and Sri Lanka. The region is surrounded by West Asia, Central Asia, East Asia, Southeast Asia, and the Indian Ocean. It is a region where cultural and religious values and beliefs merge and/or exist in tandem with each other. The major religions adopted are Hinduism, Islam, Buddhism, Christianity, Sikhism, and Jainism. Southeast Asia is situated north of Australia, south of East Asia, west of the Pacific Ocean and east of the Bay of Bengal. The region comprises countries including Brunei, Cambodia, Thailand, Vietnam, Malaysia, Myanmar, the Philippines, and Singapore. The most widely practiced religion in Southeast Asia is Islam, and people of these countries relate to it in a variety of ways, often mingling tradition with religion. Besides Islam, Buddhism and Christianity are also practiced and coexist with other lesser-practiced religions. To address women's sexuality in these two regions, one must first recognize that Asian definitions and practices are both similar to and distinct from Western conceptions of sexuality.

BRIEF HISTORY OF WOMEN IN THIS REGION

The social and cultural norms regarding women's sexuality and gender roles in many of the countries of this geographically and culturally diverse part of the world have been influenced by different religious, philosophical, and indigenous spiritualities. Hinduism, Confucianism, Islam, Christianity, and other traditional beliefs and practices are factors in local constructions of sex and gender hierarchies, norms, and values. Concepts of femininity and masculinity are historically and culturally constructed and subject to change.

Anthropological evidence suggests that there was greater gender equality across regional South and Southeast Asia in ancient times (Banu 2016). Women held politically prestigious positions in early India, as alliterated in the Vedas, the oldest Hindu scriptures (1700–500 BCE), and while the importance of women's roles in the previous Indus Valley civilization (2300–1700 BCE) has yet to be determined, numerous figurines of female goddesses have been excavated (Nadeau and Rayamajhi 2013, 10). There are documented cases of women in Southeast Asia wielding great power and authority, as queens ruling kingdoms (queendoms) in their own right (Andaya-Watson 2006). Mothers, daughters, and wives of important political figures, typically, participated in politics as peacemakers and go-betweens. European colonization, from the 16th century to the latter part of the mid-20th century, dramatically changed their status and position. Religious dancers, courtesans, concubines, female shamans, healers, and midwives, earlier held in high esteem, suddenly were disparaged and assigned a lower social status by the colonizers (Levine 2003). The latter's value judgments on, for example, purdah (hiding women from public view) and sati (wife burning) in India, painted a picture of these women as being backward in relation to so-called modern Western women. Some Western scholars made gross generalizations based on mistaken notions about the inherent characteristics and personalities of pan-Asian women. They portrayed them as being overly exotic, mysterious, and hypersexual, and their sexuality was connected to some ancient mystical past. Edward Said, a well-known and respected scholar, referred to this kind of stereotyping, as "orientalization." Orientalization is the way in which early Europeans, including those from Europe and North America, came to dominate, control, and restructure the societies and cultures of South and Southeast Asia by reimagining them into their own culturally biased and fictitious images (Nadeau and Rayamajhi 2013, 2). Thus, as histories merged, geographical and societal boundaries fluctuated, and political alliances forged—with or without the support of the colonizers—roles of women, too, began to change.

South Asia and Southeast Asia are two different and separate world regions marked by significant differences in family structures and societies.

In South Asia, the dominant model of the family derives from the patrilineal/patrilocal system. Lines of descent trace back through the male side of the family. Traditionally, upon marriage, the female leaves her birth family to join the extended family of her husband. There are exceptions: the matrilineal/matrilocal Nayar, Garos, and Khasi tribes of India, where the family lines are traced through women and inheritances are passed down to subsequent generations through daughters (von Ehrenfels 1971). In Southeast Asia, the bilineal and bilateral family model is more prevalent, where the nuclear family traces its descent through male and female lines; both sons and daughters can inherit land and properties upon the death of their parents, and bilateral ties uniting the husband's and wife's extended families, horizontally in the present, are most highly valued (Nadeau 2003a, b). Again, some matrilineal and patrilocal exceptions apply in the various social, cultural, and regional contexts of Southeast Asia, the most famous being the matrilineal Minangkabau of Indonesia, the second-largest matrilineal population in the world (Lam 2016). Thailand, largely, also is a matrilineal and matrilocal society, although authority typically rests with a senior male member of the family household (Lim 2011). Similarly, in Indonesia, where the bilineal family is common, usually the eldest male is still considered to be the patriarch. Southeast Asia, in large part, is locally perceived to be a patriarchal region (Kreager and Schroder-Butterfill 2008).

CULTURE AND ATTITUDES TOWARD SEXUALITY

The social institution of the family entails particular cultural and religious expectations and ideologies that are rooted in social values and norms and religious values and sanctions. Banu (2016, 3) documented that gender disparities, especially in South Asian countries such as Bangladesh, India, and Sri Lanka, as well as Pakistan to a lesser degree, are not correlated with income poverty: "Many studies show that often there is no correlation between per capita income and gender disparities in health and education outcomes." Rather, gender inequalities between women and men, between girls and boys, are formed in the family and household. She explained that many local women find themselves in subordinate positions to men, dependent socially, culturally, and economically. Often they are excluded from making decisions, have limited access to and control over how resources are used, and are not allowed to come and go freely. Many also live under the threat of violence from male relatives and sometimes from female relatives and in-laws. Son preference is widespread, and

The dowry system is commonly practiced in India and involves a transfer of money from the bride's to the groom's family, prior to or during the wedding. In many cases, the payment turns into a form of extortion wherein the bridegroom's family continues to ask for financial benefits from the bride's family well into the future. Such practices lead to other social ills, including sex selective abortions and violence against the wife and/or daughter-in-law. In order to halt these negative outcomes, the Dowry Prohibition Act was passed in 1961; however, it has not been effective, because many families, especially in the Hindu community, consider dowries to represent status; therefore the practice continues.

women often are considered to be a liability, due to the dowry system (Banu 2016, 4). "Dowry," defined from a Hindu perspective, refers to cash and kind that flows from the bride's family to that of the groom as a condition of the marriage.

Women who are subordinated to men are often viewed as playing a sexually subservient role and reduced to their biological bodies. The wife is there to fulfill her husband's sexual desires, without regard for her own, and to produce a male heir. The power imbalance in the patriarchal structure of the household allows men to dominate women (Nadeau and Rayamajhi 2013, 87). In this instance, women are not differentiated from each other in terms of class, caste, and ethnicity but differentiated only from the men, thereby sustaining a gendered inequality. In the public sphere, which includes the media and pornography, women are reduced to objects, their bodies sexualized and portrayed as being used for the benefit of others. When women are presented in this fashion and on such a grand scale, instances of abuse, including harassment, rape, incest, trafficking, prostitution, and other human rights violations, become normalized (Blitt 1996). Through this process of hypersexualization and subordination, the fight for women's rights is hindered, and progress toward gender equality is slowed.

RELIGION AND SEXUALITY

Marriage and sexuality across the region are largely influenced by religion. For example, among the Buddhists of Thailand, sexuality is neither perceived as sinful nor something requiring justification based on

This image shows a Malaysian dowry, which is transferred from the bride's family to the groom's upon marriage. (Mohd Haniff Abas/Dreamstime. com)

reproduction (Sponberg 2005). Suwanbubbha (2003) notes that sexual activities, which represent human desires, can only reinforce unenlightened tendencies. Most of the time, Buddhist supporters advocate for the avoidance of having too many children that could subsequently lead to poverty. A common belief among Buddhists about sexuality and fertility is that "they should focus on spreading the joy of enlightenment [the value of a small family] to others, while transmitting their genes to subsequent generations or extending their family lineage is less important" (Childs et al. 2005; Gross 1995). In Thailand, the Buddhist women have slowly reduced their fertility over time, and today, they have a lower fertility rate than local Muslim and Christian women (Suwanbubbha 2003).

By contrast, the Philippines, a predominantly Roman Catholic country, has the highest birth rate in Asia (Velasco 2018, 1). According to World Bank data, the fertility rate (total births per woman) in the Philippines was reported at 2.92 in 2017 (https://data.worldbank.org). More than 80% of the local population are Roman Catholics, and the church is one of the Philippines' most powerful institutions, holding enormous political clout and sway over social policy, including family planning (Weisshaar 2008). Natividad (2013) documented that local teenage pregnancies have steadily increased over the past 35 years. She found that Filipina teenage mothers were predominantly poor, resided in rural areas, and had low educational attainment. However, there coincided a "trend of increasing proportions of teenagers who are not poor and who have a better education, and are residents in urban areas, who also have begun childbearing in their teens" (Natividad 2013, 1). Accordingly, among the factors that contribute to explaining this trend are the younger age of menarche, premarital sex activity at a younger age, the rise of cohabiting unions in this age group, and the possible decrease in stigma of out-of-wedlock pregnancy.

SEXUAL VIOLENCE

Violence against women is a global phenomenon. The primary reason that violence is perpetrated against women is the desire for power. The UN Convention on the Elimination of all Forms of Discrimination against Women (CEDAW) adopted an international treaty in 1979 that came into effect on September 3, 1981. It was described as the international bill of rights of women. This declaration states that "violence against women is a manifestation of historically unequal power relations between men and women" and "one of the crucial social mechanisms by which women are forced into a subordinate position compared with men." There are different forms of violence against women, and often the boundary between violence and nonphysical coercion is indistinguishable. Common practices adversely affecting the well-being of women include dowry violence, rape, trafficking, female genital mutilation (FGM)—which refers to the partial or total removal of the external female genitalia or other injury to the female organ for nonmedical reasons—forced marriage, and sexual harassment. In addition to these risk factors, in South Asia, parents prefer sons over daughters because sons typically care for parents in their old age, and sons open the door to heaven for the parents. Only a son is allowed to light the funeral pyre upon a parent's death. With the birth of a son, parents are relieved of the dowry burden that must be given to daughters' (brides') new families. These cultural beliefs and practices lead parents to perform prenatal sex discrimination tests and subsequent female feticide and infanticide. Girl-child marriage is a prevalent practice in Bangladesh, Nepal, Pakistan, and Afghanistan.

The dowry system is widespread in India, Bangladesh, and parts of Nepal. When girls are married, they take with them a certain amount of wealth in cash and kind to their new homes, depending on the status and inclination of their family. Typically, the power relationship between husbands and wives and the family relates to this wealth, or dowry. The dowry practice, mainly, is the cause of local domestic violence, which may take the form of physical or nonphysical abuse, including, in extreme cases, bride burning (e.g., "kitchen accidents," as when a mother-in-law intentionally pushes the daughter-in-law against the stove, catching her sari aflame) or widow burning (when in-laws push her but say she jumped of her own accord into the funeral pyre to avoid further living expenses) (Nadeau and Rayamajhi 2019, 193). Traditionally, after a woman marries, she is considered the property of her husband and his extended family. She moves out of her birth family's home and into that of her husband. Often, in-laws expect a steady flow of wealth (dowry) over the next few years, and when this does not occur, a mother-in-law may begin to increasingly mistreat her son's wife in an effort to get more money from her parents. Dowry violence is institutionalized in many forms, for example, compelling a daughter-in-law to work for long hours doing household chores or working outside in the fields, denying her adequate food, refusing to give her medical treatments, or physically and verbally abusing her (Nadeau and Rayamajhi 2013, 95).

Honor killings are used to exercise control over female sexuality and are common in the Muslim countries of Pakistan and Afghanistan, as well as in Muslim communities in India. Honor killing is defined as intentionally committed or attempted homicides perpetrated against females to reinforce patriarchal dominance, under the guise of traditional values and family honor (Nadeau and Rayamajhi 2019, 81). It is a common misperception to connect honor killings with the religion of Islam; although they often happen in South Asian Muslim countries and communities, they do not occur in Indonesia, located in Southeast Asia, which has the world's largest Muslim population. Some honor killings are carried out in an act of revenge, such as when a woman refuses to be forced into an arranged marriage, perhaps because she has become involved with a man the family disapproves of or simply because she has become too westernized. Despite many organizations working for the welfare and empowerment of women around the world and especially in Asia, the high rates of "honor killings" have not declined significantly. Srivastava observes that "the Pakistani states adoption of the British Penal Code of 1860 with its masculinist and patriarchal biases, the implicit endorsement by the contemporary legal system of

Honor killings involve intentionally murdering women under guise of protecting traditional family values and honor. This photo shows a Chinese emperor killing his daughter. The practice remains common across several Asian countries and is even on the rise in Pakistan. (Rare Book Division, The New York Public Library. "Chinese emperor killing his daughter," New York Public Library Digital Collections. Accessed March 29, 2022. https://digitalcollections.nypl.org/items /8e05fc20-286c-0131-d0b9-58d385a7b928)

customary attitudes towards women, and the history of 'Islamization' under General Zia's rule have all contributed to the present state of affairs" (2013, 9).

Srivastava gives an example of an honor crime where an elderly man killed his young wife after finding her in a compromising position with another man. The girl's own family was involved in the attack and murder. The court did not convict them on any criminal counts or charge the elderly husband for marrying a teenager. The legal age of marriage for girls is 16, while it is 18 for boys in Pakistan (Ijaz 2018, 1). As is the case with many honor crimes, the parents and other family members were equally brutal in the attack leading to the girl's death. In order to justify these crimes, a masculinist argument is promoted, suggesting that such crimes further demonstrate the disgrace brought to the family. Honor killings are on the rise in Pakistan, and Warraich (2005, 96) notes that "cases of convictions are nominal."

Sex Trafficking and Female Feticide

The practice of female infanticide is prevalent around South Asia. In Nepal, there is a common saying: "If a boy is born, cut a goat; if a daughter is born, cut a squash" (Nadeau and Rayamajhi 2013, 87). The conventional thinking is that girls are born to be fed throughout their lifetimes, while boys are born to earn and support the whole family (Niaz and Hassan 2006). Sex selection during pregnancy, which is achieved, mainly, through abortion of female fetuses, is especially common in Hindu India. For example, the practice of female infanticide is widespread in a number of districts in Tamil Nadu. Data from primary health-care records on female infant deaths due to "social causes" (a euphemism for female infanticide) show that an average of 3,000 cases of female infanticide occur every year in Tamil Nadu (Srinivasan and Bedi 2010, 17). In many Muslim households in Pakistan, women are under pressure from their husbands and in-laws to produce a male baby. There are even instances of some women who are forced by their elders, especially mothers-in-law, to keep on giving birth until they produce a boy. In the process, a woman may end up giving birth to five or six girls before a boy is born (Nadeau and Raya-mahji 2013, 87).

In South Asia, social exclusion based on gender discrimination puts women at increased risk for trafficking. The patriarchal structure of the family has traditionally privileged boys when it comes to providing an education and allowing the use valuable household resources, although there are instances of better-off families affording daughters an education. In rural areas, parents tend to require female children to work at home or in the fields as a means of helping the family survive. Girls usually lack status within the family and community, and without access to education and general privileges, they also tend to be excluded from politics and denied access to health care (Human Rights Watch 2018; Pennington et al. 2018).

In South Asia, most of the girls and women are trafficked from Bangladesh, Nepal, and Pakistan, with India being the destination country. In addition to in-country trafficking, these girls and women are taken to other destinations within Asia and even to Europe and the Middle East. For example, young Nepali girls from the rural hills are lured by mediators into marrying men from neighboring China (Dhungana 2019). China's one-child policy, which has been repealed, has greatly impacted the socio-cultural fabric of Chinese society and disrupted the sex ratio. According to the 2015 census (as reported by Dhungana 2019, 1), "the sex ratio at birth was 113.5 boys for every 100 girls." The young girls are lured on the pretext of getting married to wealthy Chinese men. In 2015, the police arrested traffickers at Tribhuvan International Airport, rescuing 6 women who were being sent to Korea and China. The Chinese men paid as much

From 1980 to 2016, the Chinese government held a one-child policy that limited families to one child each. The patriarchal system favored boys, leading to increased rates of females being aborted, placed into orphanages, and abandoned. (Rafael Ben Ari/Dreamstime.com)

as "1.5 million [Indian Rupees] to marry Nepali women" and also to buy expensive gifts worth approximately 60,000 Nepali rupees for each potential bride. Until a decade or so ago, in Southeast Asia, girls and women were trafficked to China from Cambodia and Vietnam, but since those countries have revised their security measures, the traffickers are now targeting India, Pakistan, Bangladesh, and Nepal. Even though the Chinese men legally marry the trafficked girls, once in China, these girls are sold again and again to be used as unpaid laborers and sex slaves. Or they are repeatedly raped and held against their will. This latter strategy is used to impregnate the girls and provide an heir to the family.

Bangladesh also is used as a transit and destination country for the trafficking of young boys, girls, and women for forced labor and sex trade. To add to the already flourishing sex trade in Bangladesh, there is the added problem of thousands of Rohingya fleeing Myanmar into Bangladesh. The Rohingya community, with a stateless status, are kept in refugee camps in Cox's Bazaar in Bangladesh: "Rohingya women and girls are reportedly recruited from refugee camps for domestic work in private homes, guest houses, or hotels and are instead subjected to sex trafficking. Rohingya girls are also reportedly transported within Bangladesh to Chittagong and Dhaka and transnationally to Kathmandu and Kolkata and subjected to sex trafficking—some of these girls are 'traded' between traffickers over the internet. Some Rohingya women and girls report being subjected to sex trafficking by other Rohingya through fraudulent job or marriage proposals" (U.S. Department of State 2018, 8).

Most of these women who are recruited with other boys and men who work in stores, as fishermen, or as rickshaw pullers, are made to work as domestic helpers. But they are paid the minimum wage or not paid at all, forced to work long hours, and barred from communicating with their families (U.S. Department of State 2018).

Even though the trafficking of girls and women has been reduced in Cambodia and Vietnam compared to the past few decades, The U.S. State Department's 2018 "Trafficking in Persons Report" documented that these countries barely meet the minimum standard set by the U.S. law to combat trafficking. In spite of the increase in awareness about trafficking and the anti-awareness programs in provinces and local communities, the report explained that no "significant efforts" were made by the government to eliminate trafficking. Human trafficking for labor and the sex trade has been an ongoing problem in South and Southeast Asia. In Cambodia, sex trafficking has been described in the local press as "a lot easier and more lucrative than drug smuggling" (*Post* Staff 2000, 1). Girls from Vietnam are sold into brothels in Cambodia:

In Cambodia, women and men, children and old people alike are trafficked every day. Some are abducted and sold into forms of slavery for as little as $30. Others pay hundreds of dollars to people-smugglers who promise them a better, brighter future somewhere else. Almost all end up in precarious situations, exploited by rich and powerful trafficking lords.

The stream of the human trade flows in all directions. Young girls are brought from their villages in the provinces to brothels in Phnom Penh. . . . Vietnamese girls are bought to join their Cambodian sisters in the brothels. And Eastern European women are lured into working as nightclub escort girls—like the five Romanian and two Moldovan girls rescued from the Best Western Cangi Hotel on August 13. (*Post* Staff 2000, 1)

Though the traffickers are sometimes prosecuted, such prosecutions are rare. In November 2000, the Palermo Protocol to Prevent, Suppress and Punish Trafficking in Persons Especially Women and Children, which supplemented the United Nations Convention Against Transnational Organized Crime, was adopted. This was a very significant step in the movement against trafficking. The Protocol used "Trafficking in Persons" as an umbrella term that covered all types of trafficking offenses, from forced labor to commercial sexual exploitation. Since its adoption, it has become easier for governments of various countries to form their policies "to criminalize human trafficking and stop traffickers, protect victims and prevent victimization, and promote cooperation among countries" (U.S. Department of State 2019, 1).

REPRODUCTIVE HEALTH AND MENSTRUATION

The experiences of females in South Asia and Southeast Asia have undergone an abundance of change regarding reproductive health issues in recent times. A mere few decades ago, many young South Asian female adolescents, after their first period, or menarche, would be arranged into a marriage and have their first sexual encounter with their husband and would at some point thereafter become mothers (Nadeau and Rayamajhi 2013, chapter 3). For girls, education was not a priority, because early marriage and childbearing were the traditional norm. There has always been a gender imbalance in South Asia, where education and employment opportunities are not the same for young men and women. Young girls face family pressures to get married at an early age. Once married, they are encouraged to prove their fertility by getting pregnant. Most of the time, the childbearing gap is closely spaced, particularly when a girl is the first-born, due to preferences for a son over a daughter. This trend holds in many rural areas even today, but it is changing in urban cities, where a majority of girls complete high school and even college and tend to marry later in life. Due to their delayed marriage, young females often become sexually active before marriage. However, vast differences in these practices exist for the women because of cultural diversity and unique, individual differences.

Surveys on family planning conducted by Pachauri and Santhya (2002) in South Asia (i.e., Bangladesh, India, Nepal, Pakistan, Sri Lanka) and Southeast Asia (i.e., Indonesia, the Philippines, Thailand, Vietnam) show that couples who use contraceptives tend to have smaller families. But with early marriage practices in South Asia, early childbearing is the norm. This trend is especially common in Bangladesh, India, and Nepal, and while early marriage is generally frowned upon in Southeast Asia, teenage pregnancy rates are high in a few countries. "Sixty percent of currently married adolescent girls in the Philippines are mothers. Similarly, 52% of currently married teenage girls in Indonesia and 45% of those in Vietnam have had a child" (National Statistics Office/Philippines, Department of Health, Philippines, and Macro International 1998; National Committee for Population and Family Planning 1997).

In recent years, many local government and nongovernment organizations have begun to focus on special health programs relating to reproductive health to address the changing patterns of sex and sexuality among young girls and boys. Sex education is provided in the schools, and students, parents, teachers, and communities are all encouraged to be involved. Radio programs raise further awareness regarding reproductive health and action plans and are used as a means for reaching a larger audience, including those residing in rural areas. In spite of the strategies implemented by the region's respective governments and institutions, sex education and the use of family planning methods vary greatly from country to country (National Statistics Office/Philippines, Department of Health, Philippines, and Macro International 1998).

The subject of women and sexuality unfailingly raises the issues of abortion and sexually transmitted infections (STIs) and diseases (STDs). In Thailand in recent decades, there has been a decline in the case of abortions, HIV/AIDs, and STDs. Thailand is known for its sex tourism and has been focusing on safe sex practices since the late 20th century, when the country experienced a spike in cases of STDs. The need for higher education coupled with increasingly low marriage rates are causing women to engage in unmarried sexual relations. For men, fear of infection from commercial sex workers is motivating them to engage in noncommercial unmarried sex (VanLandingham and Trujillo 2002). Although commercial sex patronage by local men is declining in Thailand, the country continues to be a destination for sex tourism.

In the Philippines, abortion is legally prohibited, thus giving rise to unsafe abortions that lead to complications and subsequent deaths. Abortion was criminalized through the Penal Code of 1870, under the Spanish Colonial Rule (1521–1898), and later incorporated into the Revised Penal Code, under the U.S. occupation (1898–1946) of the Philippines. According to Juarez et al. (2005, 140), in 2000, 78,900 women were hospitalized for postabortion care, and 473,400 women had abortions, or 27 abortions per 1,000 women aged 15 to 44 years old. The proportion of unplanned births and pregnancies rose substantially, as did the use of traditional contraception methods (rhythm, withdrawal, and plants and herbs) in Manila and Visayas (central Philippines). In spite of the country's law against abortion, the practice is prevalent. As with other countries in the region, wealthier women find ways to carry out the procedure safely, whereas those with a lower socioeconomic background engage in more traditional and unsafe practices. This is largely because consulting nurses and doctors for medical advice is expensive, and since abortion is prohibited by law, women likely worry about the ramifications of consulting with a medical professional. Given that abortion is punishable by law, it is rarely reported. There is countrywide concern among social scientists, medical professionals, and legislators, and yet abortion remains illegal, and the rate of abortion has not declined. In rural areas, traditional abortion practices and the lack of postabortion care leads to greater numbers of deaths than in urban regions. At the same time, women and men of reproductive age lack awareness. Sex education is barely offered in schools, and no information is imparted by the government, nor is counseling provided.

Vietnam has one of the highest rates of abortion in the world. Bich (1999, 193) writes that "as many as 1,700 abortions per 1,000 live births [occurred] when the rates peaked in the mid-to-late 1990s." Most of the women seeking abortions were either married between the ages of 25 and 40 or teenage girls. In 1992, the "total abortion rate for the country was at least 2.5 per woman" (Croll 2000, 48). The government has a family policy of allowing one or two children per family. The preference for sons in Vietnam, as well as the countries of South Asia, contributes to abortion. While children of both sexes are treasured in the Philippines, government sex education campaigns in schools are rare. Sexually active youths'

A main reason for the lower fertility rate in Vietnam is the rise in abortions. For many decades, Vietnam had a two-child policy, and very little information was provided to the public about reproductive health. Schools did not offer sex education, and parents avoided talking to their children about it. Additionally, there was no free health care provided in the country. Youth therefore resorted to abortion as a form of birth control. In recent years, circumstances have improved. Health information is now freely provided, and contraceptives are widely available. Despite these changes, abortion rates remain high compared to other countries in the region.

questions regarding sex and sexuality go unanswered. The reasons for terminating pregnancies include the reluctance to use intrauterine devices (IUDs), especially in Vietnam, and the difficulty of obtaining contraceptives in the Philippines. As Peletz (2012) explained, "IUDs are ineffective in preventing the spread of sexually transmitted diseases such as HIV/AIDS; partly for this reason, Vietnam is now confronting an alarming epidemic of HIV/AIDS; the epidemic is spreading to the general population, though it is currently concentrated among sex workers, their clients, and their clients' regular partners on the one hand, and among intravenous drug users and their partners on the other; state policies are directly implicated in high rates of abortion and HIV/AIDS alike" (900).

In Nepal, due to the later age of marriage, premarital sex and unintended pregnancies and abortions are on the rise. Abortion in Nepal was legalized in 2002. It can be carried out within 12 weeks of the gestation period, before 18 weeks if the pregnancy is the result of incest or rape, and "at any time if the pregnancy poses a danger to the woman's life or physical or mental health or if there is a fetal abnormality" (Nepal Ministry of Health 2002). However, in India, a petition was submitted to the Delhi High Court in 2019 that "challenged Section 3(2)(b) of the existing Act, demanding the pregnancy period for abortions be raised to 24–26 weeks from 20 weeks, in case of a health risk to the mother or the foetus" (Gupta 2019, 1). In more than 60 countries around the world, women have the right to abortion upon request. But in the countries of South Asia, women do not have this right except in cases of medical problems with the fetus or pregnant mother.

For many girls, menstruation is associated with pain, discomfort, anxiety, and shame. This is true especially in the rural settings of South Asia and some countries of Southeast Asia, where toilets, waste disposal, and pads and tampons are unhygienic or unavailable. Many girls in South Asian rural communities stop attending school for fear of "period shaming" or due to the lack of sanitary products. An editorial in the *Lancet Child and Adolescent Health* (2018) reported:

> Because of entrenched stigma and taboos, menstruation is rarely discussed in families or schools, and menarche often arrives suddenly to girls with little or no knowledge of what is happening. A UNICEF study showed that one in three girls in South Asia had no knowledge of menstruation before their first period, and 48% of girls in Iran thought that menstruation was a disease. Often considered a shameful, dirty, female weakness, the secrecy surrounding menstruation

has permeated every aspect of society, nurturing superstitions and taboos that are passed on between generations. In many communities, menstruating girls and women are still banned from kitchens, crop fields, or places of worship. (379)

At the same time, after the girls reach menarche, their freedom is curtailed in urban and rural areas throughout South Asia and Southeast Asia. In the Islamic country of Pakistan, for example, menstrual periods are as much a taboo as in India and Nepal, where the citizens are predominantly Hindu. According to an AFP news report (2019), menstruating women in Pakistan are viewed as unclean and permitted to perform only certain household tasks during the menstruating days. In this conservative country, information about menstruation is deliberately withheld from young girls in order to protect their chastity. According to the same report, girls within a single household typically share the same menstrual rags and pieces of the same fabrics, which increases the risks of contracting urinary and reproductive tract infections. In northern Pakistan, which is more conservative than the other parts of the country, menstruation is not discussed openly. Even among women, the issue is rarely discussed; many do not know about menstruation prior to their own commencement; consequently, some believe they have contracted a disease or fallen ill. Only recently have children started receiving sex education in the schools (Fioriti and Khan 2019).

In a photo essay, Andrew Kratz addressed the Hindu practice of *Chaupadi* in Nepal. Since menstruation is considered impure, as in Pakistan, in the far western region of Nepal, menstruating girls and women are relegated to spend six or seven days in makeshift huts in the middle of fields or elsewhere, far away from the home. This practice endangers these girls and women, who are exposed to wild animals and snakes and experience assault and abduction by boys and men. When it is time for meals, food is brought by a member of the household and thrown to the girl/woman from afar. During this time, girls and women are not allowed to socialize or share their food. They are "forced away from public space and barred from using the main water source" (Katz 2014, 1), while others die from "asphyxiation or fire when trying to ward off the cold" (Katz 2014, 1). According to Cousins (2019, 1), some women, including girls as young as 12, were sent to small cubicles, the size of closets, with little room to move around in to help ward off the cold Himalayan nights. This practice of Chaupadi is deeply rooted in tradition (Himalayan News Service 2017). In traditional Hindu families, menstruating women are not allowed to enter the kitchen or the *puja* (worship) room. In traditional Muslim households, as well, menstruating females are considered to be unclean and not allowed to participate in *namaj* (prayer); however, they may enter the kitchen to prepare and cook family meals. Nepal's Supreme Court banned the practice of Chaupadi in 2005, but the segregation of menstruating women and girls remains prevalent in both rural and urban (Cousins 2019, 1).

MARRIAGE AND PARTNERSHIP

Marriage for women is culturally encouraged, and women are expected to ultimately get married. Unmarried women are still stigmatized in both rural and urban areas (Nadeau and Rayamajhi 2013, chapter 3). Though the practice is considered socially inappropriate, cohabiting unions are becoming increasingly popular among youth across the region. Intergenerational living arrangements of grown-up children and aging parents are common. However, in recent years, economic development, declining family size, and migration of adult children have caused the practice of extended intergenerational co-living to decline. Nuclear families are more common, especially in urban settings, although in the Philippine case, urban families often welcome rural-to-urban migrant relatives to move in and live together until they get financially settled enough to form a household of their own. Despite recent gains in women's rights and freedoms, young girls often are socialized to focus on their sexuality. In South Asia, "mothers become extra watchful when their daughters reach puberty. It is a markedly significant rite of passage in an adolescent woman's life and a woman who has reached puberty begins to be closely scrutinized by her mother, family members and society at large" (Nadeau and Rayamajhi 2013, 88). This transition of a South Asian girl into womanhood can therefore be stressful and difficult.

In countries such as India, Nepal, the Philippines, Malaysia, and Singapore, the population of single youth is on the rise, and the later age of marriage is closely related to urbanization, educational and job opportunities, and improved status, especially for women. According to Greenspan (1992, 1), the average age of marriage has risen from 15 years old to 18 and 19 years old for women and men, respectively. Dating and the choice of spouse is more liberal today, except in countries such as Afghanistan, Pakistan, and Bangladesh, where in most cases, marital choices are left to the parents. In India, Hindu and Muslim families typically expected girls to preserve their reputation as a demonstration of the family's honor. Such a traditional, so-called honorable family would not willingly allow women to have sex before marriage. Nevertheless, due to globalization, which has brought about unprecedented employment opportunities for new millennials of both sexes to work side by side, usually on the night shift (incidentally), in international call centers in, for example, India and the Philippines, premarital sexual relationships are on the rise. Working women, such as those operating the factories in the export processing zones of the Philippines, Malaysia, and Indonesia, have more independence and freedom of mobility than did earlier generations, who would have been under the watchful eye of a chaperone. But in India's call centers, working daughters are still closely monitored and bused back and forth between home and work (De Gulla 2010).

Everywhere around the region, contemporary women's mobility has been changing and is impacting their sexuality. In the past, mostly men traveled to other countries for education and/or employment. However, this freedom has been widely extended to contemporary women across the region. Their movement can be either seasonal or can last a few years in order to send back remittance to their families. Often, women from the rural areas or marginalized social groups travel in search of employment. Many are married and leave behind children, who are in the care of their aging parents. Young Indian and Nepalese women in their 30s and 40s, for example, who go abroad for employment may not be stigmatized, but at the same time, they do not command respect for their financial contributions. Likewise, the Papuan women of Indonesia leave their rural communities for educational and employment reasons as well as to broaden their pool of romantic partners (Butt, Munro, and Numbery 2017).

Women who leave home to improve their life opportunities are at risk for various adverse outcomes. Those who engage in sexual relationships and contract HIV/AIDS often return home and may be regarded with suspicion in terms of their sexuality and their inability to succeed financially. As Butt, Munro, and Numbery (2017, 147–48) describe the situation, "mobility away from more conservative, watchful rural sites opens up the possibility of women making decisions, however constrained, about sex and relationships in ways that challenge norms of patriarchal dominance over women's sexual engagements." Many Asian women go to the Middle East and Israel to work as domestic helpers or caregivers in hospices or the homes of senior citizens. In many cases, women household helpers have been subjected to domestic violence and had their sexuality compromised, especially in the Middle Eastern countries. Human Rights Watch (2006, 1) documented cases of female domestic workers who are starved, confined to their rooms, sexually harassed, left unpaid (in violation of their contracts), physically abused, and worked to excess. Slama (2012) notes that "in Indonesia more broadly, conservative government and Islamic influences also strongly influence gender and sexual space along boundaries of public and domestic domains" (314; see also Robinson 2009; Davies 2015).

Traditional societal norms regarding sex, sexual behavior, and women's sexuality continue to exist across the region. Families and educational institutions exercise control over the sexual behavior of unmarried girls and women. Sex and sexuality are considered private, personal matters, never to be talked about within the family and only discussed among close friends and peers. In academia, gender and sexuality are increasingly becoming popular and significant as areas of study (Rayamajhi, personal observation, 2019). South Asia is a region where sex and sexualities play pivotal roles in churning out important anecdotes, which are evoked to demonstrate the origins of sexuality. For example, several ancient Hindu epics in the Ramayana and Mahabharata include a story of King Ila, who was cursed by Shiva and Parvati, to alternate between being a man and a woman each month. After changing sex, he loses the memory of being the other one (*India Today* Web Desk 2018). Parents tend to shy away from educating their children about sex, and girls are especially sheltered from such information. The schools, too, in many parts of South Asia, are wary of introducing sex education and discussing sexual identities. Having school-aged and even college-aged children talk openly about sexuality poses a threat to the traditional values and interests of the society. Only a few decades ago, there was moral panic and fear about contracting STDs, including HIV/AIDS. Today, that fear and moral panic have transferred to

Even as late as 1996, Deepa Mehta's popular film *Fire* was denounced as obscene and offensive when it was shown in Indian movie theaters. The story of two women in the same household who turn to each other for emotional and physical solace and satisfaction was considered a Western phenomenon and not applicable to Indian society. Heterosexual marriage is still considered the only moral and honorable institution in the country, and LGBTQ+ identities remain in the margins of the societies not only in India but in most of the South Asia region.

concerns over sexualities: lesbians, gays, bisexuals, transgender/transsexuals, and queers (LGBTQ). This fear has become especially pronounced in South Asia.

Despite the diversity of sexual identities represented, the region is largely xenophobic, meaning that people espouse fears toward those who do not abide by heteronormative standards or fall into the realm of LGBTQ+. In the colonial past (1858–1947), "the British designated British homosexuality as the oriental vice, the result of excessive British immersion in India" (Bacchetta 2013, 123). The postcolonial world of South Asia has not yet freed itself from the hypocrisy of the bourgeois colonial mindset. But

> if repression has indeed been the fundamental link between power, knowledge, and sexuality since the classical age, it stands to reason that we will not be able to free ourselves from it except at a considerable cost: nothing less than transgression of laws, a lifting of prohibitions, an eruption of speech, a reinstating of pleasure within reality, and a whole new economy in the mechanisms of power will be required. For the least glimmer of truth is conditioned by politics. Hence, one cannot hope to attain the desired simply from medical practice, nor from a theoretical discourse, however rigorously pursued. (Bacchetta 2013, 5)

In colonial times, the policing, deterrence, and repression of nonheterosexual and transgender identities were common. The Victorian British mindset conceptualized women as passionless and sexually passive. Women had no sexual agency. The British surveillance team "carried out a scheme to prevent same-sex acts among the male British soldiers. Female prostitutes were brought in so that any form of sex-act whether inter-racial, or extra marital could be carried out as long as it was not homosexual. But the scheme failed. An act was passed in 1850 by which the homosexual would be sentenced to seven years in prison" (Ballhatchet 1980, 10).

In Nepal, current laws governing the rights of LGBTQ+ people are progressive (UNDP and USAID 2014). In academic compositions, sexual identities often are described as imported from the West, even though historical accounts, art, architecture, and literature portray otherwise—for example, the ancient Kama Sutra, recorded in music, sculpture, and dance. Nepal indirectly inherited the legacy of colonial rule in India and was impacted by the criminalization and illegalization of the sexual minorities. In early 2007, a reform was sanctioned that prohibited discrimination against nonheterosexual individuals. Ten years later, India also implemented such law. But prior to these laws, the Blue Diamond Society, an LGBTQ organization was established to promote the rights of sexual minorities. The small Himalayan country of Bhutan also had laws restricting the freedom of sexual minorities but, unlike Nepal and India, homosexuality and transgender individuals are socially recognized and accepted, even in rural areas. Nevertheless, it was not until June 8, 2019, that Bhutan's Parliament voted to decriminalize homosexuality. Despite recent reforms, LGBTQ+ community members still face considerable discrimination in their respective countries. The laws tend not to protect those targeted, and discrimination occurs in the schools (leading to LGBTQ+ dropouts) and even at the hands of the police (UNDP and USAID 2014).

MEDIA AND SEXUALITY

In the current technological and globalized media era, Asian women are often portrayed as sexual objects and used for voyeurism. The sites of consumption where women's images are projected are multifaceted and range from everyday advertisements to pornographic websites. Hypersexualized images of women are easily available, and the eroticization of women's bodies provide "open spaces" (public sites) for voluntary or nonvoluntary voyeuristic consumption. Lukose (2009) explained that such display of sexuality and its consumption signifies "the increasing sexualization of public space" and "female sexuality is the most problematic" (97). Mass media often presents women as slim, young, and beautiful, which is tailored to men's preferences. As Datyan-Gevorgyan (2016) notes, when commercials display "only slender long legs, prominent breasts or thighs, it is difficult to perceive that body holistically and as possessing personality" (1).

Traditionally, men have controlled the media, and therefore products were tailored to their preferences. Despite campaigns against false projections that portray women as sexual objects (being there only for men's sexual pleasure) and the numerous theories regarding women and empowerment, the beauty myth continues to be displayed in Asia. This myth refers to the fictive relationship between women's beauty and identity or how images of beauty in the media are used against women. Today's media also portrays women as powerful and independent, yet "qualities informed by sexuality continue to play a dominant role in the shaping of femininity"

(Datyan-Gevorgyan 2016, 1). In order to be considered sexually desirable, women need to look and act "sexy." But, in order to conform with traditional family and community expectations, they must suppress this aspect of their identity.

CONCLUSION

Women are bound by complex social contexts of power, class, gender, and kinship. The societies of South Asia and Southeast Asia are similar to those in other parts of the world wherein sexual cultures are produced, controlled, and more recently, contested by the women and men who live there. Thus when the sexuality claims of women span across South Asia and Southeast Asia, we see how various sociocultural assertions contribute to the construction of female sexuality, kinship expectations, the law, the community, science and health, economy, the country and above all, gender disparity. We also see in the process, how female sexuality and expectations and assumptions change as they cut across cultural and religious boundaries, until they are either embraced or negated by the respective social communities.

REFERENCES

Andaya-Watson, Barbara. 2006. *The Flaming Womb: Repositioning Women in Early Modern Southeast Asia.* Honolulu: University of Hawaii Press.

Bacchetta, Paola. 2013. "Queer Formations in (Hindu) Nationalism." In *Sexuality Studies*, edited by Sanjay Srivastava, 121–40. New Delhi, India: Oxford University Press.

Ballhatchet, Kenneth. 1980. *Race, Sex and Class under the Raj: Imperial Attitudes and Policies and their Critics, 1793–1905.* New York: St. Martin's Press.

Banu, Ayesha. 2016. "Human Development, Disparity, and Vulnerability: Women in South Asia." Global Human Development Report: Background Paper. United Nations Development Programme. Accessed July 16, 2022. https://hdr.undp.org/system/files/documents //latesteditedbanutemplateg11augustpdf.pdf.

Bich, Pham Van. 1999. *The Vietnamese Family in Change: The Case of the Red River Delta.* Richmond, UK: Curzo.

Blitt, Chela, dir. and prod. 1996. *Sisters and Daughters Betrayed: The Trafficking of Women and Girls and the Fight to End It*. Berkeley, CA: Berkeley Media.

Butt, Leslie, Jenny Munro, and Gerdha Numbery. 2017. "Adding Insult to Injury: Experiences of Mobile HIV-Positive Women Who Return Home for Treatment in Tanah Papua, Indonesia." In *Mobilities of Return: Pacific Perspectives*, edited by John Taylor and Helen Lee, 147–70. Canberra, Australia: ANU Press. Accessed June 27, 2022. https://www.jstor.org/stable/j.ctt20krz1j.9.

Childs, G., M. C. Goldstein, B. Jiao, and C. M. Beall. 2005. "Tibetan Fertility Transitions." *Population and Development Review* 31 (2): 337–49.

Cousins, Sophie. 2019. "In Nepal, Tradition Is Killing Women." Accessed July 16, 2022. https://foreignpolicy.com/2019/01/06/in-nepal-tradition-is-killing-women-chhaupadi-womens-rights-menstruation/.

Croll, Elizabeth. 2000. *Endangered Daughters: Discrimination and Development in Asia*. New York: Routledge.

Datyan-Gevorgyan, Anna. 2016. "Women and Mass Media." Heinrich Böll Stiftung [Green Political Foundation], April 8.Accessed June 27, 2022. https://feminism-boell.org/en/2016/04/08/women-and-mass-media.

Davies, S. G. 2015. "Surveilling Sexuality in Indonesia." In *Sex and Sexuality in Indonesia: Sexual Politics, Diversity and Representations in the Reformasi Era*, edited by L. R. Bennett and S. G. Davies, 30–61. London: Routledge.

Dhungana, Shuvam. 2019. "Nepali Women Are Being Trafficked to China and Sold as Wives." *Kathmandu Post*, September 9.

Fioriti, Joris, and Ashraf Khan. 2019. "Myths and Menstruation: Overcoming Pakistan's Period Taboo." Agence France-Presse, September 16.

Greenspan, A. 1992. "Age of Marriage Is Rising for Asian Men and Women, According to New Data." *Asia Pacific Population Policy*, no. 22 (September): 1–4.

Gross, R. M. 1995. "Buddhist Resources for Issues of Population, Consumption, and the Environment." In *Population, Consumption and the Environment. Religious and Secular Responses*, edited by H. Coward, 155–72. Albany: State University of New York Press.

Gupta, Rohan. 2019. "Abortion in India: Experts Call for Changes." Down to Earth, August 21. Accessed February 7, 2020. https://www

.downtoearth.org.in/news/health/abortion-in-india-experts-call-for
-changes-66369.

Himalayan News Service. 2017. "Chaupadi Exists in Urban Areas as
Well." *Himalayan Times*, May 30.

Human Rights Watch. 2006. "Swept under the Rug: Abuses against
Domestic Workers around the World." July 27. Accessed February
8, 2020. https://www.hrw.org/report/2006/07/27/swept-under-rug
/abuses-against-domestic-workers-around-world.

Human Rights Watch researcher, in consultation with Elin Martinez. 2018.
"Shall I Feed My Daughter, or Educate Her? Barriers to Girls'
Education in Pakistan." November 12. Accessed June 27, 2022.
https://www.hrw.org/report/2018/11/12/shall-i-feed-my-daughter
-or-educate-her/barriers-girls-education-pakistan.

Ijaz, Saroop. 2018. "Time to End Child Marriage in Pakistan." Human
Rights Watch, November 9. Accessed June 27, 2022. https://www
.hrw.org/news/2018/11/09/time-end-child-marriage-pakistan.

India Today Web Desk. 2018. "Homosexuality in Ancient India: 10
Instances." *India Today*, July 10.

Juarez, Fatima, Josefina Cabigon, Susheela Singh, and Rubina Hussain.
2005. "The Incidence of Induced Abortions in the Philippines:
Current Levels and Recent Trends." *International Perspectives on
Sexual and Reproductive Health* 31, no. 3 (September): 140–49.

Katz, Andrew. 2014. "The 'Untouchables': The Tradition of Chhaupadi in
Nepal." *Time*, August 11. Accessed February 7, 2020. https://time
.com/3811181/chhaupadi-ritual-nepal.

Kreager, Philip, and Elizabeth Schroder-Butterfill. 2008. "Indonesia
against the Trend? Ageing and Inter-Generational Wealth Flows in
Two Indonesian Communities." *Demographic Research* 19, article
52. Accessed June 27, 2022. http://www.demographic-research.org
/Volumes/Vol19/52.

Lam, May-Ying. 2016. "A Glimpse Inside the World's Largest Matrilineal
Society." *Washington Post*, July 6.

Lancet Child and Adolescent Health. 2018. "Normalising Menstruation,
Empowering Girls." Editorial, June 1. https://doi.org/10.1016/S2352
-4642(18)30143-3.

Levine, Philippa. 2003. *Prostitution, Race and Politics: Policing Venereal
Disease in the British Empire*. New York and London: Routledge.

Lim, May. 2011. "Women of Northeast Thailand: Privilege and Obligation." Georgetown University: Berkley Center for Religion, Peace,

and World Affairs, December 2. Accessed June 27, 2022. https://berkleycenter.georgetown.edu/posts/women-of-northeast-thailand-privilege-and-obligation.

Lukose, Ritty. 2009. *Liberalization's Children. Gender Youth and Consumer Citizenship in Globalizing India*. Durham, NC: Duke University Press.

Nadeau, Kathleen. 2003a. "Is Sex Trafficking in Asia Ancient or New? Challenge to the Churches." *East Asian Pastoral Review* 40 (2): 128–43.

Nadeau, Kathleen. 2003b. "The Philippine Family." In *International Encyclopedia of Marriage and Family*, edited by James Ponsetti, 3:1227–30. New York: Macmillan Reference USA.

Nadeau, Kathleen, and Sangita Rayamajhi, eds. 2013. *Women's Roles in Asia*. Santa Barbara, CA: Greenwood.

Nadeau, Kathleen, and Sangita Rayamajhi, eds. 2019. *Women and Violence: Global Lives in Focus*. Santa Barbara, CA: ABC-CLIO.

National Statistics Office/Philippines, Department of Health, Philippines, and Macro International. 1998. *National Demographic and Health Survey 1998*. Manila: NSO and Macro International. Accessed June 27, 2022. https://psa.gov.ph/sites/default/files/1998%20National%20Demographic%20and%20Health%20Survey%20%28NDHS%29%20-%20Philippines.pdf.

Natividad, Josefina N. 2013. "Teenage Pregnancy in the Philippines: Trends, Correlates and Data Sources." *Journal of the ASEAN Federation of Endocrine Societies* 28: 30–37.

NCPFP (National Committee for Population and Family Planning), Vietnam. 1997. *Population and Family Health Project and Macro International, Viet Nam Demographic and Health Survey*. Hanoi: NCPFP.

Nepal Ministry of Health. 2002. *National Safe Abortion Policy*. Kathmandu, Nepal: Ministry of Health. Accessed June 27, 2022. http://www.mohp.gov.np/images/pdf/policy/National%20abortion%20Policy.pdf.

Niaz, Unaiza, and Sahar Hassan. 2006. "Culture and Mental Health of Women in South-East Asia." *World Psychiatry* 5 (2): 118–20.

Pachauri, Saroj, and K. G. Santhya. 2002. "Reproductive Choices for Asian Adolescents: A Focus on Contraceptive Behavior." *International Family Planning Perspectives* 28, no. 4 (December): 186–95. Accessed March 9, 2019. https://www.jstor.org/stable/3088221.

Peletz, Michael G. 2012. "Gender, Sexuality, and the State in Southeast Asia." *Journal of Asian Studies* 71, no. 4 (November): 895–917. Accessed June 27, 2022. https://www.jstor.org/stable/23357425.

Pennington, Andy, Lois Orton, Shilpa Nayak, Adele Ring, Mark Petticrew, Amanda Sowden, Martin White et al. 2018. "The Health Impacts of Women's Low Control in Their Environment: A Theory-Based Systemic Review of Observational Studies in Societies with Profound Gender Discrimination." *Health and Place* 51 (May): 1–10.

Post Staff. 2000. "Slavery and Human Trafficking in Cambodia." *Phnom Penh Post*, September 1.

Robinson, K. 2009. *Gender, Islam and Democracy in Indonesia*. London: Routledge.

Slama, M. 2012. "'Coming Down to the Shop': Trajectories of Hadhrami Women into Indonesian Public Realms." *Asia Pacific Journal of Anthropology* 13 (4): 313–33. https://doi.org/10.1080/144422 13.2012.699089.

Sponberg, A. 2005. "Buddhism." In *Sex and Religion*, edited by C. Manning and P. Zuckerman, 41–59. Toronto: Thomson Wadsworth.

Srinivasan, Sharada, and Arjun Bedi. 2010. "Daughter Elimination: Cradle Baby Scheme in Tamil Nadu." *Economic and Policy Weekly* 45, no. 23 (June): 5–11.

Srivastava, Sanjay. 2013. "Introduction." In *Sexuality Studies,* edited by Sanjay Srivastava, 1–23. New Delhi, India: Oxford University Press.

Suwanbubbha, P. 2003. "The Right to Family Planning, Contraception and Abortion in Thai Buddhism." In *Sacred Rights: The Case for Contraception and Abortion in World Religions*, edited by D. C. Maguire, 145–65. New York: Oxford University Press.

UNDP and USAID (United Nations Development Department and United State Agency for International Development). 2014. *Being LGBT in Asia: Nepal Country Report.* Bangkok: UNDP and USAID.

U.S. Department of State. 2018. "2018 Trafficking in Persons Report: Bangladesh." June 30. Accessed June 27, 2022. https://www.state .gov/reports/2018-trafficking-in-persons-report/bangladesh.

U.S. Department of State. 2019. "Trafficking in Persons Report: June 2019." June 28. Accessed October 18, 2019. https://www.state.gov /wp-content/uploads/2019/06/2019-Trafficking-in-Persons-Report .pdf.

VanLandingham, Mark, and Lea Trujillo. 2002. "Recent Changes in Heterosexual Attitudes, Norms and Behaviors among Unmarried Thai Men: A Qualitative Analysis." *International Family Planning Perspectives* 28, no. 1 (March): 6–15.

Velasco, Ed. 2018. "Philippines' Total Fertility Rate is Highest in Asia: UN." *Manila Times*, October 18. Accessed June 27, 2022. https://www.gulf-times.com/story/609816/Philippines-total-fertility-rate-is-highest-in-Ase.

Von Ehrenfels, U. R. 1971. "Matrilineal Joint Family Patterns in India." *Journal of Comparative Family Studies* 2, no. 1 (Spring): 54–66.

Warriach, Sohail Akbar. 2005. "'Honor Killings' and the Law in Pakistan." In *"Honour" Crimes, Paradigms and Violence against Women*, edited by Lynn Welchman and Sarah Hossain, 78–110. London: Zed Books.

Weisshaar, Rachel. 2008. "The Philippines' Highest Birth Rates, Pervasive Poverty Are Linked." *New Security Beat* (blog), April 21. Wilson Center. Accessed June 27, 2022. https://www.newsecuritybeat.org/2008/04/in-the-philippines-high-birth-rates-pervasive-poverty-are-linked.

EIGHT

Oceania

Rashmi Pithavadian, Anita Ogbeide, Angelica Ojinnaka, Rubab Firdaus, Syeda Zakia Hossain, Tinashe Dune, and Pranee Liamputtong

INTRODUCTION

In this chapter, sexuality across a diverse range of countries in Oceania is discussed. Situated in the southeast of the Asia-Pacific zone, Oceania is a geographic region comprised of Australasia, Melanesia, Micronesia, and Polynesia. Spanning the Western and Eastern Hemispheres, Oceania has a land area of 8,486,460 square kilometers (3,276,639 square miles) and a population of over 42.5 million people (Worldometer 2020). When compared to continental regions, Oceania is the smallest in land area and the second smallest in population after Antarctica. The largest and most populous country in Oceania is Australia, with Sydney being the largest city of both Australia and Oceania.

Despite its size, Oceania includes a range of countries and encompasses vast diversity across all areas of life. Oceania includes developed and developing nations, some that have been extensively westernized and those that remain relatively more traditional in their social, political, and economic structures. Like many other Western nations, Australia and New Zealand rank high in quality of life and human development. Less-developed economies include countries such as Kiribati and Tuvalu, and medium-sized economies of the Pacific Islands are countries such as Palau, Fiji, and Tonga. All countries within the region were colonized, largely by Europeans, at some point in history. In some countries, the colonizers never left, and in others the colonizers stayed for varying lengths of time. In both cases, the traditions of the Indigenous peoples of Oceania, including their understanding and experiences of gender and, therefore, sexuality, were changed forever.

This chapter provides an overview of a diverse range of perspectives on women and sexuality in Oceania, starting with a brief history of the region. It also presents readers with a contemporary view on the intersection between culture and national attitudes toward sexuality. This leads into a discussion of the role of religion as a major source of community morals, gender roles, and rights. The implications of these on sexual and gender-based violence as experienced by women are also discussed. The chapter also explores how women in Oceania experience and approach their reproductive health and menstruation as well as cultural perspectives on marriage and partnerships. The chapter ends with a review of women's representations in the media and the role of those representations on Oceania women's sexuality.

TRADITIONAL WOMEN AND SEXUALITY IN OCEANIA: BRIEF HISTORY

The diversity of cultures in Oceania presents both an opportunity and a challenge in trying to summarize the history of women's sexuality in the region. With that in mind, this section features a brief history of Oceanic regions, including Australia, New Zealand, Melanesia, Micronesia, and Polynesia to introduce the relevance of history to women's sexuality.

Indigenous Australians

Indigenous Australians are the Aboriginal and Torres Strait Islander peoples who are the original inhabitants of the Australian continent and nearby islands. Aboriginal and Torres Strait Islander people are believed to have migrated from Africa to Australia around 50,000 years ago (Coper, Williams, and Spooner 2018). Aboriginal and Torres Strait Islander cultures are cited as the oldest surviving cultures in human history (Australian Human Rights Commission 2016). However, cultures (and therefore constructions of sexuality) are ever-evolving and intermingling, especially in the context of Indigenous Australia. Notably, Indigenous Australians live on a spectrum of at least two cultures, one which is Eurocentric and the other more traditionally cultural in nature. Indigenous conceptions

The period from the middle 1800s until the 1960s is called the Stolen Generations. During this period, the Australian government passed laws that allowed the removal of Indigenous children from their families in order to reform them in Christian missions before relocating some children to the homes of settler Australians. Although the legislation to enact the forcible removal of Aboriginal children from their families was repealed in 1969, the impact of European invasion and the changes it brought are permanently etched in Indigenous people's direct and indirect memories (SBS 2015). The Stolen Generations reflect a paternalistic strategy based on systemic racism and discrimination under the laws and policies of Australian federal and state governments during a large part of the 20th century.

and experiences of sexuality in scholarship and practice have been obstructed by the dominance of Eurocentric, meaning Western, conceptualizations of gender, embodiment, and intimacy. This cultural dominance is particularly significant to Indigenous women whose bodies have been vilified and violated within Australia's colonial history and practices (Moreton-Robinson 2003). Through such history and experiences, Indigenous women (re)construct sexuality over time and across generations.

The British invasion and settlement of Australia eroded the freedom and autonomy that Indigenous women enjoyed in precolonial society. In addition to the destruction of Indigenous communities, invasion deprived women of their influence, status, and role within their respective communities. The imposition of a highly patriarchal European legal and value system ensured that Indigenous women were demoted to second-class status in relation to their male counterparts (Byrd 2011). Notably, the events following 1788 (when Captain James Cook first arrived in Australia) fundamentally altered the traditional relationships between Indigenous Australian men and women. These changes wreaked havoc on established and long-standing values and cultural standards, which the Europeans perceived of as inferior and barbaric (Windschuttle 2003). The cross-cultural differences highlight tremendous historical, social, and economic changes that have been largely destructive for Aboriginal and Torres Strait Islander communities.

In addition to the widespread extermination of Indigenous peoples at the hands of the Europeans, invasion was also marked by the exploitation of men for labor and women as sexual servants (Sullivan 2017). Family and community cooperation experienced in precolonial contexts were further destroyed through Australian policy, which mandated the separation

Australian Reconciliation Day celebration. (Rozenn Leard/Dreamstime.com)

of families and children (particularly those of mixed Aboriginal and white heritage) from their communities, language, land, lore, and law. Within the missions, young Indigenous women were often restricted to domestic duties. Those who were "adopted" out to settler families were relegated to domestic work and rearing the settlers' children. Indigenous women in these circumstances were thus under the complete control of the settlers and restricted from any opportunities that could catalyze their agency and autonomy (Ruttan, Laboucane-Benson, and Munro 2008). During this period, Indigenous people were considered by the Europeans as incapable of autonomous decision-making and in need of their guidance to reduce what the Europeans referred to as uncivilized traits, behavior, values, and beliefs (Armitage 1995).

Although a lot has changed in the past five decades to better address the prejudices and inequity that Indigenous Australians face, discrimination toward this population persists in all areas of life. Sadly, the Australian Institute of Health and Welfare (AIHW 2013) found that Indigenous children are 10 times more likely to be removed than non-Indigenous children under the current "out-of-home-care" policy. While this all continues to impact Indigenous Australian women in terms of gender and sexuality, the resilience of Indigenous Australians and their cultures is demonstrated by their dedication to reclaim their lives and heritage.

The Māori

The Māori are the Indigenous people of New Zealand, or *Aotearoa*, which is the Māori name for New Zealand. After the onset of European colonization in New Zealand, Māori became the minority in a predominantly European majority, as did the Indigenous peoples of Australia. It is often assumed that leadership was primarily the domain of men and that they exercised power over women in Māori culture. However, evidence abounds that refutes the notion that traditional Māori society attached greater significance to men's roles than to women's roles. In fact, before the colonization of New Zealand, Māori women held a range of roles and responsibilities in their societies (Kenney 2011). The colonial imposition of English law changed the way of life and experiences of sexuality for Māori peoples, particularly women. According to English common law, the husband/father was the head of the family in control of the household (Blackstone 2016). As girls reached adulthood and married, they changed from being the property of their fathers to being the property of their

Māori women cooking. (Awcnz62/Dreamstime.com)

husbands (Blackstone 2016). The imposition of such patriarchal English laws impacted the Māori way of life, and Māori women increasingly occupied more subordinate roles that mirrored the colonizers' way of life. The vestiges of this common law approach have remained apparent in many aspects of New Zealand (and Oceanic) law. Therefore, the view that Western, English law brought by colonization wholly liberated Māori people, especially women, must be recognized as a misconception.

Before European colonization, traditional Māori were accepting of sexual diversity and difference and sought to embrace them as part of sexuality rather than exclude them (Aspin and Hutchings 2007). The Christianity of colonialism denounced same-sex homosexuality and promoted abstinence from sex outside marriage. It changed traditional Māori understandings of sexuality where previously, Māori people, including women, were able to freely act on their sexual desire outside of heterosexual monogamy. As time has passed, contemporary Māori are becoming more aware of how colonization transformed their ancestors' traditional views of sexuality (Aspin and Hutchings 2007). Māori people, particularly women, are seeking to reclaim and express discarded aspects of traditional Māori sexuality. In doing so, Māori are now rejecting Western descriptors of sexuality and "use the term *takatapui* to describe non-heterosexual forms of sexual expression" (Aspin and Hutchings 2007, 422). Unlike the Western terms of "gay" and "lesbian," which are markers of sexual identity, *takatapui* can be used by Māori women (and Māori peoples more generally) to represent their sexual relations with other women and transgender and transsexual people without having to identify as gay (Aspin and Hutchings 2007). In these ways, Māori are seeking to overcome the sexual and gendered oppression that colonialism brought to New Zealand, and as such, they are sexually empowering Māori women.

Polynesia

Polynesia is an ethno-geographic subgroup of Oceania that includes Hawaii (United States), Tonga, Western Samoa, American Samoa, Cook Islands, New Zealand (Māori), French Polynesia, Easter Island, Tuvalu, Niue, Tokelau, Pitcairn Island, Clipperton Island, and Wallis and Fatuna. More than 1,000 islands in the central and southern Pacific Ocean constitute Polynesia. The countries in Polynesia fall under the governance of Australia, New Zealand, the United States, and France. The predominant religion in the Polynesian region is Christianity. Therefore, while there are cultural differences between countries in Polynesia, there are shared cultural values, social structure, language, and beliefs due to a similar history of European colonization and the Christian faith that it spread.

Traditional gender roles were already established prior to European contact. While women would work within the home to cook, clean, and raise children, men would provide the food from fishing or gardening. However, gender roles were of equal value and not fixated to a sex. Men and women could perform both gender responsibilities if needed (Helu 1995). Also, the position of women varied between Polynesian cultures. For example, women had a generally high social ranking in Tonga, but this was not the case in other Polynesian societies (Spano 2000). It does not seem that before colonization, women were pressured to endure hardship in their marriages, as it was acceptable for marriages to end should the relationship dissolve (Helu 1995). Women could then return to their village and remarry (Helu 1995). However, women's virginity was sometimes an indication of social class, as noble women remained virgins until marriage (James 1994).

From records of European colonizers' observations of Polynesian society, it seems that Polynesian people, including women, freely engaged from adolescence in sexual activity and homosexual relations, which made Europeans uncomfortable (Tcherkézoff 2009). After the colonization and the Christianization of the Polynesian Islands by the missionaries in the 18th century, open and unreserved attitudes toward sex moved into the private sphere as Christian values and morals infiltrated the Polynesian culture and continue on to the present. Nonetheless, traditional values still shape women's position in Polynesian societies; for example, Tongan women continue to have high societal positions due to the country's partly matriarchal structure (Spano 2000). However, the Western influence of colonization and its Christian teachings has been used in ways to oppress many Polynesian women into fixed gendered positions and has repressed their sexuality.

Melanesia

The Oceania subregion of Melanesia consists of the four independent countries of Fiji, Solomon Islands, Vanuatu, and Papua New Guinea; the French collectivity of New Caledonia; and parts of Indonesia. Gender roles in traditional Melanesian societies were historically polarized. Women's duties mainly focused on producing food for their communities. Yet women also participated in rituals because of their perceived reproductive and productive power (Keesing and Kahn 2014). Melanesian societies were organized into local groups or kinships based on extended family relations and descent (Keesing and Kahn 2014). Intermarriage between kinships were important to foster and maintain ties. Such marriages between kinships could be used to at least temporarily reconcile with enemies. However, it was the women in the kinship groups who were offered as part of forging links between different kin. If the labor of the woman's children and family were to be transferred to her husband, her family would be compensated with bridewealth in the form of goods, pigs, or other services (Keesing and Kahn 2014).

From the 17th century, the Netherlands, Britain, Japan, Germany, and Australia established colonial claims in different parts of Melanesia. British colonialism led to Indians being brought to Fiji as indentured laborers. Their descendants form the present Indo-Fijian population of Fiji, while the major Indigenous Fijian group are the iTauki people. During European colonization in the 20th century, European settlers occupied the top positions in government and most other fields, which restricted Melanesian women's growth in many areas (Macintyre and Spark 2017). The impacts of colonialism, and the Christianity it brought, continue to influence the gender and sexual expectations of modern Melanesian women (Macintyre and Spark 2017).

Micronesia

Thousands of small islands constitute Micronesia, in the western Pacific Ocean. The four main archipelagos are the Caroline Islands, consisting of the two republics of the Federated States of Micronesia (Micronesia) and Palau; the Gilbert Islands, which form the Republic of Kiribati; the Mariana Islands, which are divided into the two jurisdictions of the Northern Mariana Islands and Guam; and the Marshall Islands. Nauru and Wake Island are separate island nations. There are also many other islands in the Micronesia subregion. The diverse Indigenous peoples across the different parts of the subregion have been colonized by Spain, Germany, Japan, Britain, and the United States from the 17th century onward. Micronesian families follow a large kinship structure. Historically, older men have been entitled to have sex with the wives of younger male kin or even other women or girls within the kin (Rauchholz 2016).

Younger kin felt compelled to oblige their older male kin's sexual desire out of respect to their higher position in the hierarchical kinship structure. In the past, it was reported that men had sex with prepubescent girls as young as four or five years of age (Rauchholz 2016). While the majority of people in Micronesia will publicly condemn such acts, sexual relations between men and young girls within kinship structures continue to be tolerated as part of traditional norms (Rauchholz 2016). Even in cases where young teenage girls respond positively to the sexual advances of older men, the problem lies in the fact that girls have been "groomed" for sexual exploitation.

Other contemporary traditions that shape Micronesian women's sexuality are also grounded in historical practices. Even before colonization, it was common for kin to sexually exchange female family members for shell money, goods, and other valuables. However, such practices were recognized and "amplified during the colonial period" (Rauchholz 2016, 344). During colonialism, American sailors and local men sexually exchanged Micronesian women for goods, and "Japanese government officials requested young girls for sex whenever they travelled through the communities" (Rauchholz 2016, 345). Even though the sharing and exchange of women's sexuality as goods within the community has continued to the present, it has been recognized as violating the United Nations (UN) declaration of Human Rights and UN Convention on the Rights of the Child. The latter has been ratified by the Micronesian island state governments despite the fact it opposes culturally held views and practices (Rauchholz 2016). The government also raised the legal age of consent for sexual relations in the Micronesian islands of Pohnpei in 2008, and in Chuuk in 2014 (Rauchholz 2016). Therefore, it cannot be said or assumed that all men in Micronesian cultures continue to take advantage of women's sexuality. Many men living in Micronesian islands take no part in such traditions. Rather, it is important to note how traditional Micronesian practices continue to exploit women's sexuality.

CULTURE AND ATTITUDES TOWARD SEXUALITY

Given the cultural diversity and traditional differences across Oceanic countries, the attitudes held toward sexuality vary through time and cultures in the region. This means that there are no uniform attitudes about sexuality and what it encapsulates, such as sexual expression and sexual orientation,

> The *aiga* socialize children to align their behavior and attitudes with what is upheld by the elders. For example, unmarried women are considered to be a reflection of the cultural status of the village. As a result, the aiga strictly police women's sexual behavior from when they begin menstruation (Tupuola 1996). The male relatives control young women to ensure that they have limited (if any) contact with other men. In this way, the men of the aiga exert control over young women's sexuality to ensure that they do not engage in socially unacceptable sexual behavior, which could tarnish the status of the aiga.

in Oceania. There is a mixture of conservative, liberal, changing, and unique attitudes toward sexuality that exist simultaneously throughout the Oceania region at present. Some conservative attitudes are grounded in traditional cultural values and beliefs. For example, due to strict traditions, Samoan society has a hierarchical structure with authoritative positions of the *aiga*, which translates to "family" that "extends beyond the nuclear family . . . incorporating uncles, aunties, both sets of grandparents and many cousins" (Tupuola 1996, 62). Social hierarchies in the iTauki culture in Fiji also restrict young unmarried women from exercising sexual agency (Mitchell and Bennett 2020a). This is because "premarital sex is not socially sanctioned for women," and women cannot challenge men's authority (Mitchell and Bennett 2020a, 1558).

Men's sexuality is not controlled in the same way, even though premarital sex is taboo in the discussed cultures (Tupuola 1996; Mitchell and Bennett 2020a). Nonetheless, young people in Oceanic cultures that uphold conservative attitudes experience little to no sexual freedom before marriage (which is often arranged) (Tupuola 1996; Heard et al. 2019). This, in turn, hinders youth, especially women, from understanding their sexual and reproductive health. It is worthwhile to note that conservative attitudes can be identified when certain behavior is restricted and socially unacceptable. Therefore, the social unacceptability for young Samoan and iTauki women to explore their sexuality reflects the ways that cultural traditions can restrict their sexual expression. This discussion of cultural attitudes toward Samoan and iTauki women's sexuality is not intended to represent all conservative attitudes toward women but rather offer a glimpse into how more traditional cultural values shape attitudes toward sexuality in Oceanic countries.

It cannot be assumed that culture and attitudes toward sexuality are fixed and homogenous even in the Oceanic countries with prevailing conservative values. In fact, attitudes toward sex are changing in some parts of Oceania. A study found that some young iTauki women in Fiji selectively choose when and where to express and explore their sexuality (Mitchell and Bennett 2020b). To avoid bringing shame to themselves or their families, these women employ several strategies, such as engaging in secret relationships, publicly presenting themselves as sexually innocent, and limiting sexual activity to their university campus, dormitories, night-clubs, house parties, motels, and public parks (Mitchell and Bennett 2020b). This indicates how some women's attitudes are changing in ways to discreetly challenge dominant cultural values in order to act on their sexual desire. However, the increasing rates of teenage pregnancy in Fiji indicate that youth (Varani-Norton 2014), especially women, are unable to access and gain sexual health literacy due to the taboo of discussing such sexual topics. This poses a barrier for youth with transgressive sexual views against safely exploring their sexuality.

The spread of the sexual revolution and women's and gay liberation movements to countries around the world from the 1960s onward led to more liberal cultural attitudes toward sexuality. In the Oceania region, it was largely felt in Australia and New Zealand. During the peak of these concurrent movements, queer men and women began to publicly express their sexuality by openly living with their same-sex partners, and they explored new types of intimate relationships in emerging gay spaces such as "the bar scene in Sydney" (Arrow and Woollacott 2019, 3–4). The new sexual and feminist politics encouraged people's sexual experimentation in nonmonogamy, shared households, and communal living (Arrow and Woollacott 2019). In a nutshell, "the old taboos about sex began to break down" and were replaced by "a new emphasis on sexuality as a form of self-expression and as a source of pleasure" (Arrow and Woollacott 2019, 5). Such liberal attitudes toward sexuality continue in dominant contem-porary Australian culture; research has shown that premarital sex is largely socially acceptable and people are becoming sexually active at younger ages (Rissel et al. 2003). Moreover, the Sydney Gay & Lesbian Mardi Gras is the largest Pride event in Oceania to celebrate queer expressions of sexuality.

However, such liberal attitudes to sexuality are not uniform within cul-tures. Dominant Australian culture historically positioned Indigenous Aus-tralian women as paradoxically exotic, erotic, and desired, as well as savage, promiscuous, and primitive, which continues to have implications for atti-tudes toward Indigenous Australian women's sexuality today (Sullivan

2017, 397). The colonial representation of Indigenous Australian women as "prostitutes" partly stemmed from European observations that it was socially acceptable for Aboriginal women's bodies to be exchanged for survival, bargaining, or partnership in Aboriginal cultures (Sullivan 2017). However, it was disregarded that Aboriginal women exercised sexual agency and offered themselves as they desired. Instead, the sexual coercion and sexual objectification of Aboriginal women during colonization were justified by pointing to a biased Western interpretation of Aboriginal cultures (Sullivan 2017). This has led to current representations of the sexually passive and victimized Indigenous Australian woman, which must be pushed aside as it occludes discussions on ways that Indigenous Australian women have expressed their sexuality for "power, love, intimacy and sexual desire" (Sullivan 2017, 407). This example also indicates how conflicting liberal and problematic attitudes toward sexuality can exist within a society such as Australia's.

The notion of "liberal" attitudes is a Western construct that should not be simplistically used in a binary with "conservative." A Western, or Eurocentric, lens must be removed in order to understand the unique attitudes held toward sexuality in the cultures of some countries in Oceania. While "drag shows" are common performances in the Cook Islands, their meaning is different from that of Western drag shows (Alexeyeff 2000, 298). Although performers in the drag shows in the Cook Islands publicly enact sexual practices in dance, with women's hips bumping men's torsos and "grinding sex moves" on stage, these are not intended to simply be expressions of sexuality. Rather, the shows express Cook Islands norms of public and private behavior, social roles, and individual desires (Alexeyeff 2000, 298). For instance, to visually narrate land being pushed out of water, a performer pulled on the coconut bra they were wearing (Alexeyeff 2000, 302). Moreover, in Samoa, while *fa'afafine* are born male at birth, *fa'afatama* are born female at birth. *Fa'afafine* and *fa'afatama* express and regularly transition between both masculine and feminine traits. *Fa'afafine* and *Fa'afatama* are a recognized third gender in Samoan culture that does not conform to binary gender nor the more permanent transitioning from one gender to another that the concept "transgender" signifies in Western culture. Therefore, Western concepts of sexual expression are not entirely relevant to understand the cultural attitudes to sexuality in the non-Western societies of Oceania. Given the numerous cultures across countries in Oceania, it is not possible to detail the distinct cultural attitudes toward sexuality in the region. Instead, this discussion has sought to provide a broad snapshot to capture the complex, changing, and different attitudes toward sexuality that sometimes coexist within cultures in Oceania.

RELIGION AND SEXUALITY

Christianity is the dominant religion in Oceania, and it shapes sexual moralities particularly for women in many countries in the region. Given the shared history of European colonialism in Oceania, the evangelical mission of colonialization succeeded in largely converting the population of people in Oceanic countries to denominations of Christianity. While DFAT (2016) reported that around 95% of people in the Pacific Islands identify as Christian, about 52% of Australians and 37% of New Zealanders identify as Christians (ABS 2017a; 1 News 2019). Biased interpretations of the Bible have been used by clergy and religious figures to continue to condemn premarital sex, same-sex relations, and contraceptive use, and to condone the subordinate positions of women to men and their husbands. Such teachings are internalized by the large Christian populations of countries in Oceania. It has led to Christian doctrines being used to assert patriarchal authority in many parts of Oceania and to dissuade young women from exploring their sexuality and acting on their sexual desire (Heard et al. 2019; Mitchell and Bennett 2020a). Research shows that unmarried women are afraid of being labeled a "bad Christian" if they engage in premarital sex and it becomes public knowledge (Mitchell and Bennett 2020b). Some iTauki Fijian women who were secretly sexually active before marriage still feared that they would face consequences for their "sinful behaviour" in the afterlife (Mitchell and Bennett 2020b). It indicates that even when women challenge cultural sexual norms to explore their sexuality, their Christian upbringing causes them to experience guilt for what they perceive as sexual transgressions.

There are significant minorities of Hinduism and Islam in Oceania, except in Fiji, where Hinduism is the second most dominant religion in the country. Over 27% of the Fijian population, who are largely Indo-Fijian, were found to be Hindu (Fiji Bureau of Statistics 2007). Hinduism and Islam uphold similar teachings to Christianity on promoting sex only in marriage (Naz 2013). This religious mentality often encourages women to repress their sexuality and pleasure, which is detrimental to their sexual health and well-being. In fact, in Oceania, countries with declining religion such as Australia, research indicates that women with no religious beliefs express greater sexual liberalism and permissiveness toward premarital sex, homosexuality, and engaging in an active sex life for well-being (Rissel et al. 2003). This further reflects the correlation between the dominance of religion in women's lives and their sexual agency.

Moreover, research indicates that the families of many women in the Pacific Islands, such as Fiji, raise their daughters to believe that contraception use is "un-Christian" (Mitchell and Bennett 2020b, 510). In response, young women resort to church-sanctioned forms of contraception, such as withdrawal, more commonly known as the "pull-out method" (Mitchell and Bennett 2020b). This poses serious risks to young people's, especially women's, sexual and reproductive health by increasing their chance of contracting STDs or becoming pregnant. As such, in certain parts of Oceania religion, particularly Christianity, has shaped social norms that restrict women's sexual freedom in ways that can have adverse health impacts if they choose to be sexually active.

However, the Micronesian government ratification of the UN Convention on the Rights of the Child and raising the age of sexual consent in response to young girls being sexually exchanged and exploited in some islands of Micronesia (as previously discussed in the section on Micronesia) have been fueled by women's groups that have local key actors following Christianity and its condemnation of the sexual exploitation of children (Rauchholz 2016). Herein, the Christian religion has been positively utilized to reconstruct accepted sexual moralities in ways to stop the sexualization and exploitation of young girls in Micronesia (Rauchholz 2016). In any case, these conditions highlight the power of religion in shaping the very structure of society and its responses toward women's sexuality in Oceania.

SEXUAL VIOLENCE

Sexual violence against women in Oceania is a significant health and social concern. Even in developed Oceanic countries such as Australia and New Zealand, women continue to be susceptible to sexual violence. Based on the Personal Safety Survey (PSS) by the ABS, it is estimated that 1 in 6 women and 1 in 25 men have experienced at least one incident of sexual assault from 15 years of age on in Australia (ABS 2017b; AIHW 2020). One in 2 women and 1 in 4 men have experienced sexual harassment, according to the PPS (ABS 2017b). Even though only 2.1% of people in New Zealand were victims of a sexual offense, women were much more likely than men to experience it, according to the New Zealand Crime and

Safety Survey (Ministry of Justice 2014). Therefore, while men certainly experience sexual violence, there is a significantly higher likelihood for women to be victims of it. In multicultural societies such as Australia and New Zealand, there may be language and cultural barriers that inhibit migrant women and even Indigenous women from reporting or seeking support services for sexual violence (AIHW 2020). Moreover, it was found that 1 in 4 Australian women who experienced sexual assault did not report it to the police due to feeling ashamed (AIHW 2020). This highlights that there are sociocultural barriers that not only make it difficult to discern the true number of women who face sexual violence but also inhibit women from accessing the help that they need for their sexual health and well-being.

Research has indicated that poor knowledge and attitudes toward sexual assault may contribute to the incidence of sexual violence against women in developed Oceanic countries. For example, the findings from the 2017 National Community Attitudes toward Violence against Women Survey (NCAS) in Australia indicate that 19% of Australians did not know that nonconsensual sex in marriage is against the law, 42% believed that "it was common for sexual assault accusations to be used as a way of getting back at men," and 33% responded that "rape resulted from men not being able to control their need for sex" (AIHW 2020). It is therefore apparent that such poor sexual-health-and-safety literacy is another barrier for women that compromises their sexual agency.

In other parts of Oceania, it has been estimated that 60% to 80% of women in the Pacific Islands of Polynesia, Melanesia, and Micronesia will experience physical or sexual violence during their lifetime (Asian Pacific Institute on Gender-Based Violence 2018). The rates of women in this region experiencing physical and/or sexual violence by an intimate partner range from 25% in Palau to 68% in Kiribati (Asian Pacific Institute on Gender-Based Violence 2018). Research has also shown that from the age of 15, 6% of women in Tonga and a whopping 47% of women in Nauru have experienced sexual violence by a nonpartner (Asian Pacific Institute on Gender-Based Violence 2018). Due to the diversity in cultures, language, and lack of research in the Oceania region, figures of women's experiences of sexual violence in Oceania vary per country. Nonetheless, the existing research has indicated that gender-based violence is very high in the Pacific Islands (Thomas 2017).

Research shows that there is low gender equity in the justice systems in the Pacific Islands of Oceania. The practices for sentencing, and barriers for survivors of sexual and/or partner violence, hinder the reporting of perpetrators (Christie, Singh, and Singh 2015). For instance, the Law Reform Commission discovered that in Papua New Guinea, both men and women and, often, even the officials from support services, all held problematic views that wife-beating is legal and normal and domestic violence is a private issue that should not warrant interference from outsiders, including the authorities (Thomas 2017; Counts 1990). This uncovers how the mentality and pervasive beliefs and cultural values held by the majority of society members construct the responses of a nation's justice system.

High incidence of sexual violence, including, rape correlates to societies that permit gender-based violence. It has been found that Christian religious leaders, who are perceived as role models in their communities, encourage women to tolerate violence through their teachings of the Bible in some of the Pacific Islands in Oceania (Meo 2003; Smith 2019). However, Fijian theologian Meo (2003) calls for women to reclaim and promote sections in the Bible that praise women who challenge authority to improve their quality of life. Christian scripture and faith should be interpreted and utilized in ways that encourage women to respond to their physical and sexual violence and resist it, according to Meo (2003). These are promising initiatives that seek to reduce gender-based physical and sexual violence against women.

However, the true scale of sexual violence in Oceania is difficult to discern due to the diversity of the region, limited available of data, and lack of reporting. The few existing studies on this topic tend to combine the data collected from the Pacific Islands with Asia (Thomas 2017). This hinders the identification of the unique sexual violence issues that exist and need to be addressed in the Pacific Islands. Hence, there is need for continuous efforts to research, design, and promote intervention and prevention strategies to manage this issue. All systems need to work together to make a major difference to the prevalence and impact of sexual violence

---

The Pacific Women Shaping Pacific Development is working with the Pacific Council of Churches, Uniting World, and the Anglican Church to increase women's leadership opportunities in religious spaces and challenge the traditional patriarchal interpretations of the Bible to allow more inclusivity and motivate women to assert themselves against violence (DFAT 2016).

against women in order for the women who have experienced it to rebuild their lives.

REPRODUCTIVE HEALTH AND MENSTRUATION

Reproductive Health

Regarding women's reproductive health, access to contraception and information about family planning, abortion, and pregnancy continue to be issues in Oceania. "Reproductive health" does not simply imply the absence of disease but indicates that people can have a safe sex life, the capability to reproduce, and freedom to decide on matters of sexuality. In developed countries such as Australia and New Zealand, women are significantly more likely to play the major role in contraceptive decision-making to have safe sex. In Australia, about 81% of women use some form of contraception (Ministers: Department of Health 2020). Yet about 50% of Australian women have an unplanned pregnancy, which suggests poor contraception use, such as not correctly following instructions for using contraceptives (Family Planning NSW [FPNSW] 2018). It reflects that engaging in safe sex is not only having access to contraception but also using contraception correctly and following family planning for good reproductive health.

On the other hand, women's internalization of men's higher societal position informs their use of contraception in other parts of Oceania. For example, research has indicated that in Fiji, women's perceptions of female subservience to males in Fijian society inhibit their use of contraception (Lincoln, Mohammadnezhad, and Khan 2018). This is especially true among the largely Hindu Indo-Fijian population, which reflects that it is not solely Christianity that drives ideas of female subservience to men (Lincoln, Mohammadnezhad, and Khan 2018). Rather, a complex enmeshment of religion, culture, and social structures of gender positions influences many Oceanic women's choices on whether to engage in safe sex for their reproductive health.

Moreover, the incidence and impact of poor sexual and reproductive health vary among different population groups according to sociodemographic factors such as age, sex, socioeconomic background, and geographic location. For example, young women, women living in rural areas, Aboriginal and Torres Strait Islander women, women with disabilities, and same sex and trans/transgender women are most at risk to experiencing poor sexual and reproductive health. This increased risk is due to discrimination, difficulty with accessing health services, and previous bad experiences hindering future attempts to seek help for reproductive health. For instance, research has shown that the iTauki women in New Zealand and Fiji have significantly lower levels of contraceptive use and family planning methods (20% and 22%, respectively) compared to the national prevalence in both countries (of 72% and 45%, respectively) (Cammock et al. 2018). Such findings reflect the impact of the sociodemographic factor of education level, as the iTauki women who had received tertiary education had higher contraceptive and family planning awareness (Cammock et al. 2018). In another study, with 325 women participating from Suva, Fiji, only 54% of participants were aware that missing contraceptive pills for more than three days can result in a pregnancy (Lincoln, Mohammadnezhad, and Khan 2018). This reflects how reproductive health literacy regarding contraception and family planning is another pertinent sociodemographic factor that determines the sexual and reproductive health of women and contributes to health inequalities in various regions of Oceania.

Women's ability to access abortion is key for good reproductive health. The right to abortion varies per country in Oceania. Abortion is legal in all states and territories of Australia, although specific laws apply in each state and territory (FPNSW 2018). Abortion termination costs are paid out of pocket, while the public system remains largely unresponsive to helping with the cost or subsidized care. Other countries in the Oceania region, such as Papua New Guinea, Solomon Islands, Tuvalu, and Vanuatu have great legal restrictions on women's rights and choice to have abortions (Center for Reproductive Rights 2020). Women's right to abortion to preserve their own health is also legally denied in Tuvalu and the Solomon Islands (Center for Reproductive Rights 2020). All the aforementioned countries legally allow abortion only to save the woman's life if it is at risk due to the pregnancy. Even in developed countries in Oceania, abortion has only been recently decriminalized (March 2020) and removed from the 1961 Crimes Act in New Zealand, and there are still restrictions on abortion in the state of South Australia at the time of this writing. Despite the varied legislation regarding abortion in Oceania, women still lack full autonomy and agency over their bodies regarding abortion and, in effect, their reproductive health. More legislation and attitudes toward abortions have to change in Oceania to enable women to access abortions simply on request. Only then can women be free of paternalistic governing structures that attempt to dictate what is best for them and their bodies.

Disparities between the experiences of pregnancies between the ethnic/ Indigenous and non-Indigenous women in Oceanic countries have been observed in their reproductive health. Many Aboriginal and Torres Strait Islander women in Australia experience healthy pregnancies and have healthy babies. However, inequalities persist and, overall, Aboriginal women are more likely to experience teenage pregnancies than non-Aboriginal mothers are (Boyle and Eades 2016). Aboriginal women also experience twice the rates of preterm birth and low birthweight, and "five times the maternal mortality rate of non-Aboriginal women" (Boyle and Eades 2016). Undernutrition, smoking, and increased BMI are more likely to be experienced by Aboriginal women during pregnancy, which reflects how compromised reproductive health impacts their overall holistic health (Boyle and Eades 2016).

Similarly, women from other ethnic groups in the Oceania countries face difficulties in their reproductive health surrounding pregnancy. A study found that compared to white women, Hawaiian Pacific Islander women and Samoan women had more sociodemographic risk factors such as teenage pregnancies or lacking health insurance (Chang et al. 2015). While Native Hawaiian women were found to give birth to babies with lower birth weights, Samoans had very high risk of macrosomic—meaning much heavier than average—birth weights for babies (Chang et al. 2015). Pacific Islander women tend to have a higher incidence of preeclampsia and gestational diabetes compared to the average female population (Chang et al. 2015). The reasons for these persisting health inequalities are complex. Compared with other non-Indigenous or non–ethnically diverse women, Indigenous women in the discussed island countries of Oceania experience greater socioeconomic disadvantage, higher rates of imprisonment, lower levels of health literacy, and a lack of culturally appropriate and available services. Therefore, women of Indigenous descent in areas of Oceania may have to maneuver more challenges than non-Indigenous /white women do, to be able to attain good reproductive health.

Menstruation

The age of the onset of menstruation (also known as menarche) and social perceptions of menstruation vary across Oceania. A longitudinal study reported mean age of menarche of Australian women as 13.6 years and the median age as 14 years (Giles et al. 2010). The reported mean age of menarche for girls is 12.9 years in New Zealand (St. George, Williams, and Silva 1994) and 15.8 years in Papua New Guinea (Groos and Smith 1992).

In many traditional non-Western or Indigenous cultures, menstruation is associated with myths, taboos, and stigma. Restrictions are imposed on the participation of menstruating girls and women in social, cultural, and religious activities as well as on their mobility. Research has found that menstrual blood and menstruating women are perceived as "dirty" or "unclean" in parts of Oceania, such as rural parts of Papua New Guinea and Solomon Islands (Mohamed et al. 2018). Consequently, women in these parts face disruptions to their daily lives, as they are expected to refrain from cooking or cleaning to avoid bringing "bad luck" to the health and physical strength of the men around them (Mohamed et al. 2018). The mobility of menstruating women in these areas is also restricted, as they are expected to not sit close to men or walk in front of them and must avoid places frequented by men or boys (Mohamed et al. 2018).

The stigma and taboo surrounding menstruation in these parts of Oceania have also been influenced by Christianity. In Fiji, many participants in a study, including religious and community leaders, rationalized the exclusion and aversion of menstruating women by citing the Bible's book of Leviticus to "not approach a woman during her uncleanliness period" (Mohamed et al. 2018). In Solomon Islands, menstruating women either do not attend church due to being "dirty" or only sit at the back of the church service on a bench allocated for them and do not deliver Bible readings or receive Holy Communion (Mohamed et al. 2018). It is therefore important to note that the traditions of social ostracization, taboo, and stigma of menstruating women in non-Western cultures are not wholly grounded in historical traditions but encapsulate interpretations of Christianity.

There are differences in girls' experiences of menstruation and menstrual health and hygiene (MHH) throughout Oceania. Members of Indigenous Australian communities, girls from low socioeconomic backgrounds, those experiencing homelessness, and those living with disabilities face challenges to practice good MHH due to differences in beliefs about and attitudes toward menstruation, barriers to accessibility and availability of resources, stigma, and social norms. For example, in many Indigenous Australian cultures, menstruation is considered private "women's business," making it a particularly sensitive topic for discussion. Furthermore, due to taboos and stigma, many girls in Oceania frequently manage their menses in ways that are considered unhygienic and harmful. A study found that menstruating women from both urban and rural areas of Papua

New Guinea and Solomon Islands dry the cloths that they use to manage menstrual bleeding on an outside clothesline under another piece of cloth so they are out of direct sunlight, while others are more secretive and dry cloths inside the house to avoid shame (Mohamed et al. 2018). Such stigma and shame restrict women's ability to hygienically wash and dry reusable absorbent materials in direct sunlight. This may increase the risk of reproductive tract infections (Sumpter and Torondel 2013). Several studies show that girls use inappropriate menstrual absorbents in the absence of, or limited access to, disposable commercial sanitary products and practice poor disposal methods and incorrect or infrequent cleaning of external genitalia. Apart from infections, the unhygienic management of menstruation can lead to gynecological issues that adversely affect the reproductive health of adolescent girls as they transition through puberty.

Various initiatives have been taken to provide better access to menstrual hygiene products. The Australian government recently removed the goods and services tax (GST) on menstrual hygiene products, which will ease the financial burden associated with menstruation (Cook 2018). The Australian Government Department of Foreign Affairs and Trade (DFAT 2017) funded the research project The Last Taboo: Research on Menstrual Hygiene Interventions in the Pacific. The research investigated barriers to women's access to menstrual hygiene in Fiji, Solomon Islands, Papua New Guinea, and Bougainville (DFAT 2017). The findings will be used to develop DFAT-funded menstrual hygiene management programs in that region of Oceania. While these incentives indicate that positive steps are being taken in Oceanic countries to improve women's access to menstrual hygiene, strategies and programs also need to be designed to target dismantling the stigma and shame associated with menstruation. It will only then be possible to address the attitudes and beliefs that perpetuate barriers to women's access to menstrual hygiene in order to encourage them to practice good reproductive health.

MARRIAGE AND PARTNERSHIPS

The nature of marriage and partnerships for women greatly vary across the different regions of Oceania. In Australia, marriage is regulated by the federal government, and the Marriage Act 1961 applies to all states and territories. Australian law recognizes only monogamous marriage, including same-sex marriage, but does not recognize other forms of union such as traditional Aboriginal or polygamous marriages. Same-sex marriage was recognized in Australian law in 2017, and it was legalized in New Zealand in 2013. However, same-sex marriage and same-sex unions are not recognized or legalized in countries such as Fiji, Papua New Guinea, Solomon Islands, Vanuatu, Micronesia, Kiribati, Marshall Islands, Nauru, American Samoa, Cook Islands, Samoa, Tonga, and Tuvalu. This means that many queer women in these countries are denied the right to legalize their commitment to a same-sex partner. It may deter queer or questioning women from acting on their feelings for other women for fear that a long-term relationship may be difficult to sustain in societies where same-sex unions are not accepted. Not being able to openly embrace their sexuality or legalize their same-sex relationships as heterosexual individuals do can be potentially detrimental to the mental, emotional, and sexual well-being of queer or questioning women who live in parts of Oceania that do not recognize same-sex unions.

Oceania has unique marriage practices throughout the region. The past English practice of "dowry," where the groom receives payment from the bride's family for the marriage, is not currently common even in Oceanic countries that have strong cultural ties to their British colonizers. The notion of engaging in partnerships and marriage out of romantic love is the dominant ideology in developed Oceania nations. However, in parts of Melanesia, such as Papua New Guinea and Solomon Islands, bridewealth, also known as bride-price, is practiced when grooms offer money and other items in exchange for a bride (Eves 2019). As Eves (2019) notes, bride-price is a cultural practice that should not be viewed as inherently harmful simply because it is so different to Western marriage practices. Some women from poorer families are able to gain much needed finances from the bride-price paid by the husband. However, bride-price is harmful to women when they are deprived of agency and forced to follow their husband's orders during the course of their marriage because of the payment that was made (Eves 2019).

MEDIA AND SEXUALITY

Mainstream Media

Mainstream media has served to spread societal expectations of gender and sexuality in Oceania. Movies, television shows, and the internet frequently portray women in ways that relate to motherhood, parenting, or seeking love and commitment to eventually fulfill a lifelong dream to

Tiwi women checking phone. (Nikol Senkyrikova/Dreamstime.com)

"start a family." Research has indicated that even educational media such as university medical textbooks in Australia depict women's sexuality with a "heterosexual perspective, with marriage and mothering the 'natural' aspirations of all women" (Koutroulis 1990, 73). Koutroulis (1990, 78) argues that women in Australia are still seen as "mothers who are almost entirely responsible for the ills of their offspring or kin." If women continue to be viewed in this way, their sexuality and sexual experiences will continue to be stereotyped as limited to functions of reproduction. The repetition of the stereotype of the maternal woman in various forms of media normalizes societal perceptions that women's sexuality is somehow connected to motherhood. When such stereotypes are internalized by members of society, even in developed Oceania countries, the sexual choices of women who do not want to ever become mothers are scrutinized and criticized.

The popular media has also continually demonstrated unrealistic and stereotypical images of the "perfect" body type, which has affected the self-esteem of many girls and women. Many young women feel the pressure to conform to an "ideal body size" or to "beauty" norms as a result of certain photos being advertised in numerous media outlets such as billboards and fashion magazines (Calogero and Thompson 2010). The media tends to promote Eurocentric or "white" ideals of beauty and sexual attractiveness, which can have a detrimental impact on the self-esteem of non-European-looking women who cannot conform to such ideals. It is not surprising, then, that Indigenous women from Oceania have largely been excluded from the beauty norms circulated by the media. Recently, Aboriginal women Samantha Harris and Magnolia Maymaru from Australia have been given media exposure as successful and beautiful models, which is a welcome break from the usual "all buxom, blonde, blue-eyes beauties" circulated in the media (Mulholland 2019, 211). While this is a start, there is still not nearly enough diversity in the media to represent all the different Indigenous types of beauty in Oceania. The media's portrayal of a few Indigenous figures as beautiful among countless European-looking beauty and sex icons reinforces social norms that feminine beauty and sex appeal are most common within the default and dominant white European women.

The media also acts as a globalizing influence throughout Oceania. For example, the two dominant cultures of Indo-Fijian and Indigenous Fijian had distinct ideals of beauty and sexual attractiveness rooted in respective cultural traditions (Becker 1995). This meant that simultaneous and sometimes conflicting ideals of feminine beauty coexisted. However, with the global influence of Western media, one particular type of ideal feminine beauty and sexual attractiveness has begun to permeate Fiji and other countries such as Hawaii, which reflect contemporary Western standards of beauty (Kong 2007; Meyerhoff 2020). This highlights how the Western media has a homogenizing global effect on beauty and, consequently, on ideals of what is considered "sexy" that are constructed for women in Oceania. It can be presumed that more traditional ideals of feminine beauty and sexual attractiveness would continue to exist in Oceania countries that have not been greatly influenced or exposed to Western popular media.

Social Media

Social media has also been utilized to bring issues pertaining to women's sexual rights and freedoms to the forefront. For instance, Indigenous Australian women Marlee Silva and her sister Keely Silva, from the Kamilaroi Aboriginal nation, launched the Instagram platform Tiddas 4 Tiddas

(*tiddas* is an Aboriginal word for "sister"). Their aim was to offer a platform that encourages young Aboriginal and Torres Strait Islander Australian women to share their untold stories and experiences (Sardya 2019), which offers a space for Indigenous Australian women to freely discuss issues pertaining to their gender struggles and sexuality. The "It's Your Choice, Have a Voice" campaign by the Aboriginal Health and Medical Research Council also utilized social media through Facebook to educate Indigenous youth on making informed decisions about their sexual and reproductive health (Rice et al. 2016).

Given the previously discussed higher rates of teenage pregnancy and maternal mortality that Aboriginal women experience, the campaign's use of social media would have been engaging and empowering for Indigenous women to follow health literacy in ways that allowed them to express their sexuality while upholding their own sexual and reproductive well-being. Māori and other New Zealander women have used Instagram to embrace their unique bodies, post about the unique struggle of being "brown" women, and share experiences of their own sexuality, such as masturbation (Casey 2019). While there is unclear research on the impacts of social media on health (Walker, Palermo, and Klassen 2019), social media provides an outlet for Oceania women, and those who identify as Indigenous women, to share their diverse and similar experiences and learn more about their sexuality from each other.

Pornography

Pornography has become widely accessible, cost effective, and diverse, with increased internet access in the 21st century. Such access has increased worldwide concerns, even in Oceania, of the negative effect on health and well-being. These concerns include watching any sexually explicit content that depicts violence against women, which could normalize and influence real-life sexual aggression and violence against women (Quadara, El-Murr, and Latham 2017). About 37% to 88% of mainstream pornography scenes involve acts of physical violence (mostly gagging and spanking), most usually aimed at women (Lim, Carrotte, and Hellard 2016). Papua New Guinea was found to have the highest percentage of searches for "porn" and "pornography" compared to the number of overall searches in the country (Cochrane 2015). Incidentally, Papua New Guinea also has some of the highest rates of sexual violence and domestic violence against women in the world (Cochrane 2015). Senior lecturer and researcher in pornography from University of Wollongong, Dr. Michael Flood, argues that "violent pornography—is associated with a tolerance for sexual violence, a tolerance for rape" (Cochrane 2015). However, pornography should not be mistaken as the sole cause of the high sexual violence against women in Oceania countries such as Papua New Guinea (Flood, cited in Cochrane 2015). Rather, in countries with already high levels of all forms of violence, high use of (especially violent) pornography may increase or influence the incidence of sexual violence against women (Cochrane 2015).

Conversely, despite negative portrayals of women and their sexuality, some women in Australia described having positive experiences to watching pornography (Ashton, McDonald, and Kirkman 2019). These women indicated that pornography provided visual and mental stimulation for them to engage in the solo pleasure of masturbation, which sexually empowers them to explore and enjoy their own bodies (Ashton, McDonald, and Kirkman 2019). Pornography also enables women to discover and explore new sexual desires on their own or with partners (Ashton, McDonald, and Kirkman 2019). In these ways, pornography is a double-edged sword that can sexually disempower women by potentially encouraging gendered sexual violence or, alternatively, can sexually empower women to explore and enhance their experiences of pleasure. This more broadly reflects how the media is a tool that can be used to sexually educate and liberate the traditional and Indigenous women of Oceania, or reinforce gender, beauty, and sexual stereotypes that can be detrimental to Oceania women's sense of self.

CONCLUSION

This chapter covers issues concerning the lives of women in the Oceania region and how society and social structures have impacted their lives by exposing them to violence and exploiting their sexuality via the institution of religion, marriage, and media. There is limited data available on the diverse experiences of women across every nation in Oceania, which makes it difficult to gain a nuanced and comparative understanding of all these women's experiences. Nonetheless, this chapter has attempted to broadly cover women and sexuality in Oceania. It must be noted that due to the diversity of Oceania, generalized assumptions about women's experiences should be avoided, as each country has its own culture, beliefs, and values. More research needs to be undertaken in the countries of Polynesia,

Melanesia, and Micronesia to gain better knowledge on women's sexuality, sexual freedom, and sexual and reproductive health and rights. However, it is easier said than done, as strict religious values and traditions in Oceanic countries may hinder women's ability to engage with researchers and share their story. Hence, the initiatives and strategies to target patriarchal traditions, religious beliefs, and perceptions of menstruation are steps in the right direction. While there appear to be more overall freedoms for women in the developed countries in Oceania, women in other parts of Oceania are beginning to challenge sexually repressive attitudes, albeit in secret. More research, programs, and initiatives need to be spearheaded and funded to support and work with women in the Oceania region in order to join their struggle to achieve gender equality and the right to sexually explore themselves.

REFERENCES

ABS (Australian Bureau of Statistics). 2017a. "Media Release: 2016 Census Data Reveals 'No Religion' Is Rising Fast." Accessed on October 23, 2020. https://www.abs.gov.au/AUSSTATS/abs@.nsf/mediarelea sesbyReleaseDate/7E65A144540551D7CA258148000E2B85.

ABS (Australian Bureau of Statistics). 2017b. "Personal Safety, Australia." Accessed on October 23, 2020. https://www.abs.gov.au/statistics /people/crime-and-justice/personal-safety-australia/latest-release.

AIHW (Australian Institute of Health and Welfare). 2013. "Australia's Welfare 2013." Accessed June 27, 2022. https://www.aihw.gov.au /getmedia/64b51173-927f-405a-83cc-985a3d699e8c/15448.pdf.

AIHW (Australian Institute of Health and Welfare). 2020. "Sexual Assault in Australia." Accessed June 27, 2022. Australian Government. https://www.aihw.gov.au/getmedia/0375553f-0395-46cc-9574 -d54c74fa601a/aihw-fdv-5.pdf.

Alexeyeff, Kalissa. 2000. "Dragging Drag: The Performance of Gender and Sexuality in the Cook Islands." *Australian Journal of Anthropology* 11 (3): 297–97. https://doi.org/10.1111/j.1835-9310.2000.tb00045.x.

Armitage, Andrew. 1995. *Comparing the Policy of Aboriginal Assimilation: Australia, Canada, and New Zealand.* Vancouver, Canada: University of British Columbia Press.

Arrow, Michelle, and Angela Woollacott. 2019. "Revolutionising the Everyday: The Transformative Impact of the Sexual and Feminist Movements on Australian Society and Culture." In *Everyday*

Revolutions: Remaking Gender, Sexuality and Culture in 1970s Australia, edited by Michelle Arrow and Angela Woollacott, 1–20. Canberra, Australia: ANU Press. Accessed June 27, 2022. http:// www.jstor.org/stable/j.ctvq4c17c.4.

Ashton, Sarah, Karalyn McDonald, and Maggie Kirkman. 2019. "Pornography and Women's Sexual Pleasure: Accounts from Young Women in Australia." *Feminism & Psychology* 29, no. 3 (March): 409–32. https:// doi.org/10.1177/0959353519833410.

Asian Pacific Institute on Gender-Based Violence. 2018. "Fact Sheet: Pacific Islanders and Domestic & Sexual Violence." Accessed June 27, 2022. https://www.api-gbv.org/resources/dvfactsheet-pacificislander.

Aspin, Clive, and Jessica Hutchings. 2007. "Reclaiming the Past to Inform the Future: Contemporary Views of Maori Sexuality." *Culture, Health & Sexuality* 9, no. 4 (July–August): 415–27. https://doi.org /10.1080/13691050701195119.

Australian Human Rights Commission. 2016. "Aboriginal and Torres Strait Islanders: Australia's First Peoples." Accessed June 27, 2022. https://humanrights.gov.au/our-work/education/aboriginal-and -torres-strait-islanders-australias-first-peoples.

Becker, Anne E. 1995. *Body, Self, and Society: The View from Fiji*. Philadelphia: University of Pennsylvania Press.

Blackstone, William. 2016. *Commentaries on the Laws of England*. Oxford: Oxford University Press.

Boyle, Jacqueline, and Sandra Eades. 2016. "Closing the Gap in Aboriginal Women's Reproductive Health: Some Progress, but Still a Long Way to Go." *Australian and New Zealand Journal of Obstetrics and Gynaecology* 56, no. 3 (June): 223–24. https://doi.org/10.1111/ajo.12470.

Byrd, Jodi A. 2011. *The Transit of Empire: Indigenous Critiques of Colonialism*. Minneapolis: University of Minnesota Press.

Calogero, Rachel M., and J. Kevin Thompson. 2010. "Gender and Body Image." In *Handbook of Gender Research in Psychology*, edited by Joan C. Chrisler and Donald R. McCreary, 153–84. New York: Springer.

Cammock, Radilaite, Patricia Priest, Sarah Lovell, and Peter Herbison. 2018. "Awareness and Use of Family Planning Methods among iTaukei Women in Fiji and New Zealand." *Australian and New Zealand Journal of Public Health* 42, no. 4 (January): 365–71. https://doi.org/10.1111/1753-6405.12761.

Casey, Alex. 2019. "Positive Influencers: The Kiwi Women Changing the Face of Instagram." The Spinoff. Acccessed June 27, 2022. https://thespinoff.co.nz/partner/womens-health-action/08-05-2019

/positive-influencers-the-kiwi-women-changing-the-face-of-instagram.

Center for Reproductive Rights. 2020. "The World's Abortion Laws." Accessed October 9, 2020. https://reproductiverights.org /worldabortionlaws.

Chang, Anne Lee, Eric Hurwitz, Jill Miyamura, Bliss Kaneshiro, and Tetine Sentell. 2015. "Maternal Risk Factors and Perinatal Outcomes among Pacific Islander Groups in Hawaii: A Retrospective Cohort Study Using Statewide Hospital Data." *BMC Pregnancy & Childbirth* 15 (October): 239. https://doi.org/10.1186/s12884-015-0671-4.

Christie, Emily, Hansdeep Singh, and Jaspreet K. Singh. 2015. "An Analysis of Judicial Sentencing Practices in Sexual & Gender-Based Violence Cases in the Pacific Island Region." *ICAAD.* Accessed June 27, 2022. http://138.25.65.49/other/general-materials/ICAAD -Analysis-of-Judicial-Sentencing-Practices-in-SGBV-Cases.pdf.

Cochrane, Liam. 2015. "PNG Tops Porn Searches on Google, Experts Divided over Link between Pornography and Violence." ABC News. Last modified February 26, 2016. Accessed June 27, 2022. https://www .abc.net.au/news/2015-02-25/papua-new-guinea-tops-google-porn -searches/6262028.

Cook, Lauren. 2018. "Removing GST on Feminine Hygiene Products." Parliament of Australia. Last modified November 29, 2018. Accessed June 27, 2022. https://www.aph.gov.au/About_Parliament/Parliamentary _Departments/Parliamentary_Library/FlagPost/2018/November /Removing_GST_on_feminine_hygiene_products.

Coper, Alan, Alan N. Williams, and Nigel Spooner. 2018. "When Did Aboriginal People First Arrive in Australia?" UNSW Sydney Newsroom. Accessed June 27, 2022. https://newsroom.unsw.edu .au/news/science-tech/when-did-aboriginal-people-first-arrive -australia.

Counts, Dorothy Ayers. 1990. "Domestic Violence in Oceania: Conclusion." *Pacific Studies* 13 (3): 225–54.

DFAT (Department of Foreign Affairs and Trade). 2016. "Case Study: Faith in Gender Equality in the Pacific." Australian Government. Accessed June 27, 2022. https://www.dfat.gov.au/news/news /Pages/faith-in-gender-equality-in-the-pacific.

DFAT (Department of Foreign Affairs and Trade). 2017. "The Last Taboo: Research on Menstrual Hygiene Management in the Pacific (Solomon Islands, Fiji and Papua New Guinea)." Australian Government. Accessed June 27, 2022. https://www.dfat.gov.au/about-us

/publications/Pages/the-last-taboo-research-menstrual-hygiene
-management-pacific.

Eves, Richard. 2019. "Full Price, Full Body: Norms, Brideprice and Intimate Partner Violence in Highlands Papua New Guinea." *Culture, Health & Sexuality* 21, no. 12 (January): 1367–80. https://doi.org/10.1080/13691058.2018.1564937.

Family Planning NSW. 2018. "Unplanned Pregnancy: Abortion." Accessed on October 22, 2020. https://www.fpnsw.org.au/factsheets/individuals/abortion/unplanned-pregnancy-abortion.

Fiji Bureau of Statistics. 2007. "1.10 Population by Religion and Province of Enumeration, Fiji: 2007 Census." Accessed on October 23, 2020. http://www.statsfiji.gov.fj/index.php/document-library/doc_download/426-population-by-religion-province.

Giles, Lynn C., Gary F. V. Glonek, Vivienne M. Moore, Michael J. Davies, and Mary A. Luzcz. 2010. "Lower Age at Menarche Affects Survival in Older Australian Women: Results from the Australian Longitudinal Study of Ageing." *BMC Public Health* 10: 341. https://doi.org/10.1186/1471-2458-10-341.

Groos, A. D., and T. A. Smith. 1992. "Age at Menarche and Associated Nutritional Status Variables in Karimui and Daribi Census Divisions of Simbu Province." *PNG Medical Journal* 35, no. 2 (June): 84–94. Accessed June 27, 2022. https://pubmed.ncbi.nlm.nih.gov/1509816.

Heard, Emma, Lisa Fitzgerald, Sina Va'ai, Fiona Collins, Maxine Whittaker, and Allyson Mutch. 2019. "'In the Islands People Don't Really Talk about This Stuff, so You Go through Life on Your Own': An Arts-Based Study Exploring Intimate Relationships with Young People in Samoa." *Culture, Health & Sexuality* 21 (5): 526–42. https://doi.org/10.1080/13691058.2018.1492021.

Helu, Futa. 1995. "Brother/Sister and Gender Relations in Ancient and Modern Tonga." *Journal de la Société des Océanistes* 100–101: 191–200. https://doi.org/10.3406/jso.1995.1963.

James, Kerry E. 1994. "Effeminate Males and Changes in the Construction of Gender in Tonga." *Pacific Studies* 17, no. 2 (June): 39–69. Accessed June 27, 2022. https://contentdm.lib.byu.edu/digital/collection/PacificStudies/id/218/rec/45.

Keesing, Roger M., and Miriam Kahn. 2014. "Melanesian Culture." *Britannica*. Accessed October 23, 2020. https://www.britannica.com/place/Melanesia.

Kenney, Christie M. 2011. "Māori Women, Maternity Services and the Treaty of Waitangi." In *Always Speaking: The Treaty of Waitangi and Public Policy*, edited by Veronica Tawhai and Katarina Gray -Sharp, 127. Wellington, New Zealand: Huia Publishers.

Kong, Melissa. 2007. "Beauty Ideals & Body Image: Suva, Fiji." *Independent Study Project Collection* 217. Accessed June 27, 2022. https://digitalcollections.sit.edu/isp_collection/217.

Koutroulis, Glenda. 1990. "The Orifice Revisited: Women in Gynaecological Texts." *Community Health Studies* 14, no. 1 (March): 73–84. https://doi.org/10.1111/j.1753-6405.1990.tb00024.x.

Lim, Megan S. C., Elise Carrotte, and Margaret E. Hellard. 2016. "The Impact of Pornography on Gender-Based Violence, Sexual Health and Well-Being: What Do We Know?" *Journal of Epidemiology and Community Health* 70 (1): 3–5. https://doi.org/10.1136/jech-2015-205453.

Lincoln, Jay, Masoud Mohammadnezhad, and Sabiha Khan. 2018. "Knowledge, Attitudes, and Practices of Family Planning Among Women of Reproductive Age in Suva, Fiji in 2017." *Journal of Women's Health Care* 7, no. 3 (May): 100431. https://doi.org/10.4172/2167-0420.1000431.

Macintyre, Martha, and Ceridwen Spark, eds. 2017. *Transformations of Gender in Melanesia*. Canberra, Australia: ANU Press. Accessed June 27, 2022. https://press-files.anu.edu.au/downloads/press/n2310/pdf/book.pdf.

Meo, Ilisapeci. 2003. "Asserting Women's Dignity in a Patriarchal World." In *Weavings: Women Doing Theology in Oceania*, edited by Lydia Johnson Joan Alleluia Filemoni-Tofaeno, 150–60. Suva, Fiji: Weavers, South Pacific Association of Theological Schools.

Meyerhoff, H. 2020. "America the Beautiful U.S. Imperial Beauty Politics in Hawaii, from WWII to Statehood." Diss., Haverford College. Accessed June 27, 2022. http://hdl.handle.net/10066/22680.

Ministers: Department of Health. 2020. "More Contraceptive Choice for Australian Women." Australian Government. Accessed June 27, 2022. https://www.health.gov.au/ministers/the-hon-greg-hunt-mp/media/more-contraceptive-choice-for-australian-women.

Ministry of Justice (New Zealand). 2014. "2014 New Zealand Crime and Safety Survey: Main Findings." Accessed June 27, 2022. https://www.justice.govt.nz/justice-sector-policy/research-data/nzcass/resources-and-downloads/#report.

Mitchell, Elke, and Linda Rae Bennett. 2020a. "Pressure and Persuasion: Young Fijian Women's Experiences of Sexual and Reproductive Coercion in Romantic Relationships." *Violence against Women* 26, nos. 12–13 (October): 1555–73. https://doi.org/10.1177/10778 01219882505.

Mitchell, Elke, and Linda Rae Bennett. 2020b. "Young Women's Perceptions and Experiences of Sexual Risk in Suva, Fiji." *Culture, Health & Sexuality* 22 (5): 504–19. https://doi.org/10.1080/1369105 8.2019.1614669.

Mohamed, Yasmin, Kelly Durrant, Chelsea Huggett, Jessica Davis, Alison Macintyre, Seta Menu, Joyce Namba Wilson et al. 2018. "A Qualitative Exploration of Menstruation-Related Restrictive Practices in Fiji, Solomon Islands and Papua New Guinea." *PLoS ONE* 13, no. 12 (December): e0208224. https://doi.org/10.1371/journal.pone .0208224.

Moreton-Robinson, Aileen. 2003. "Researching Whiteness: Some Reflections from an Indigenous Woman's Standpoint." *Hecate* 29 (2): 72–85.

Mulholland, Monique. 2019. "Sexy and Sovereign? Aboriginal Models Hit the 'Multicultural Mainstream." *Cultural Studies* 33, no. 2 (June): 198–222. https://doi.org/10.1080/09502386.2018.1473457.

Naz, Rafia. 2013. "Sex Education in Fiji." *Sexuality & Culture* 18: 664–87. https://doi.org/10.1007/s12119-013-9204-3.

1 News. 2019. "'No Religion' Officially Overtakes Christianity in New Zealand Census Stats." Accessed on October 22, 2020. https:// www.tvnz.co.nz/one-news/new-zealand/no-religion-officially-overtakes -christianity-in-new-zealand-census-stats.

Quadara, Antonia, Alissar El-Murr, and Joe Latham. 2017. "The Effects of Pornography on Children and Young People." Australian Government: Australian Institute of Family Studies. Accessed June 27, 2022. https://apo.org.au/sites/default/files/resource-files/2017-12 /apo-nid127771_5.pdf.

Rauchholz, Manuel. 2016. "Masculine Sexuality, Violence and Sexual Exploitation in Micronesia." *Asia Pacific Journal of Anthropology* 17, nos. 3–4 (July): 342–58. https://doi.org/10.1080/14442213.2016.1196724.

Rice, Emma S., Emma Haynes, Paul Royce, and Sandra C. Thompson. 2016. "Social Media and Digital Technology Use among Indigenous Young People in Australia: A Literature Review." *International Journal for Equity in Health* 15 (May): 81. https://doi .org/10.1186/s12939-016-0366-0.

Rissel, Chris E., Juliet Richters, Andrew E. Grulich, Richard O. de Visser, and Anthony M. A. Smith. 2003. "Sex in Australia: Attitudes toward Sex in a Representative Sample of Adults." *Australian and New Zealand Journal of Public Health* 27 (2): 118–23.

Ruttan, Lia, Patti Laboucane-Benson, and Brenda Munro. 2008. "'A Story I Never Heard Before': Aboriginal Young Women, Homelessness, and Restoring Connections." *Pimatisiwin: A Journal of Aboriginal and Indigenous Community Health* 69 (3): 31–54. Accessed June 27, 2022. https://www.homelesshub.ca/resource/%E2%80%9C -story-i-never-heard-%E2%80%9D-aboriginal-young-women -homelessness-and-restoring-connections.

Sardya, Ali. 2019. "Building a Community for Change Sister to Sister." Western Sydney University. Accessed June 27, 2022. https://www .westernsydney.edu.au/newscentre/news_centre/story_archive /2019/building_a_community_for_change_sister_to_sister.

SBS. 2015. "Timeline: Stolen Generations." Last modified February 26, 2015. Accessed June 27, 2022. https://www.sbs.com.au/news /timeline-stolen-generations.

Smith, Sarah A. 2019. "Gender, Relationships and Sexual Violence in the Lives of Women from Chuuk." *Micronesia, Journal of Aggression, Maltreatment & Trauma* 28, no. 2 (July): 146–65. https://doi.org/10 .1080/10926771.2018.1494236.

Spano, Susan. 2000. "In Tonga, Women Cloak Their Power under Mother Hubbard Dresses." *Los Angeles Times*, June 11. Accessed June 27, 2022. https://www.latimes.com/archives/la-xpm-2000-jun-11-tr -39675-story.html.

St. George, Ian M., Sheila Williams, and Phil A. Silva. 1994. "Body Size and the Menarche: The Dunedin Study." *Journal of Adolescent Health* 15, no. 7 (November): 573–76. https://doi.org /10.1016/1054-139x(94)90141-O.

Sullivan, Corrinne Tayce. 2017. "Indigenous Australian Women's Colonial Sexual Intimacies: Positioning Indigenous Women's Agency." *Culture, Health & Sexuality* 20, no. 4 (July): 397–410. https://doi.org/10 .1080/13691058.2017.1349930.

Sumpter, Colin, and Belen Torondel. 2013. "A Systematic Review of the Health and Social Effects of Menstrual Hygiene Management." *PLoS One* 8, no. 4 (April): e62004. https://doi.org/10.1371/journal .pone.0062004.

Tcherkézoff, Serge. 2009. "A Reconsideration of the Role of Polynesian Women in Early Encounters with Europeans: Supplement to

Marshall Sahlins' Voyage around the Islands of History." In *Oceanic Encounters: Exchange, Desire, Violence*, edited by Margaret Jolly, Serge Tcherkézoff, and Darrell Tryon, 113–60. Canberra, Australia: ANU Press. Accessed June 27, 2022. https://www.jstor .org/stable/j.ctt24h8jn.

Thomas, Erin. 2017. "Domestic Violence and Sexual Assault in the Pacific Islander Community: Understanding the Pacific Islands." Asian /Pacific Islander Domestic Violence Resource Project. Accessed June 27, 2022. https://www.api-gbv.org/resources/dv-sa-pacific -islander-community-bydvrp.

Tupuola, Anne-Marie. 1996. "Learning Sexuality: Young Samoan Women." *Women's Studies Journal* 12 (2): 59–76.

Varani-Norton, Eta. 2014. "'It's Good to Teach Them, but . . . They Should Also Know When to Apply It': Parents' Views and Attitudes towards Fiji's Family Life Education Curriculum." *Sex Education* 14 (6): 692–706. https://doi.org/10.1080/14681811.2014.934443.

Walker, Troy, Claire Palermo, and Karen Klassen. 2019. "Considering the Impact of Social Media on Contemporary Improvement of Australian Aboriginal Health: Scoping Review." *JMIR Public Health and Surveillance* 5, no. 1 (February): e11573. https://doi.org /10.2196/11573.

Windschuttle, Keith. 2003. "The Fabrication of Aboriginal History." *Sydney Papers* 15, no. 1 (Summer): 20–29. Accessed June 27, 2022. https://search.informit.com.au/documentSummary;dn=839662676 745905;res=IELHSS.

Worldometer. 2020. "Oceania Population (LIVE)." Accessed June 27, 2022. https://www.worldometers.info/world-population/oceania -population.

Bibliography

Aldama, Frederick L. 2018. *The Routledge Companion to Gender, Sex, and Latin American Culture.* New York: Routledge.

Alvarez, Carmen, Jose A. Bauermeister, and Antonia M. Villarruel. 2014. "Sexual Communication and Sexual Behavior among Young Adult Heterosexual Latinos." *Journal of the Association of Nurses in AIDS Care* 25 (6): 577–88. https://doi.org/10.1016/j.jana.2014.06.005.

Arnfred, Signe, ed. 2004. *Re-thinking Sexualities in Africa.* Uppsala, Sweden: Nordic Africa Institute.

Arrow, Michelle, and Angela Woollacott. 2019. "Revolutionising the Everyday: The Transformative Impact of the Sexual and Feminist Movements on Australian Society and Culture." In *Everyday Revolutions: Remaking Gender, Sexuality and Culture in 1970s Australia*, edited by Michelle Arrow and Angela Woollacott, 1–20. Canberra, Australia: ANU Press. Accessed June 27, 2022. http://www.jstor.org/stable/j.ctvq4c17c.4.

Ashton, Sarah, Karalyn McDonald, and Maggie Kirkman. 2018. "Women's Experiences of Pornography: A Systematic Review of Research Using Qualitative Methods." *Journal of Sex Research* 55 (3): 334–47. https://doi.org/10.1080/00224499.2017.1364337.

"Asia and the Pacific." 2018. Global Slavery Index. Accessed June 27, 2022. https://www.globalslaveryindex.org/2018/findings/regional-analysis/asia-and-the-pacific.

Asian Pacific Institute on Gender-Based Violence. 2018. "Fact Sheet: Pacific Islanders and Domestic & Sexual Violence." Accessed June 27, 2022. https://www.api-gbv.org/resources/dvfactsheet-pacificislander.

Aspin, Clive, and Jessica Hutchings. 2007. "Reclaiming the Past to Inform the Future: Contemporary Views of Maori Sexuality." *Culture, Health & Sexuality* 9, no. 4 (July–August): 415–27. https://doi.org /10.1080/13691050701195119.

Bennet, Jane, and Sylvia Tamale, eds. 2017. *Research on Gender and Sexualities in Africa.* Dakar, Senegal: Codesria.

Binard, Florence. 2017. "The British Women's Liberation Movement in the 1970s: Redefining the Personal and the Political." *Revue Francaise de Civilisation Britannique XXII Hors série.* Accessed July 19, 2022. https://journals.openedition.org/rfcb/1688.

Bishop, Ryan, and Lillian S. Robinson. 1998. *Night Market: Sexual Cultures and the Thai Economic Miracle.* New York and London: Routledge.

Błuś, Anna. 2018. "A Wave of Women Fighting Rape across Europe." Amnesty International. Accessed June 27, 2022. https://www .amnesty.org/en/latest/news/2018/11/a-wave-of-women-fighting -rape-across-europe.

Bose, Brinda, and Subhabrata Bhattacharyya, eds. 2007. *The Phobic and the Erotic: The Politics of Sexualities in Contemporary India.* Calcutta, India: Seagull Books.

Bott, Sarah, Alessandra Guedes, Mary Goodwin, and Jennifer A. Mendoza. 2012. *Violence against Women in Latin America and the Caribbean: A Comparative Analysis of Population-Based Data from 12 Countries.* Washington, DC: Pan American Health Organization.

Boyle, Jacqueline, and Sandra Eades. 2016. "Closing the Gap in Aboriginal Women's Reproductive Health: Some Progress, but Still a Long Way to Go." *Australian and New Zealand Journal of Obstetrics and Gynaecology* 56, no. 3 (June): 223–24. https://doi.org/10.1111 /ajo.12470.

Bradbury, Thomas N., and Benjamin R. Karney. 2019. *Intimate Relationships.* 3rd ed. New York: W. W. Norton & Company.

Burki, Talha. 2016. "Sex Education in China Leaves Young Vulnerable to Infection." *Lancet Infectious Diseases*, no. 1. https://doi.org/10.1016 /S1473-3099(15)00494-6.

Byerly, Carolyn M. 2011. "Global Report on the Status of Women in the News Media." International Women's Media Foundation. Accessed May 29, 2019. https://www.iwmf.org/wp-content/uploads/2018/06 /IWMF-Global-Report.pdf.

Cammock, Radilaite, Patricia Priest, Sarah Lovell, and Peter Herbison. 2018. "Awareness and Use of Family Planning Methods among iTaukei Women in Fiji and New Zealand." *Australian and New Zealand Journal of Public Health* 42, no. 4 (January): 365–71. https://doi.org/10.1111/1753-6405.12761.

Campbell, Kelly, David W. Wright, and Carlos Flores. 2015. "Newlywed Women's Marital Expectations: Lifelong Monogamy?" *Journal of Divorce and Remarriage* 53 (2): 108–25.

Chatterji, Angana P. 2016. "Gendered and Sexual Violence in and beyond South Asia." *ANTYAJAA: Indian Journal of Women and Social Change* 1 (1): 19–40. https://doi.org/10.1177/2455632716646278.

Chopra, Radhika, Caroline Osella, and Filipo Osella, eds. 2004. *South Asian Masculinities: Context of Change, Sites of Continuity*. New Delhi: India: Kali for Women.

Coleman, David. 2013. "Partnership in Europe; Its Variety, Trends and Dissolution." *Finnish Yearbook of Population Research* XLVIII: 5–49.

Contreras, Juan M., Sarah Bott, Alessandra Guedes, and Elizabeth Dartnall. 2010. *Sexual Violence in Latin America and the Caribbean: A Desk Review*. Sexual Violence Research Initiative. Accessed July 19, 2022. https://ciaotest.cc.columbia.edu/wps/svri/0024041/f_0024041_19595.pdf.

Cook, Lauren. 2018. "Removing GST on Feminine Hygiene Products." Parliament of Australia. Last modified November 29, 2018. Accessed June 27, 2022. https://www.aph.gov.au/About_Parliament/Parliamentary_Departments/Parliamentary_Library/FlagPost/2018/November/Removing_GST_on_feminine_hygiene_products.

Crais, Clifton, and Pamela Scully. 2011. *Sara Baartman and the Hottentot Venus: A Ghost Story and a Biography*. Princeton, NJ, and Oxford: Princeton University Press.

Curtis, Debra. 2009. *Pleasures and Perils: Girls' Sexuality in a Caribbean Consumer Culture*. New Brunswick, NJ: Rutgers University Press.

Dalby, Liza. 2008. *Geisha*. Updated with a New Preface. Berkeley: University of California Press.

Davison, Tamara. 2019. "Latin America Has a Child Marriage Crisis." *Latin America Reports* (blog), April 29. Accessed January 14, 2021. https://latinamericareports.com/latin-america-has-a-child-marriage-crisis/1831.

DeLamater, John, and Rebecca F. Plante. 2015. *Handbook of the Sociology of Sexualities*. New York: Springer.

De Schrijver, Lotte, Tom Vander Beken, Barbara Krahé, and Ines Keygnaert. 2018. "Prevalence of Sexual Violence in Migrants, Applicants for International Protection, and Refugees in Europe: A Critical Interpretive Synthesis of the Evidence." *International Journal of Environmental Research and Public Health* 15, no. 9 (November): 1979. https://doi.org/10.3390/ijerph15091979.

Dickson, Sean, and Steve Sanders. 2014. "India, Nepal and Pakistan: A Unique South Asian Constitutional Discourse on Sexual Orientation and Gender Identity." In *Social Difference and Constitutionalism in Pan-Asia*, edited by Susan H. Williams, 316–48. Cambridge: Cambridge University Press. https://doi.org/10.1017/CBO9781139567312.017.

Donnelly, Kristin, and Jean M. Twenge. 2017. "Masculine and Feminine Traits on the Bem Sex-Role Inventory, 1993–2012: A Cross-Temporal Meta-Analysis." *Sex Roles: A Journal of Research* 76, nos. 9–10: 556–65.

Dragadze, Tamara. 1993. "The Domestication of Religion under Soviet Communism." *Socialism: Ideals, Ideologies, and Local Practice* 31: 141.

Epprecht, Marc. 2004. *Hungochani: The History of a Dissident Sexuality in Southern Africa*. Montreal, Canada: McGill-Queen's University Press.

Epprecht, Marc. 2008. *Heterosexual Africa? The History of an Idea from the Age of Exploration to the Age of AIDS*. Athens: Ohio University Press.

Essayag, Sebastian. 2017. *From Commitment to Action: Policies to End Violence against Women in Latin America and the Caribbean*. Panama: UN Development Programme and UN Entity for Gender Equality and the Empowerment of Women.

"Estimating the Costs of Gender-Based Violence in the European Union." 2019. European Institute for Gender Equality, March 7. Accessed May 30, 2019. https://eige.europa.eu/gender-based-violence/estimating-costs-in-european-union.

Eves, Richard. 2019. "Full Price, Full Body: Norms, Brideprice and Intimate Partner Violence in Highlands Papua New Guinea." *Culture, Health & Sexuality* 21, no. 12 (January): 1367–80. https://doi.org/10.1080/13691058.2018.1564937.

Gil, Rosa M., and Carmen I. Vazquez. 1996. *The Maria Paradox*. New York: Perigee Book.

Giles, Lynn C., Gary F. V. Glonek, Vivienne M. Moore, Michael J. Davies, and Mary A. Luzcz. 2010. "Lower Age at Menarche Affects Survival in Older Australian Women: Results from the Australian Longitudinal Study of Ageing." *BMC Public Health* 10: 341. https://doi.org/10.1186/1471-2458-10-341.

Gilman, Sander. 1985. "Black Bodies, White Bodies: Towards an Iconography of Female Sexuality in Late Nineteenth-Century Art, Medicine and Literature." *Critical Inquiry* 12 (1): 204–42.

Girls Not Brides. 2017. *Child Marriage in Latin America and the Caribbean.* London: Girls Not Brides.

Hare, Denise, Li Yang, and Daniel Englander. 2008. "Land Management in Rural China and Its Gender Implications." *Feminist Economics* 13, nos. 3–4: 35–61. https://doi.org/10.1080/13545700701445298.

"Health." 2019. European Institute for Gender Equality. February 24. Accessed May 31, 2019. https://eige.europa.eu/gender-mainstreaming/policy-areas/health.

Higgins, Louise T., Mo Zheng, Yali Liu, and Chun Hui Sun. 2002. "Attitudes to Marriage and Sexual Behaviors: A Survey of Gender and Culture Differences in China and United Kingdom." *Sex Roles* 46, nos. 3–4: 75–89. https://doi.org/10.1023/a:1016565426011.

Huang, Grace Hui-Chen, and Mary Grove. 2012. "Confucianism and Chinese Families: Values and Practices in Education." *International Journal of Humanities and Social Science* 2, no. 3 (February): 10–14. https://doi.org/10.1007/978-3-319-16390-1_3.

Hulshof, Karin. 2016. "Let's Talk about Sex: Why We Need Sexuality Education in Asia-Pacific." UNICEF East Asia & Pacific, September 1. Accessed June 27, 2022. https://blogs.unicef.org/east-asia-pacific/lets-talk-sex-need-sexuality-education-asia-pacific.

Hutchinson, Elizabeth Q. 2003. "Add Gender and Stir? Cooking Up Gendered Histories of Modern Latin America." *Latin American Research Review* 38 (1): 267–87.

Jeffreys, Elaine, and Haiqing Yu. 2015. *Sex in China.* Cambridge: Polity.

Jolly, Susie, Andrea Cornwall and Kate Hawkins. 2013. *Women, Sexuality and the Political Power of Pleasure.* London and New York: Zed Books.

Jung, Patricia B., Mary E. Hunt, and Radhika Balakrishnan. 2005. *Good Sex: Feminist Perspectives from the World's Religions.* New Brunswick, NJ: Rutgers University Press.

Kempadoo, Kamala. 2004. *Sexing the Caribbean: Gender, Race, and Sexual Labor.* New York: Routledge.

Kimmel, Michael. 2017. *The Gendered Society.* New York: Oxford University Press.

Kinsey, Alfred C., Wardell B. Pomeroy, Clyde E. Martin, and Paul H. Gebhard. 1953. *Sexual Behavior in the Human Female.* Philadelphia: W. B. Saunders.

Laumann, Edward O. 1994. *The Social Organization of Sexuality: Sexual Practices in the United States*, Chicago: University of Chicago Press.

Lewis, Myrna I. 1980. "The History of Female Sexuality in the United States." In *Women's Sexual Development*, edited by Martha Kirkpatrick, 19–43. Boston: Springer.

Lim, Megan S. C., Elise Carrotte, and Margaret E. Hellard. 2016. "The Impact of Pornography on Gender-Based Violence, Sexual Health and Well-Being: What Do We Know?" *Journal of Epidemiology and Community Health* 70 (1): 3–5. https://doi.org/10.1136/jech-2015-205453.

Lipka, Michael, and David Masci. 2019. "Where Europe Stands on Gay Marriage and Civil Unions." Pew Research Center, May 30. Accessed June 24, 2019. https://www.pewresearch.org/fact-tank/2019/05/30/where-europe-stands-on-gay-marriage-and-civil-unions.

Magubane, Zine. 2001. "Which Bodies Matter? Feminism, Poststructuralism, Race, and the Curious Odyssey of the 'Hottentot Venus.'" *Gender & Society* 15 (6): 816–34.

Masters, William, and Virginia Johnson. 1966. *Human Sexual Response.* New York: Bantam.

metoomvmt.org. n.d. Accessed February 20, 2020. https://metoomvmt.org.

Mijalković, Saša. 2014. "'Sex-Espionage' as a Method of Intelligence and Security Agencies." *Bezbednost Beograd* 56 (1): 5–22.

Miller, Rowland S. 2018. *Intimate Relationships.* New York: McGraw Hill Education.

Mistreanu, Simina. 2019. "China's #MeToo Activists Have Transformed a Generation." Foreign Policy, January 10. Accessed June 27, 2022. https://foreignpolicy.com/2019/01/10/chinas-metoo-activists-have-transformed-a-generation.

Mitchell, Elke, and Linda Rae Bennett. 2020. "Pressure and Persuasion: Young Fijian Women's Experiences of Sexual and Reproductive Coercion in Romantic Relationships." *Violence against Women* 26, nos. 12–13 (October): 1555–73. https://doi.org/10.1177/1077801219882505.

Molony, Barbara, Janet Theiss, and Hyaeweol Choi. 2016. *Gender in Modern East Asia, China, Korea*. Boulder, CO: Westview Press.

Morrison, Andrew, Mary Ellsberg, and Sarah Bott. 2007. "Addressing Gender-Based Violence in the Latin American and Caribbean Region: A Critical Review of Interventions." *World Bank Researcher Observer* 22 (1): 25–51.

Mulholland, Monique. 2019. "Sexy and Sovereign? Aboriginal Models Hit the 'Multicultural Mainstream.'" *Cultural Studies* 33, no. 2 (June): 198–222. https://doi.org/10.1080/09502386.2018.1473457.

Nadeau, Kathleen, and Sangita Rayamajhi. 2013. *Women's Roles in Asia*. Santa Barbara, CA: Greenwood.

Nadeau, Kathleen, and Sangita Rayamajhi, eds. 2019. *Women and Violence: Global Lives in Focus*. Santa Barbara, CA: ABC-CLIO.

Naz, Rafia. 2013. "Sex Education in Fiji." *Sexuality & Culture* 18: 664–87. https://doi.org/10.1007/s12119-013-9204-3.

Niemann, Yolanda F. 2004. "Stereotypes of Chicanas and Chicanos: Impact on Family Functioning, Individual Expectations, Goals, and Behavior." In *The Handbook of Chicana/o Psychology and Mental Health*, edited by Leticia M. Arellano, Brian McNell, and Roberto J. Velasquez, 61–82. Mahwah, NJ: Lawrence Erlbaum Associates.

Nye, Robert A., ed. 1999. *Sexuality*. New York: Oxford University Press.

Nyeck, S. N., and Mark Epprecht, eds. 2013. *Sexual Diversity in Africa: Politics Theory and Citizenship*. Montreal, Canada: McGill-Queen's University Press.

Ong, Aihwa, and Michael G. Peletz. 1995. *Bewitching Women, Pious Men, Gender and Body Politics in Southeast Asia*. Oakland: University of California Press.

Parkin, David, and David Nyamwaya, eds. 1987. *Transformations of African Marriage*. Manchester, UK: Manchester University Press.

Pattanaik, Devdutt. 2014. *Shikhandi and Other Tales They Don't Tell You*. New Delhi, India: Zubaan and Penguin Books.

Paxton, Pamela Marie, Melanie M. Hughes, and Tiffany Barnes. 2020. *Women, Politics, and Power: A Global Perspective*. Lanham, MD: Rowman & Littlefield.

Peletz, Michael G. 2012. "Gender, Sexuality, and the State in Southeast Asia." *Journal of Asian Studies* 71, no. 4 (November): 895–917.

Pew Research Center. 2018. "Eastern and Western Europeans Differ on Importance of Religion, Views of Minorities, and Key Social Issues."

Accessed June 27, 2022. https://www.pewforum.org/2018/10/29/eastern-and-western-europeans-differ-on-importance-of-religion-views-of-minorities-and-key-social-issues.

Rathus, Spencer A., Jeffrey S. Nevid, and Lois Fichner-Rathus. 2018. *Human Sexuality in a World of Diversity.* 10th ed. New York: Pearson Education.

Rauchholz, Manuel. 2016. "Masculine Sexuality, Violence and Sexual Exploitation in Micronesia." *Asia Pacific Journal of Anthropology* 17, nos. 3–4 (July): 342–58. https://doi.org/10.1080/14442213.2016.1196724.

Rice, Emma S., Emma Haynes, Paul Royce, and Sandra C. Thompson. 2016. "Social Media and Digital Technology Use among Indigenous Young People in Australia: A Literature Review." *International Journal for Equity in Health* 15 (May): 81. https://doi.org/10.1186/s12939-016-0366-0.

Rissel, Chris E., Juliet Richters, Andrew E. Grulich, Richard O. de Visser, and Anthony M. A. Smith. 2003. "Sex in Australia: Attitudes towards Sex in a Representative Sample of Adults." *Australian and New Zealand Journal of Public Health* 27 (2): 118–23.

Rodriguez, Barbara, Sofia Shakil, and Adrian Morel. 2018. "Four Things to Know about Gender-Based Violence in Asia." Asia Foundation, March 14. Accessed June 27, 2022. https://asiafoundation.org/2018/03/14/four-things-know-gender-based-violence-asia.

Roth, Kenneth. 2018. "World Report 2018: Rights Trends in Georgia." Human Rights Watch, January 18. Accessed June 27, 2022. https://www.hrw.org/world-report/2018/country-chapters/georgia.

Sarikakis, Katharine. 2013. "Media and the Image of Women." Council of Europe, November.

Schmitt, David P., and John F. Dovidio. 2003. "Universal Sex Differences in the Desire for Sexual Variety: Tests from 52 Nations, 6 Continents, and 13 Islands." *Journal of Personality and Social Psychology* 85 (1): 85–104.

Senior, Olive. 1991. *Working Miracles: Women's Lives in the English-Speaking Caribbean.* Bloomington: Indiana University Press.

Sethi, Dinesh, and Dimitrinka Jordanova Peshevska. 2014. "Preventing Interpersonal Violence in Europe." *Macedonian Journal of Medical Sciences* 2 (2): 350. https://doi.org/10.3889/oamjms.2014.060.

Shah, Svati P. 2019 "Sedition, Sexuality, Gender, and Gender Identity in South Asia." *South Asia Multidisciplinary Academic Journal.* Accessed May 2, 2019. http://journals.openedition.org/samaj/5163.

Shin, Kyung Rim, Hyojung Park, and Chiyoung Cha. 2011. "Sex Education during the School-Aged Years Influences Sexual Attitudes and Sexual Health in College: A Comparative Study from Korea." *Nursing & Health Sciences* 13 (3): 328–34.

Shirinian, Sanan. 2010. "Domestic Violence against Women in Armenia." United Human Rights Council, May 26. Accessed June 27, 2022. http://www.unitedhumanrights.org/2010/05/domestic-violence-against-women-in-armenia.

Soh, Sarah. 2008. *The Comfort Women, Sexual Violence and Post-Colonial Memory in Korea.* Chicago: University of Chicago Press.

Solod, Darina. 2019. "In Uzbekistan, Women's Rights Are Changing—but Not Fast Enough." Open Democracy, July 4. Accessed June 27, 2022. https://www.opendemocracy.net/en/odr/uzbekistan-gender-ineauity-violence-en.

Stevens, Evelyn P. 1973. Machismo and Marianismo. *Society* 10: 57–63. https://doi.org/10.1007/BF02695282.

Sturdevant, Sandra Pollock, and Brenda Stoltzfus, eds. 1992. *Let the Good Times Roll: Prostitution and the US Military in Asia.* New York: New Press.

Swieca, Arianne. 2013. "LGBT Rights and the Long Road to Democracy in Georgia." Foreign Policy, May 17. Accessed June 27, 2022. https://foreignpolicy.com/2013/05/17/lgbt-rights-and-the-long-road-to-democracy-in-georgia.

"Tackling the Taboo of Menstrual Hygiene in the European Region." 2018. World Health Organization, November 8. Accessed June 27, 2022. http://www.euro.who.int/en/health-topics/environment-and-health/pages/news/news/2018/11/tackling-the-taboo-of-menstrual-hygiene-in-the-european-region.

Tai, Crystal. 2019. "Period Drama: How Asian Women Broke the Menstruation Taboo." *South China Morning Post*, April 14. Accessed June 27, 2022. https://www.scmp.com/week-asia/society/article/3005765/menstrual-misconceptions-how-asian-attitudes-towards-periods-are.

Tamale, Sylvia. 2011. *African Sexualities: A Reader.* Cape Town, South Africa: Pambazuka/Fahamu.

Tcherkézoff, Serge. 2009. "A Reconsideration of the Role of Polynesian Women in Early Encounters with Europeans: Supplement to Marshall Sahlins' Voyage around the Islands of History." In *Oceanic Encounters: Exchange, Desire, Violence*, edited by Margaret Jolly,

Serge Tcherkézoff, and Darrell Tryon, 113–60. Canberra, Australia: ANU Press. Accessed June 27, 2022. https://www.jstor.org/stable/j.ctt24h8jn.

Træen, Bente, Ana Alexandra Carvalheira, Gert Martin Hald, Theis Lange, and Ingela Lundin Kvalem. 2018. "Attitudes towards Sexuality in Older Men and Women across Europe: Similarities, Differences, and Associations with Their Sex Lives." *Sexuality & Culture* 23 (1): 1–25. https://doi.org/10.1007/s12119-018-9564-9.

Walker, Troy, Claire Palermo, and Karen Klassen. 2019. "Considering the Impact of Social Media on Contemporary Improvement of Australian Aboriginal Health: Scoping Review." *JMIR Public Health and Surveillance* 5, no. 1 (February): e11573. https://doi.org/10.2196/11573.

Warraich, Sohail Akabar. 2005. "Honor Killings and the Law in Pakistan." In *"Honour" Crimes: Paradigms, and Violence against Women*, edited by Lynn Welchman and Sara Hossain, 79. London: Zed Books.

Welborn, Amy. 2017. "Women and the Protestant Reformation." *Catholic World Report*. Accessed June 27, 2022. https://www.catholicworldreport.com/2017/10/28/women-and-the-protestant-reformation.

Welchman, Lynn, and Sara Hossain, eds. 2005. *"Honour" Crimes, Paradigms, and Violence against Women*. London: Zed Books.

"What Is Gender-Based Violence?" 2019. European Institute for Gender Equality, February 27. Accessed May 30, 2019. https://eige.europa.eu/gender-based-violence/what-is-gender-based-violence.

Willetts, Marion C., Susan Sprecher, and Frank D. Beck. 2004. "Overview of Sexual Practices and Attitudes within Relational Contexts." In *The Handbook of Sexuality in Close Relationships*, edited by John H. Harvey, Amy Wenzel, and Susan Sprecher, 57–85. Mahwah, NJ: Erlbaum.

Windschuttle, Keith. 2003. "The Fabrication of Aboriginal History." *Sydney Papers* 15, no. 1 (Summer): 20–29. Accessed June 27, 2022. https://search.informit.com.au/documentSummary;dn=839662676745905;res=IELHSS.

Zimmerman, Cathy, Mazeda Hossain, Katherine Yun, Vasil Gajdadziev, Natalia Guzun, Maria Tchomarova, Rosa Angela Ciarrocchi et al. 2008. "The Health of Trafficked Women: A Survey of Women Entering Posttrafficking Services in Europe." *American Journal of Public Health* 98 (1): 55–59. https://doi.org/10.2105/ajph.2006.108357.

About the Editors and Contributors

THE EDITORS

KELLY CAMPBELL, PhD, is an Interim Vice Provost at California State University, San Bernardino. Since 2008, she worked as a professor of Psychology and has directed the Psychology Honors program, served as the associate director for the Institute for Child Development and Family Relations, and codirected a study-abroad program to South Africa. Her research examines couple relationships and friendships, and she has taught courses on intimate relationships, gender, positive psychology, and race and racism.

M. L. PARKER is a licensed marriage and family therapist and assistant professor at Florida State University. She earned her doctoral degree in child and family development with an emphasis in marriage and family therapy from the University of Georgia. Her research focuses on collaborative health care, illness, and disabilities in the practice of couples and family therapy. Parker has taught undergraduate and graduate courses in couples therapy, medical family therapy, research methods, diversity in family therapy, and psychopathology. She is a member of the American Association for Marriage and Family Therapy (AAMFT) and is an AAMFT-approved supervisor.

THE CONTRIBUTORS

TINASHE DUNE, PhD, is a multiaward-winning academic in the areas of health sociology and public health. Her passion is working in a holistic framework, which takes into account the whole system around and within clients. Her most recent book is *Culture Diversity and Health in Australia: Towards Culturally Safe Health Care* (2021).

TATJANA M. FARLEY, PhD, is a marriage and family therapist and a faculty instructor and supervisor at Appalachian State University in Boone, North Carolina. She earned her doctoral degree in marriage and family therapy from Florida State University. Her research examines anger and aggression among youth through a developmental trauma framework. Her research has been published in distinguished journals such as *Journal of Family Violence, Journal of Aggression Maltreatment and Trauma, Social Science and Medicine, Child and Youth Care Forum*, and *Journal of Child and Family Studies*.

RUBAB FIRDAUS is a sessional academic at Western Sydney University. She has publications in migrant populations as well as in sexual marginalization and health inequities. She is also a physiotherapist in the aged-care setting with a particular focus on improving the health of the elderly population and on falls prevention.

JESSICA GOMEZ, PhD, is an instructor in behavioral sciences at Drury University in addition to serving as an online instructor for both Glendale Community College and Ozarks Technical Community College. She has published articles focusing on decision-making and risk-taking among adolescents and emerging adults, with an emphasis on cultural and religious influences on young women. She enjoys facilitating her students' exploration of this intersectionality through courses such as "Psychology of Sexuality" and "Psychology and Culture."

SYEDA ZAKIA HOSSAIN, PhD, is an associate professor at the School of Health Sciences, University of Sydney, Australia. She is an expert in women's health, with a primary focus on reproductive health and chronic disease of migrants and refugee women in the Asia-Pacific region. She uses mixed methods and publishes widely in peer-reviewed journals.

TIFFANY FAWN JONES, PhD, is a professor of African history and the department chair of the history department at California State University, San Bernardino. She has published extensively on ideas of health, race, gender, sexuality, and power structures in Africa and has a particular interest in the history of mental health in South Africa.

PRANEE LIAMPUTTONG, PhD, is an adjunct professor at the Translation Health Research Institute at Western Sydney University, Australia. Her research includes sexual and reproductive health of migrants/refugees and women in Asia. She is a qualitative researcher and has published several books on qualitative methodologies.

MARISSA A. MOSLEY, PhD, is a marriage and family therapist and assistant professor at the University of New Hampshire. She earned her doctoral degree in marriage and family therapy from Florida State University. Her research focuses on adult attachment and gender differences in technology use in romantic relationships. Dr. Mosley's work has been published in journals such as *Sexual and Relationship Therapy* and the *Journal of Family Therapy*.

KATHLEEN NADEAU, PhD, professor emeritus, California State University, San Bernardino, is the author, most recently, of *The History of the Philippines* (Second Edition, 2020) and editor of *Women and Violence, Global Lives in Focus* (2019).

ANITA OGBEIDE is an emerging public health scholar with interest and expertise in research with minority populations. Her most recent publication is "Ageing in Indigenous Australians," in *Aging Across Cultures: Growing Old in the Non-Western World* (2021).

ANGELICA OJINNAKA is a master of research candidate in the Centre for Transforming Early Education and Child Health (TeEACH) at the Translational Health Research Institute, Western Sydney University, Australia. Angelica's research primarily focuses on minority populations, particularly youth and women's engagement in social and health environments.

FRANCESCA OTERO-VARGAS, MA, is a marriage and family therapy doctoral candidate at Florida State University. Her research focuses on the integration of family therapy into the education system, and she is among the few Hispanic women in this academic field.

RASHMI PITHAVADIAN, MRes, is a sessional academic and research officer in the School of Health Sciences at Western Sydney University, Australia. Rashmi's award-nominated teaching and research utilize a multidisciplinary approach to support the holistic well-being of marginalized populations in sexual health.

SANGITA RAYAMAJHI, PhD, is a professor of Asian Studies at the Institute of Advanced Communication Education and Research (IACER), Pokhara University, Nepal. She also directs the Center for Advanced Studies in South Asia (CASSA) and the South Asian Foundation for Academic Research (SAFAR). She coauthored/edited two books for ABC-CLIO: *Women's Roles in Asia* and *Women and Violence: Global Lives in Focus.*

QIONG WU, PhD, is an assistant professor of marriage and family therapy at Florida State University. Her scholarly interests focus on maternal and child mental health. Her most recent publication is "A Developmental Hierarchical-Integrative Perspective on the Emergence of Self-Regulation: A Replication and Extension," in the journal *Child Development* (2021).

Index

Page numbers in *italics* indicate photos.

Lightning Source UK Ltd.
Milton Keynes UK
UKHW011827020123
414736UK00006B/121